FROM THE REVOLUTION TO THE MAQUILADORAS

AMERICAN ENCOUNTERS /
GLOBAL INTERACTIONS

A series edited by Gilbert M. Joseph
and Emily S. Rosenberg

FROM THE REVOLUTION TO THE MAQUILADORAS

GENDER, LABOR, AND GLOBALIZATION IN NICARAGUA

Jennifer Bickham Mendez

DUKE UNIVERSITY PRESS   DURHAM AND LONDON 2005

© 2005 DUKE UNIVERSITY PRESS

ALL RIGHTS RESERVED

PRINTED IN THE UNITED STATES OF

AMERICA ON ACID-FREE PAPER ∞

DESIGNED BY REBECCA GIMÉNEZ

TYPESET IN ADOBE MINION BY

KEYSTONE TYPESETTING, INC.

LIBRARY OF CONGRESS CATALOGING-

IN-PUBLICATION DATA APPEAR

ON THE LAST PRINTED PAGE

OF THIS BOOK.

2ND PRINTING, 2007

CONTENTS

**AMERICAN ENCOUNTERS /
GLOBAL INTERACTIONS**
A series edited by Gilbert M. Joseph
and Emily S. Rosenberg

This series aims to stimulate critical
perspectives and fresh interpretive frameworks for scholarship on the history of the
imposing global presence of the United
States. Its primary concerns include the
deployment and contestation of power,
the construction and deconstruction of
cultural and political borders, the fluid
meanings of intercultural encounters, and
the complex interplay between the global
and the local. American Encounters seeks
to strengthen dialogue and collaboration
between historians of U.S. international
relations and area studies specialists.

The series encourages scholarship based
on multiarchival historical research. At the
same time, it supports a recognition of the
representational character of all stories
about the past and promotes critical inquiry into issues of subjectivity and narrative. In the process, American Encounters
strives to understand the context in which
meanings related to nations, cultures,
and political economy are continually
produced, challenged, and reshaped.

PREFACE

In 1996, just before I left for a research trip to Nicaragua, my seventeen-year-old brother-in-law William died suddenly and unexpectedly while exercising in a PE class at school. Like many Nicaraguan migrants in the 1990s, my husband's family was spread between his home town of Jinotepe and several cities in the United States. Upon hearing of his brother's death, we traveled to Miami to make the funeral arrangements and join the rest of his U.S.-based family members to mourn this tragedy. After the funeral, as we packed to return to California, my mother-in-law began going through her recently deceased son's belongings. "*Tomá, hija*," she said to me. "It would be a shame to waste these new blue jeans. They've never even been worn. Take them to Nicaragua and give them to my cousin Agenor." As I placed the jeans in my suitcase, I noticed the label: "Made in Nicaragua."

As I reflected on the intersecting movements of this piece of clothing and the people who would come in contact with it, I came to see this garment as a powerful symbol of the intersections between globalization and the daily lives of ordinary people. Contrary to the abstract notion of globalization as best understood through macro-level analysis, the experiences of everyday people—people like William—have much to tell us about global and transnational processes. These do not simply happen to the economy or to political systems. People on the ground engage and participate in these processes—in effect, making them happen.

U.S. cotton stitched together by Nicaraguan women in the Free Trade Zone, William's Levi's must have traveled to a distributor in the States (probably in New York or Los Angeles) and finally to a retailer in Miami. There they were sold for approximately a week's wages of the workers who produced them and were purchased for a teenage boy in Miami who himself had made this voyage on more than one occasion.

William was conceived in the late seventies, just before his mother came to the United States, where she gave birth to him. The only U.S.-born child in the family, William would return to Nicaragua with the rest of the family just after the Revolutionary triumph occurred in 1979 only to migrate once again to the States in 1981. In 1990 William, along with his mother and sister, would return to a much-changed Nicaragua, where the newly formed Chamorro government had recently displaced the revolutionary party of the FSLN. During this visit with extended family, he would have to adapt to speaking in Spanish, not just responding in English as he and his brothers and sisters were accustomed to doing at home. William would never wear the jeans assembled in his parents' homeland. The garment, however, would make the return trip to be worn by an older cousin who had recently been deported from the Unites States and whose unemployment left him no way to provide for his many children.

The "Made in Nicaragua" label on William's jeans tells a familiar story about globalization. Economic production has "gone global," and a new international division of labor has emerged in which the manufacturing of many goods has been moved to sites in the developing world. Global commodity chains link the economies of various nation-states, and the countries of the Global South provide transnational corporations with inexpensive labor in the assembly of goods like garments, toys, and electronics. Central America's proximity to the United States, the world's largest market for clothing, as well as the high levels of unemployment throughout the region, which have driven down wages, make it an attractive location for production of garments for transnational corporations. This economic story, however, only reveals a small piece of what is a larger and more complex plot. Looking "behind the label," as the saying from the anti-sweatshop movement goes (see Bonacich and Appelbaum 2000), can reveal how people engage with global processes—participate in them, accommodate them in different ways in their daily lives, and sometimes actively *resist* them.

To use a popular Latin American image, resisting the negative consequences of economic globalization for women and working people is "ants' work." This book is about the "ant-like" effort of one group of women. The case of the Working and Unemployed Women's Movement, "María Elena Cuadra" (MEC) and its efforts to improve the lives of unemployed women and women workers in *maquila* factories brings gender and power to the forefront in considering the intricate ways in which local actors participate in, react to, create, and influence transnational processes.

The efforts of this group have occurred as part of a larger phenomenon of transnational political activity. Social movements' struggles for social justice have also gone global. For example, transnational networks of nongovernmental organizations (NGOS), unions, religious groups, women's organizations, and student groups have coalesced around the issue of sweatshops. In 1999 the global justice movement was born, with a wide spectrum of groups mobilizing in Seattle, Washington, to decry global injustices and the antidemocratic practices of the World Trade Organization. The early 2000s saw mass mobilizations to protest globalization occurring in Washington, Davos, Genoa, Quebec City, and other cities where global decision-makers came together. The transnational antisweatshop movement was a loud and important voice at these protests.

Although smaller in scale than these mass mobilizations, the story of resistance (and sometimes accommodation) that this book recounts is equally important. By focusing on the "ants' work" of a relatively small group of women within a broader national and international context, I hope to show how this case contributes to a clearer understanding of the complexities involved in social justice struggles in an era of globalization.

ACKNOWLEDGMENTS

A colleague once said to me, "A book will break your heart." Although the written book has broken my heart many times over, the book's many unwritten texts tell a story of deep and fulfilling connections with colleagues, family, and friends who have enriched a decade of my life and work. First and foremost, this project would not have been possible were it not for the generosity of the women of MEC who took me into their lives, work, and world and taught me so many valuable lessons about solidarity, justice, and the power of collectivism. Though confidentiality does not permit me to thank the women of the MEC collective by name, I am honored and humbled to tell their story and can only hope that these pages do it justice. The woman I call Sara Rodríguez deserves my deepest and heartfelt gratitude. Her courage, commitment to social justice, and tireless efforts give me hope for the possibility of a more equitable world.

The research for this project was funded by a Fulbright Study Abroad Fellowship, the University of California Humanities Institute, the University of California Pacific Rim Research Program, Soroptimist International, and Sigma Xi. Generous financial support for the writing of this book came from the University of California, Davis, and The College of William and Mary.

There would be no book without Gül Ozyegin. She read countless drafts of the entire manuscript, providing comments and feedback with sisterly patience and love. During the long revisions, she pulled me back from the brink of despair many times. Diane Wolf believed in this book well before it was written and has always believed in me even when I lost faith in myself. Kate Slevin deserves my warmest thanks for keeping this project and myself afloat during the years it took to write this book. Her reminders to be "kind to myself" mattered in infinite ways. Michael Lewis and Tom Linneman consistently awed me with their good-natured willingness to read the manuscript—*again*. Ronald Köpke's unflagging encouragement kept this project alive through these years. This book has benefited from his intellect, his frank criticism, and his unwavering generosity, but most of all from his political ideals, which he lives in his personal life, scholarship, and actions.

My colleagues at The College of William and Mary are deserving of my thanks: Cindy Hahamovitch, Timmons Roberts, Dee Royster, and Sal Saporito. Heartfelt abrazos go out to my colleague and *comadre* Silvia Tandeciarz for her translation expertise and for always knowing what matters. Everyone should be so fortunate to have colleagues like these! I am grateful to the many people who shared their comments on all or sections of the manuscript— Victoria Gonzalez, Luis Guarnizo, Charlie Hale, and Vicki Smith all helped a dissertation grow into a book. Gay Seidman and two anonymous reviewers at Duke University Press devoted amazing effort to reading and commenting on this manuscript. There is no question that this is a vastly improved book because of their insights. I wish to thank the editorial staff at Duke University Press, especially Valerie Millholland and Miriam Angress; their professionalism and conscientiousness never wavered. Leela Tanikella is a skilled and patient indexer.

Family and friends have seen this project along a rocky road. In Nicaragua Marvin Vargas and Cecilia Velasquez were my daily companions, confidantes, and much loved *primos políticos*. Marvincito, *mi ahijado*, Evelyn Vargas, and Eloisa kept me grounded in myriad ways and never let me forget the humanity that is at the root of this project. Other members of *mi familia política* took me under their wings and opened their homes to me—I'm grateful to Melvin Hernández, Francisca Sotelo, Mayra Hernández, and Angela Hernández for welcoming this *gringa* into their family. Special thanks in this regard are reserved for Hayda Mendez who smoothed my transition to daily life in Nicaragua. She is an expert cross-cultural advisor and social critic, and I am indebted to her for her complete acceptance of me and for her patient teachings of how to negotiate transnational family relations. I am indebted also to my parents and grandparents for my education and formation as a scholar. Heartfelt thanks go out to my father and mother, Stephen and Nancy Bickham, who taught me how to stand up for my principles and who always believed that I could do anything. I am grateful to my grandparents Ursula and Fred Orazio and Howard and Lavarre Bickham for the high value they placed on my education. Other family members, David Bickham, Leela Tanikella, and Arlene, Danae, and Javier Mendez, were constant sources of strength. My thanks to German Santiago Mendez, whose love and support over the years made the dream of this book a reality. Finally, William and Sofia Mendez are the sun of my days and the stars of my nights. I dedicate these pages to them and to the hope that a better world is possible.

AN EARLIER VERSION of material presented in chapter 4 appeared as "Organizing a Space of their Own?: Global/Local Processes in a Nicaraguan Women's Organization" in *Journal of Developing Societies*, 18 (2–3; 2002): 196–227.

An earlier version of a portion of chapter 5 appeared as "Creating Alternatives from a Gender Perspective: Central American Women's Transnational Organizing for Maquila Workers' Rights" in *Women's Activism and Globalization: Linking Local Struggles and Transnational Politics*, edited by Nancy A. Naples and Manisha Desai, pp 121–41 (Routledge, 2002).

Material from select portions of chapter 5 appeared in "A Place of Their Own?—Women Organizers Negotiating the Local and Transnational in the Maquilas of Nicaragua and Northern Mexico," an article coauthored with Joe Bandy in *Mobilization* 8 (2; 2003): 173–88.

An earlier version of material presented in portions of chapter 6 appeared under the title "Gender and Citizenship in a Global Context: The Struggle for Maquila Worker's Rights in Nicaragua" in *Identities: Journal of Culture and Power* 9 (2002): 7–38.

FROM THE
REVOLUTION
TO THE
MAQUILADORAS

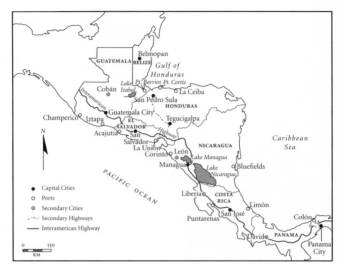

MAP 1

Central America

MAP 2

Nicaragua

1 "Just Us and Our Worms": The Working and Unemployed Women's Movement, "María Elena Cuadra"

Organizers from the Working and Unemployed Women's Movement, "María Elena Cuadra" (MEC) like to talk about how nervous and insecure they felt in their early days as members of a newly formed autonomous women's organization. They were intensely aware that "no one knew who we were." They felt like "cuatro loquitas hablando allí" (four crazy women talking there) when they attended public events organized by national and international organizations or meetings with government officials—a labor conference organized by the Nicaraguan labor movement and its international supporters, an audience with the Ministry of Labor, an international women's conference, or a forum organized by international NGOs. The story goes that at such an event someone in a position of authority would ask the women, "Who are you? Whom do you represent?" (In other words, "What gives you the right to participate in this event?") To which the women would reply defiantly (and this is the reoccurring phrase that they would repeat in different renditions of the same narrative), "Sólo nosotras y nuestras lombrises"—"Just us and our worms."

The Working and Unemployed Women's Movement, "María Elena Cuadra" was born in May 1994, when it emerged as an autonomous women-only organization from a deep-seated crisis within the Sandinista Workers' Central (CST), the largest trade union confederation in Nicaragua. Since its birth as an independent organization, much of MEC's work has revolved around organizing women workers in the country's free trade zones (FTZs) and working to improve conditions in *maquiladora* factories.[1] In addition, MEC's programs provide job training and income-generating opportunities to unemployed women and sensitize women to gender issues such as domestic violence and reproductive health while teaching them about their rights. In their work in the FTZs, MEC has struggled to raise national, regional, and international public awareness regarding the situation of *maquila* workers and to lobby for pressure on *maquila* factory owners to uphold workers' human rights and comply with local labor laws. Since 1994 over seven thousand female maquila workers have participated in MEC's programs (Köpke 2002). Although currently workers in the FTZs number around forty thousand (*Observador Económico* 2002), no other organization in the country can claim to have reached so many workers—men or women. MEC's struggle to improve conditions for maquila workers has transcended national borders, and the organization coordinates its efforts with other Central American women's organizations through a regional network that lobbies state officials and factory owners in several countries in the region.

Although I interviewed and had regular contact with women at different levels of the MEC organization—unemployed women who participated in MEC's job-training and microcredit programs; maquila workers who acted as "promoters" (*promotoras*) within FTZ factories; and workers who participated in MEC's workshops or whom MEC assisted in filing grievances after experiencing violations of their human or labor rights—the major actors portrayed in this book are the teams that made up MEC's leadership. I worked closely as an international volunteer, or *cooperante*, with these organizers, who numbered approximately twenty-five (with some fluctuation as some women left and others joined over the course of my research).

Why write a book about this relatively small organization? *From the Revolution to the Maquiladoras* offers an ethnographic account of the strategies and practices of the Working and Unemployed Women's Movement, "María Elena Cuadra" in order to demonstrate the implications of this case for the study of grassroots engagements—both resistance and accommodation—to economic globalization. Three large-scale political and economic phenomena set the stage for the story that unfolds in this book: (1) the dramatic growth of global capitalism and its incorporation of women as assembly workers; (2) political and economic transition within Nicaragua from a revolutionary socialist regime with a state-centered economy to a neoliberal "market democracy" (Robinson 2003) that emphasizes free trade, privatization, and the reduction of the public sector; and (3) the growth of women's autonomous political organizing in Latin America and around the world.

Gender is an integral component of globalization, with gender-specific consequences for women's lives. The worldwide shrinking of public services that has occurred under the global hegemony of neoliberalism has increased women's labor burden as they struggle to meet the needs of their families. More women participate in the paid labor force than ever before,[2] and women increasingly take on breadwinner roles in the global economy in ways that both draw on and undermine traditional gender roles (Peterson and Runyan 1999: 130–47; Mies 1998: 112–44). In search of an ever cheaper, more docile workforce, transnational corporations locate production in the developing world, targeting a young female labor force for employment in assembly factories where they face long workdays, harsh working conditions, sexual harassment, and other human and labor rights violations. The International Labor Organization (2003b: 21) estimates that some 42 million people are employed in FTZS around the world and that 90 percent of the workforce is female, prompting some to hail women workers as the "paradigmatic subjects" of the international division of labor (Spivak 1988: 29).

Although there have been many excellent studies about women workers in the global economy, far fewer studies examine women's movements in a global context.[3] A primary theoretical goal of *From the Revolution to the Maquiladoras* is to examine how transnational, national, and local processes interact in complex ways to shape the politics of local actors and how local movements participate in and sometimes reconfigure aspects of globalization. In order to do so, this book explores both structural and cultural elements of MEC and applies a gender analysis to the politics of resistance and accommodation under globalization.

THE WORKING AND UNEMPLOYED WOMEN'S
MOVEMENT, MARÍA ELENA CUADRA

MEC's birth was precipitated by repeated conflicts between the CST's national and regional women's secretariats, on the one hand, and union federation and national confederation leaders on the other, regarding the administration of project funds and program priorities. Such conflicts came to a head at the CST's 1994 national congress, when to the horror and outrage of the membership of the women's secretariats, the CST's national leadership (all male) failed to appoint to the national executive council even one of the seven women nominated at the women's national congress, held a month earlier. Even more shocking—the secretariats' elected choice for the next director of the National Women's Secretariat lost in favor of the rumored lover of a CST leader. In addition, the national executive council revoked the financial autonomy of the National Women's Secretariat, making all of its projects and programs subject to administration by the CST (male) leadership.

Disillusionment stemming from the election results fueled plans by a group of disgruntled women unionists and former leaders of the women's secretariats—among them Sara Rodríguez, who had recently announced her resignation as the director of the National Women's Secretariat—to form an independent working women's organization.[4] In May 1994 former leaders of the women's secretariats, along with approximately four hundred women workers and unemployed women, voted to create a new, autonomous women's organization. Following the Sandinista custom of naming a group for a hero or martyr, they chose the name the Working and Unemployed Women's Movement, "María Elena Cuadra," after a domestic worker and union organizer who had recently been killed by a drunk driver.

The general secretary of the CST was quick to react with a bitter defamatory campaign against these women, which was whipped into a national "scandal," resulting in the issuance of a warrant for the arrest of two former secretariat leaders. The CST also ousted all the women who were working on the various projects that the former secretariat had implemented, closing the clinics and day-care centers opened by the local secretariats, ousting women from small businesses established through the secretariat's micro-credit program, and expelling the domestic workers' union from the CST's national office.

As one MEC leader contends, then, the organization was "born out of a storm"—a storm resulting from a group of women claiming their own voices as leaders and asserting their autonomy as political actors. But what is the significance of this case? Sociologists often worry about the issue of generalizability—that is, can we learn anything from an n of one? All over the world women have organized around their multiple identities as mothers, workers, nationalists, and members of racial minorities; and each case helps build a better understanding of possibilities for struggle and action (Basu 1995). The struggle of the women of MEC who created a space for "just ourselves and our worms" deserves to be a focus of intellectual inquiry because of what it represents—a group of women from poor backgrounds, from the second poorest country in Latin America, who have taken up the struggle to improve women's lives under global capitalism. But beyond this, MEC stands at the intersections of some key theoretical debates regarding globalization, the global hegemony of neoliberalism, and women's organizing in postsocialist contexts.

MEC's efforts as an autonomous organization that deals with working women outside of the framework of unionism raises important questions for scholars, students, and activists interested in the struggles of women and workers under global capitalist conditions and in the intersections of feminism and labor organizing. What does it mean to organize and support women workers as both women *and* workers in this context? What kinds of local, national, and transnational struggles have resulted as women are increasingly incorporated into the global economy and organize to defend their rights?

In order to counter the mobility of transnational corporations, MEC has engaged in political strategies and practices that span national borders. Through its membership in the Central American Women's Network in Solidarity with Maquila Workers, a transnational association of women's organizations that addresses issues facing women in maquila factories, MEC coordinates with other women's organizations to lobby state officials and negotiate with factory owners in Nicaragua as well as in other parts of Central America. Furthermore, MEC's formation and continued existence have been supported and sustained by the organization's transnational linkages with NGOs and solidarity groups in Europe and North America, upon which the group depends for financial support. Global discourses, such as human rights, and global trends, such as transitions to neoliberal democracies and the accompanying importance of national discourses of rights and citizenship, have shaped MEC's strategic orientation and informed its practices.

Exploring deeper subtextual meanings behind MEC organizers' self-description as representing only themselves and their "worms" (*lombrises*) elucidates some of the complexities regarding these women's identities and perceptions of themselves as political actors. For example, it is perhaps significant that the Spanish word *lombriz*, a general word for *worm* in Nicaragua and most of Latin America is used here, as opposed to *parásito* (parasite), which, as in English, refers more specifically to crea-

"María Elena Cuadra" **5**

tures that reside in the human body. On the surface, the word choice of *lombriz* in "just us and our worms" simply reflects a common saying in Nicaraguan Spanish—comparable to "no one here but us chickens." But "lombriz" can also refer to earthworms or any other kind of worm, and the organizers' association with the humble, but hard-working, worm carries symbolic significance. The parasite connotes a disgusting creature that feeds off the lifeblood of its victim, but any gardener knows how beneficial it is to have earthworms in one's flower garden. Parasites suck the life out of their hosts, but the earthworm's productive and largely invisible activities create the possibility for life. The rather crude mention of being afflicted with worms also reflects these women's stubborn identification with the poor. The women of MEC see and talk about themselves in this way to portray the work that they carried out within the popular organizations of the Sandinista National Liberation Front (FSLN), and they see themselves continuing this kind of "grassroots" work with and as *mujeres de base* (grassroots women) in the autonomous, women-only space of MEC.[5]

But MEC cannot be understood without considering its historical and geographical location. Nicaragua's relatively late integration into the global economy of the latter part of the twentieth century, as well as its history as a postrevolutionary society makes it an ideal site for the study of oppositional initiatives under globalization. Emerging four years after the ruling Sandinista party was defeated at the polls, MEC is illustrative of the shifting challenges and opportunities that Nicaraguan social justice groups confront. In some ways the case is unique, as MEC is the only organization in that country that applies a gender perspective in its efforts to organize maquila workers and address their needs. On the other hand the case of MEC is representative of a larger process that is occurring throughout Central America and, indeed, in many parts of the developing world where societies are undergoing transitions to democracy. Social justice movements have shifted their orientations away from the revolutionary goal of state takeover and, instead, make claims based on rights and citizenship, addressing not only state, but also global institutions, such as the United Nations, and even multilateral lending organizations, such as the World Bank and the International Monetary Fund (IMF).

In this study I employ the research strategy of "global ethnography"

(Burawoy et al. 2000) and use local participant observation to theorize "the global." This approach recognizes that the "global" and the "local" are not separate realms (Freeman 2001; Grewal and Kaplan 1994), nor are global conditions merely ethnographic backdrop for a local case study. Rather, globalization itself becomes an object of study, and micro-level processes are seen as an expression of the macro (Burawoy 2000: 27, 29). This research strategy calls for the examination of local movements within a "global here and now," "strategically situated" within a national and globalized political economy (Marcus 1995: 111).

This approach specifies the ways in which power and inequalities, particularly those based on gender, shape transnational politics. Contrary to the cooperative image of a global village, what emerges is a picture of transnational political fields that are also arenas of struggle, presenting the actors in social movements with daunting obstacles as well as sometimes surprising opportunities.

Although over the years MEC organizers have been successful in obtaining funding and building their organization, they face continual challenges. As the upcoming chapters will explain in detail, they face a constant struggle to have their programs viewed favorably by NGOs and other donor organizations. They also contend with conflicts that emerged beginning in 1996 with unions and with their sponsoring federations, most of which have close ties to the Sandinista Workers' Central (CST) and to the Sandinista party and which to a certain extent vie with MEC for legitimacy as representatives of maquila workers. Organizations and activists in the United States and Europe who made up the solidarity movement with Central America during the 1980s were accustomed to dealing with unions and labor federations and other organizations tied to revolutionary fronts, like the FSLN. As the transnational anti-sweatshop movement emerged and gained strength in the late 1990s, these solidarity organizations expected that the union federations would be the logical partners to provide with assistance and funding, despite the fact that in Nicaragua the labor federations had neglected the maquilas and their predominately female labor force during their negotiations with the state in the early 1990s. Finally, MEC is dependent on international NGOs and the Canadian and European labor organizations that fund its initiatives. With this dependency come inequalities and in some cases the reproduction of neocolonial relations. Faced with traditional leftist views about unions and union organizing, MEC sometimes finds it difficult to defend its position as an independent working women's organization that is not a union.

An ethnographic approach to MEC and its strategies and practices that situates them within larger national, regional, and global contexts broadens the scope of analysis to reveal how MEC both responds to and participates in global and transnational processes. For example, when MEC organizers address state officials and call for state enforcement of the National Labor Code in the garment-assembly factories within the FTZ, such lobbying might appear to be a national strategy. But, in their claims to the state, MEC organizers use discursive tools that are globally recognized, such as human rights, and draw from international ordinances, such as the Universal Declaration on Human Rights and the Convention on the Elimination of All Forms of Discrimination Against Women (CEDAW). Indeed, the very act of addressing state agents as a social justice strategy and the accompanying emphasis on civil society which occurs under transitions to neoliberal democracy suggest its more regional and global significance.

In one case detailed in a later chapter of this book, MEC organizers activated their personal networks of contacts established during the Sandinista years to gain access to the Minister of Labor in order to lobby for his support of the campaign to establish a code of ethics within the factories of the FTZ. Their long history within the popular organizations of the Sandinista party meant that they had worked closely with many of the individuals who were current officials in the Ministry of Labor, and these networks gave them influence in this office which eventually resulted in organizers' being granted permission to enter the restricted area of the FTZ as necessary in order to meet with workers.

MEC, however, did not engage in this lobbying effort on its own. Its efforts were bolstered by its participation in a transnational network of women's organizations, the Central American Women's Network in Solidarity with Maquila Workers (the Network), and it was pressure garnered through media attention surrounding this transnational initiative that helped MEC achieve leverage with the Ministry of Labor. The Network's campaigns and strategies cross borders, as members launch public opinion and lobbying campaigns in several countries at once, traveling to different Central American countries to lobby state representatives and factory owners. The Network and all its activities are funded by Canadian and European NGOs, and Network organizers travel on a regular basis to Canada, Europe, and the United States in order to participate in activities of the larger transnational anti-sweatshop movement. Organizers, like Josefina from MEC and María Angela from the Honduran Women's Collective (CODEMUH), take part in speaking tours, conferences, and workshops organized by organizations like Global Exchange in the United States, the Central American Women's Network of Great Britain, and the European Clean Clothes Campaign.

The transnational politics of MEC, through its activities as a member of the Network and as a participant in the wider transnational anti-sweatshop movement, are made possible by several "global" phenomena such as the Internet and increasingly accessible air travel. The transfer of information through e-mail enables MEC to maintain its contact with the international NGOs that fund its local activities and organize international workshops and sessions, bringing together organizations from around the world that work on sweatshop issues. A global discourse of human rights, the existence of international conventions like CEDAW, and the near global reach of feminist discourses (thanks in part to the UN conferences on women) create an internationally recognized framework for building arguments that MEC can employ in demanding improvements in work conditions in the maquilas.

NICARAGUA IN THE AGE OF GLOBALIZATION

During the last thirty years Latin American countries have experienced a gradual, contradictory, and conflictive reorientation toward the global economy. Facilitated by multilateral institutions like the International Monetary Fund and the World Bank, neoliberal political and economic agendas have spread among Latin American state regimes to facilitate the mobility of capital, reduce the role of the state in economic decisions, and promote free trade through structural adjustment. To achieve these goals and reduce inflation, neoliberalism prescribes the privatization of state-owned enterprises and the drastic reduction of the public sector and state-supplied social services (Robinson 1997). Multilateral institutions have touted the establishment of free trade zones as part of the solution to the persisting debt crises of countries in the region.

The globalization of capitalism has been accompanied by sweeping political transitions in Central America. In the late 1980s and early 1990s many Central American military dictatorships gave way to elected governments. As early as 1980, Honduras's military dictatorship was deposed. And in the 1990s, civil wars ended in Nicaragua and El Salvador, and a peace treaty was reached in Guatemala.

Nominally democratic, these neoliberal state regimes engage in heavy competition to attract foreign investment. Free trade zones have been seen as a way to provide desperately needed jobs. The transnational apparel industry plays off the state's desire to provide employment by selling its operations to the country that offers the most benefits and the cheapest production costs. Indeed, the expansion of this industry in the region has prompted some to observe that Central American countries are quickly leaving behind their status as "banana republics" to become "sewing republics" (Fonseca Tinoco 1997a: 22), what one researcher deems the United States' new garment district (Rosen 2002).

Nicaragua's path to economic globalization has in many ways been unique within the region as it experienced a transition from an authoritarian to a revolutionary regime and then to a neoliberal democracy. Thus, the country moved away from and then back to a global capitalist system and has only relatively recently fully reinserted itself into the global economy (Robinson 2003: 71). In 1990 the revolutionary FSLN lost at the electoral polls to a coalition of opposition parties, the National Union of Opposition (UNO), and a new neoliberal regime, headed by President Violeta Chamorro, took power. This transition in state rule brought with it dramatic changes in Nicaragua's political economy. The consumer subsidies and emphasis on public welfare of the Sandinista era gave way to the privatization of state-owned enterprises and the drastic reduction of public spending.

The new government strove to stimulate economic growth by reinserting Nicaragua into the global economy. To this end and as a response to austerity measures imposed by the World Bank and the IMF, the Chamorro government issued new legislation to attract foreign investment and increase export production. A series of 1991 laws established the existence of free trade zones in Nicaragua, and the state-owned Free Trade Zone "Las Mercedes" opened the following year, with eight factories in operation (Renzi 1996).

This trajectory continued with the 1996 electoral victory of the Nicaraguan Liberal Alliance's candidate, Arnoldo Alemán, the former mayor of Managua. The new president quickly made it clear that his administration's political and economic policies would be squarely in line with neoliberal principles. In a 1997 television interview he remarked: "Nicaragua is open, is ready for globalization. The doors of the country are open to foreign investment. . . . They will not be charged a cent until they recuperate their initial investment" (quoted in Fonseca Tincoco 1997a: 24). Since coming to power, the Liberal Alliance regime, which has continued with the 2001 election of former Vice President Enrique Bolaños, has worked to further dismantle the country's previously extensive cooperative system (particularly peasant-held land in agricultural regions), privatize worker-owned and state-owned enterprises, and diminish the public sector in an effort to promote the market economy.

And yet the changes of the last decade also set the stage for Nicaraguan women's autonomous political organization, as a broad-based and vibrant women's movement emerged out of the mass organizations of the FSLN. Ironically, the postrevolutionary context opened spaces for women's increased entrance in the political sphere, as they construct alternative resistance strategies and new ways of doing politics (Babb 2001, 1997; Criquillon 1995).

Despite the continued politicization of civil society within postrevolutionary Nicaragua, export-oriented production remains central to the country's economic development plans. Since the first state-owned FTZ was opened in 1992, five other privately owned zones have been established. By late 2001 there were forty-four assembly factories in operation, the great majority of which produced garments for the U.S. market (*Observador Económico* 2002: 5). The number of workers employed in export-processing has grown exponentially from a little over a thousand in 1992 (*Observador Económico* 2002: 1) to nearly forty thousand in 2002 (Comisión Nacional de la Zona Franca 2002; *La Prensa* 2002), and about 90 percent of these are women (ILO 2003a: 9). Export production through the free trade zones has increased from $2.9 million in 1992 to $230 million in 2000, to an estimated $250 million in 2001, or 30 percent of all exports from the country (*Observador Económico* 2002: 1).

Notwithstanding, the country continues to face enormous social and economic challenges. Although Nicaragua has experienced some economic growth (9.3 percent average annual growth in GDP in 1998 and 7.3 percent in 1999; World Bank 2000), recent UN statistics estimate 80 percent of the population lives on less than $2 per day, with undernourished people making up 29 percent of the total population (UN Development Programme 2003).

THE STUDY

I first met MEC organizers from Managua in 1994, shortly after the group's succession from the CST. I was in Nicaragua conducting Master's-level research on domestic workers and their unionization. It was through the domestic workers union that I learned of the formation of this new autonomous organization and decided that it should be the subject of a more in-depth research project that would become my dissertation. I designed my research to allow me to observe and analyze both cultural and structural dimensions of MEC. The research incorporates three main components: (1) in-depth individual and group interviews with MEC leaders and MEC program participants and beneficiaries, including maquila workers; (2) participant observation as a *cooperante* in the daily events and activities of MEC; and (3) the collection of public statements, speeches, and texts written by MEC and the Network.

The first component of my research involved interviews with MEC organizers. In 1994 I met MEC organizers for the first time and conducted semi-structured intensive group and individual interviews with five of the movement's founding members. I returned to Nicaragua the following summer to conduct participant observation in MEC's Managua office as well as to continue interviewing MEC leaders. During this summer, as well as during the first half of an eleven-month research stint in 1996–97, I conducted several more interviews with movement organizers in Managua as well as Granada, León, Chinandega, El Viejo, and Chichigalpa.

I also conducted individual interviews with participants in MEC programs and collected "testimonials" through small group meetings. I interviewed nine participants in MEC's programs, including promotoras from the FTZ. I conducted six group sessions with program participants, such as participants in MEC's job-training and microcredit programs. Finally, I conducted eight nonrandom structured interviews with maquila workers, and I also surveyed forty-one maquila workers, administering a questionnaire that I had developed as part of the initial stages of a diagnostic study that MEC was in the process of conducting and that it later published (MEC 1999). The survey queried workers about working conditions, benefits, and salaries within their factory. The questionnaires, as well as numerous meetings, informal discussions with maquila workers, and trips to the FTZ, made me familiar with their experiences on and off the shop floor.

While I initially relied on interviews to examine participants' and organizers' experiences in the organization, their shifting identities, and their subjective perceptions as political actors, in the end participant observation proved a better strategy for effective data collection. As my time in the field progressed, I noticed that in many cases interviewees were unaccustomed to analyzing their own biographies and engaging in deliberate self-reflection. It would take considerable probing and redirection to prompt participants to reflect on their own thoughts and perceptions. I learned this was a symptom of a larger problem. The "language of identity," reflecting Western individualist assumptions, was not a good match with the experiences and perspectives of MEC participants (Rouse 1995a). In some cases, I believe it obstructed my ability to hear what the *compañeras* were telling me[6]—which often came from outside this individualist framework. Framing questions of identity in terms of self-reflection turned out not to be the best strategy for gaining an understanding of organizers' perspectives, and the artificial format of the interview contributed to its clumsiness as a methodological tool in this case.

Eventually, I discontinued conducting formal interviews in favor of engaging almost exclusively in participant observation, in which I concentrated on listening to MEC participants when they talked to me and to each other about their work and their experiences as political actors; later I would record this information in detailed field notes. These informal dialogues occurred while participants were in the midst of their daily routines, rather than in interviews, which are a space created outside of everyday activities (Snow and Andersen 1993). I would sometimes ask clarifying questions or engage in long informal conversations about some subject, but I opted to continue interviewing only maquila workers as part of MEC's study on working conditions in order to obtain testimonials about workers' experiences for use in MEC's campaigns.

Participant observation with MEC and the Network comprised the main component of my research and involved my working nearly seven days a week as a volunteer or international cooperante in MEC's Managua office and, less frequently, in the Granada office. In 1994 I proposed to MEC organizers that I seek funding both to volunteer for and to study the organization, and I worked closely with the organization during the summer of 1995 and for the eleven month stay in 1996–97.

Like the other two cooperantes who worked with MEC during the time of my research, I acted as a kind of consultant and participated in strategy-planning meetings, wrote grant proposals, collaborated on reports and media releases, translated documents, and did general office work. I also gradually became MEC's "official" interpreter as the organization began to receive increasing numbers of English-speaking delegations of church and student groups. I regularly attended all of the organization's meetings and strategy-planning sessions. I observed and participated in workshops and activities for participants in MEC's programs, and I accompanied MEC organizers to events and activities organized by other groups and held outside the office.

My daily presence as a researcher and cooperante involved continual interactions and discussions with MEC organizers and program participants that often carried over into informal social settings. I spent a great deal of time with MEC organizers, moving to the daily rhythms of the office with them. We spent countless hours talking informally about issues in the organization, current events in Managua, international politics, and our families. Every morning we sat at conference tables and read the daily newspapers together, and a few of us often gathered next door at Doña Cecilia's makeshift cafeteria for lunch. We would sit at the tables in front of her house and *pulpería* (small grocery store) and chat about the day's events as we waited for steaming bowls of *sopa de albondigas* (chicken dumpling soup) to cool enough to eat.

I developed relationships with all the women of the Managua and Granada offices; some remained that of cordial co-workers, while others became longer-lasting friendships. I visited the homes of different MEC organizers and spent the night on more than one occasion. I traveled with the families of the Granada team to picnic on the famous *isletas* in Lake Nicaragua. Sara and I took some trips together, including a harrowing adventure in which we boarded a dilapidated ferry and traveled to the Isla de Ometepe, where we climbed part way up the skirt of a volcano amid banana trees and screaming howler monkeys to visit a peasant-run coffee cooperative.

I also attended and participated in three meetings of the Network, which took place in Guatemala, Nicaragua, and Honduras. At these meetings I interviewed Network organizers and held numerous informal discussions with members of the Network regarding their experiences, strategies, and vision for change. In late 1997 I made another trip to Central America—this time to Honduras—to attend the fourth meeting of the Network and to conduct follow-up research with MEC organizers and other members of the Network. This trip generated important data for this component of the research, for MEC and the Network had produced several new publications and organizers related developments regarding the organization's struggle within the FTZ.

A final component of this research involved the collection and documentation of public statements, speeches, and texts written by MEC and the Network. I participated in the meetings and activities of other networks (for example the Network of Women Against Violence Against Women and Children) of which MEC was an organizational member. Observation in these settings allowed me to document MEC participants' actions and statements within different public spaces.

Thanks to the very transnational and global processes that this study analyzes, I was able to continue some aspects of the research while in the United States. Since the completion of my fieldwork, the transnational anti-sweatshop movement has emerged and grown, and MEC organizers have been active participants. I was able to attend two events held in the States in which MEC's coordinator and other members of the Network participated. The first was a conference organized by Global Exchange, a San Francisco–based NGO, to generate strategies and ideas for a campaign promoting a living wage. The second was a teach-in regarding the strategies and work of the anti-sweatshop movement, organized by Campaign for Labor Rights, an NGO based in Washington, D.C. This event was held in conjunction with the Mobilization for Global Justice, which occurred in Washington in April 2000 to protest the policies and practices of the

IMF and the World Bank. These events, my continued e-mail correspondences with MEC, and the follow-up trip to Honduras have added a longitudinal perspective to this research.

GLOBAL ETHNOGRAPHY

Ethnography allows understandings of globalization to "land with both feet on the ground," as Sara, MEC's coordinator would say. Ethnographic research with MEC brought into focus the ways in which the multilayered internal realities of this organization fit into a larger, indeed, a global scheme, and it was only by digging further in as a participant observer that I was able to make connections with the larger external world.

At strategy-planning meetings it was impossible to participate without being struck by the ways in which global forces framed our discussions. MEC participants very consciously drew from ideas, language, and documents obtained from other social movement organizations in other geographical contexts. In these sessions, organizers very explicitly discussed the opportunities and dangers that presented themselves in the larger national and transnational political arena. For example, when Sara, Laura, and the others obtained information from the Clinton-endorsed Apparel Industry Partnership (AIP), they quickly reformulated the drafted code of ethics that they planned to present to state officials and factory management so that it would include points from the AIP's code of conduct.

Although it seemed obvious that MEC's political strategies in the FTZ would involve a transnational dimension, as these factories are squarely situated within the global assembly line, it soon became clear to me that globalization and transnational processes also shaped MEC's daily existence. MEC's tiny office received a constant flow of international visitors (myself included). Those who came as NGO funders or potential funders and collaborators were also transnational brokers of information, bringing publications and reports from other groups from both the North and other parts of the South.

Organizers' constant references to "before" (the Sandinista years) and "after" (post-1990) quickly took on new meaning within this more globally oriented framework. In Nicaragua the 1990s brought with them not only a new political regime, but a new orientation toward the global economy, which was itself being restructured on neoliberal terms. Relations between oppositional organizations in Nicaragua and the U.S. solidarity movement changed, as new autonomous organizations, such as women's organizations like MEC, formed outside of the FSLN.

DILEMMAS AND POSSIBILITIES OF FEMINIST RESEARCH: NOTES FROM A NORTHERN FEMINIST IN THE GLOBAL SOUTH

Rather than claiming the voice of the objective observer, whose own presence in the field remains unexamined, feminist researchers explicitly consider the impact of their own positionalities and the dilemmas, issues, and advantages arising from them (Stacey 1991). That is, feminist ethnographers strive to recognize and reflect on the ways that power shapes our relationships with those we study, and we attempt to be cognizant of the inevitable incompleteness of our accounts, presenting our studies as "situated knowledge" (Haraway 1988), particular truths that are embedded in historical contexts and are told from a standpoint shaped by the subjectivity of the researcher (Freeman and Murdock 2001: 423).

During my field research I acted as a cooperante, a role carved out during the revolutionary period in Nicaragua when solidarity workers from the North worked closely with the mass organizations of the FSLN. I was actively engaged in MEC's political work, but my position in the organization was rather more ambiguous than that of the other North American cooperantes who were present at MEC when I conducted my fieldwork. For one thing, I did not receive a salary from MEC, nor did my stipend depend on my work as a cooperante. Unlike the other cooperantes, I could not claim to be completely uninterested in the organization's "internal" dynamics, and indeed, those events form a large part of the data for my study. Ethnography, it turns out, is nosy business, and my researcher's curiosity made me more interested in observing and taking part in certain activities than the other North Americans were.

As a participant-observer, I was constantly struggling to balance on the thin line between insider and outsider, trying to avoid both extremes (see Wolf 1996b). This was a constant frustration, for sometimes I did not have enough to do for either my research or my work as a cooperante, and at other times, I was overloaded with work for MEC, which took time away from recording field notes and conducting interviews. Of course, being a *chela* (a light-skinned or white woman; see Lancaster 1992) and a *gringa* (North American from the United States) always set me apart from the other *Nica* members of the collective;[7] my flexible schedule and obvious greater income also contributed to my "outsiderness."

An outsider who often appeared in insider spaces, I was both a novelty and, at times, a nuisance. I found myself constantly alert to respect what MEC organizers would call "internal" meetings or spaces in which no outsiders were permitted. I spent a good deal of time evaluating whether or not I was present in a space where I did not belong, which was made more difficult because there was not always consensus within the collective as to when and where my direct participation was appropriate or desired. At times this generated uncomfortable situations—for myself as well as others. Furthermore, as I came to increasingly identify with MEC's work and with the compañeras (indeed, two months into my third trip to Nicaragua in my field notes I began to refer to MEC organizers not as "they," but as "we"), my role as researcher caused me to experience what for me were painful feelings of exclusion—something that I am sure affected my interactions with the women who were both my co-workers and my respondents.

My insider/outsider position was further complicated by my marriage into a Nicaraguan working-class family, with whom I lived during my fieldwork. During my longest research stint I lived outside of Managua in Jinotepe, the town where my husband grew up and where the majority of his mother's family still resides. Like scores of Nicaraguans who reside in *los pueblos*, I joined the large number of daily commuters from nearby small towns to the city. This living arrangement meant that I participated in Nicaraguan community life in a way that would have been impossible had I opted to live by myself in Managua. Despite the many differences that existed between me and the participants of MEC, in many ways my day-to-day life followed some of the same rhythms.

Like the MEC organizers who lived in Tipitapa, the town to the northeast of Managua where many workers from the assembly plants of the country's FTZs reside, my days were punctuated with the trials of securing public transportation and braving the overcrowding, flat tires, unscrupulous fare-collectors, and muggers as I traveled back and forth between MEC's Managua and Granada offices and home. I became versed in the many complicated bus routes within Managua and between Managua and other towns, as well as the landmarks (rather than street names and numbers) used in Nicaraguan addresses. Opting not to purchase a car, I also became skilled at *pidiendo ray* (hitching a ride). On more than one occasion I found myself stranded on the very rural road between Granada and Jinotepe and made my way home on the backs of trucks or motorcycles. During the transportation strike in 1997, I shared the panic of being stuck behind the *tranques* (blockades) with no way to get between home and "work."

Like Evelyn, a MEC organizer who was raised in Diriamba (a town that neighbors Jinotepe) and whose parents and brothers and sisters still lived there, I attended the religious festivals and saint's days activities within the department of Carazo. And like most Nicaraguans, I went to the outdoor market to buy food, usually in the company of one or more small children who clung to my hand, having begged their mothers for the privilege of accompanying their "tía Yení," as they called me. On the way home we would stop for *gaseosa* (soda pop), and as we walked along sipping Coca-Cola from plastic bags full of the much-coveted liquid, it was hard not to think about the marked differences in the ways that "global" culture and globally marketed products are quite literally consumed.

Participating in such a way in Nicaraguan community life gave me lived familiarity with many of the cultural issues around which MEC's work centered. For example, when organizers discussed cultural notions regarding women and domestic violence or issues facing Nicaraguan women who work to support their families, I related them not only to my own experiences in the United States but to examples from my husband's family and my mother-in-law's network of friends. In Jinotepe I witnessed the daily struggles of women with children whose earnings often supported not only the needs of the household but their spouses' or partners' taste for alcohol and the entertainment of *queridas* (other women; literally, "dear ones").

Residing with my *familia política* (family by marriage), I often was present when violence broke out within households, an endemic problem under the long-term conditions of scarcity that Nicaragua has experienced. My status as insider/outsider and gringa protected me to a large degree and made me seem a neutral party, so I was sometimes called upon to help remove from the scene a child or a spouse who was the victim of violence in order to give the parent or husband time to cool off. In this way, my fieldwork transcended the public/private divide, as I participated in, analyzed, and discussed many of the same issues in my home life as I did through my work as a cooperante in MEC's offices.

In part because of my in-between position, neither outsider nor insider, participant observation as a research method began to feel intrusive and contributed to some feelings of distrust on the part of some of the women of MEC and to moments of loneliness and rejection on my part. I began to feel a bit schizophrenic and developed a distaste for this "paparazzi-like" aspect of my role.

For the most part, on both sides, these tensions were carefully hidden behind a wall of silence. I learned early on that openly broaching the subject was futile, as my initial, very gringa efforts to "clear the air" and get everything out into the open were always met with assurances that no problems existed. As my time with the compañeras continued, however, the members of the collective would sometimes let slip clues about their feelings regarding my role within the organization. A few incidents took me by surprise.

One occurred at an informal gathering. One of the Canadian cooperantes, who had spent ten years in Nicaragua and had worked with some of the members of the MEC team even before the group's inception, was returning to Canada. We celebrated with a cake, and a few of us grabbed several glass bottles from MEC's stash and headed to *la venta*, the small store across the street, to have them filled with the ever-popular gaseosa or the unpalatably sweet *rojita*, a red soft drink whose flavor resembles something between cough syrup and the red licorice whips that I used to eat as a child.

Since I did not have a desk of my own, I often carried my notebooks and work materials with me around the office. That day I had been conducting interviews, so I also had my hand-held tape recorder. As we conversed and joked informally, suddenly one of the compañeras remarked, "Cuidado, la Jennifer anda la grabadora y te puede grabar." (Watch out, Jennifer has her tape recorder and might tape you.) Everyone laughed. I blushed, mostly because these kinds of remarks had never been made openly in front of me, and I made some comment about being quite a nuisance (*necia*). Another woman chimed in jokingly, "Aqui se dice: Tal vez no es necia . . . pero ¿qué jode? ¡¡Que jode!!" (Loosely translated: Here we have a saying: She might not be a nuisance, but is she a pain in the ass?—She is a *pain* in the ass!)[8] Here my slight blush must have turned a deep red, since I sensed the barb underlying this comment. Everyone giggled at my discomfort and reminded me that this expression was very *Nica*—I shouldn't take it the wrong way. Though I clearly understood a message about the presence of the tape recorder, I also came to see this moment as one in which I had crossed some kind of threshold as a member of the group. Significantly, it was at that point—several months into my longest research stint—that I discontinued conducting taped interviews.

Still, as much as I wanted to fit in and be just another compañera within the MEC organization, I could not escape the power dynamics of race, national origin, and class that also shaped my ethnographic work (Wolf 1996a). Although arguably all fieldworkers face contradictions stemming from power differentials, my close collaborations with MEC organizers and participants and my feminist orientation brought contradictions even more dramatically to the fore.

My race and national origin represented both a major barrier between me and the other compañeras but also "social capital" for the MEC organization.[9] As a chela and a foreigner, to the women of MEC I represented the "eyes of the North." This contradictory relationship was compounded by an affiliation with the U.S. embassy that my Fulbright Fellowship granted me. Because the organizers did not like airing MEC's "dirty laundry" in front of the cheles, on a number of occasions I was invited to attend certain internal meetings precisely because my presence would temper the potential for open conflict.

At one meeting an organizer asked me to leave. Although I had repeatedly requested that MEC organizers alert me if my presence was not desired, I left the meeting somewhat puzzled. For Sara herself, MEC's coordinator, had asked me to call and organize the meeting—probably for quite political reasons. Later, two of the compañeras confided to me that there had been a rather heated argument after I had left and that the organizer had been sharply admonished for requesting that I leave and for mistreating a compañera who had been *solidaria* (in solidarity) with the Movement. The organizer fired back that I was a *gringa metiche* (nosy or meddlesome North American). And, indeed, when I heard her claim, I thought to myself that she was probably right.

This dispute highlights some of the power dimensions that underlay my complex relations with MEC and MEC participants. My connection to the North symbolized by my whiteness contributed to MEC organizers' feeling compelled to put up with the *joderera* (screwing around) of this gringa metiche. But MEC also mentioned me in funding proposals as well as reports, and I frequently appeared in MEC's photos used to document its activities.

My involvement with MEC represented an example of a larger, thorny dilemma for the organization. MEC's dependence on NGO funding meant that the organization and its leaders had a love/hate relationship with solidarity organizations and other funders and representatives from the North. Sara and the others constantly struggled with the need to court new funders and report to current ones, while not compromising MEC's autonomy and ability to create and structure programs and projects according to the needs of its participants. Although my role was perhaps unique in some ways, in other ways I was just another knot in the transnational web of individuals and organizations upon which MEC depends for its financial survival. I was a taker, a giver, and a linker. I had the opportunity to connect MEC with some organizations that resulted in the funding of specific projects; I wrote a number of grant proposals, some of which were successful.

Whereas in some areas, my relationship with MEC organizers was largely reciprocal, there were other areas in which the balance of power was tipped entirely in my favor. After all, I have exercised authority over the choice of how and when to use the words of MEC organizers and participants. The women of this study are represented through my editorial decisions, translations, and written descriptions of them.

The problems of hierarchy, exploitation, and the reproduction of colonial structures that can accompany the representation of "Third World" women by privileged First World academics is a contradiction that has been hotly contested, particularly by Third World feminists (Mohanty 1991; Trinh 1989; Ong 1988; Spivak 1988).[10] While some have experimented with different strategies of representation in order to de-center their own authority and re-center the experience and voice of research participants (Abu-Lughod 1993; Tsing 1993), others have questioned if feminist ethnography is even possible (Stacey 1991).

And yet it would be inaccurate to suggest that power flowed only one way in my relationship with the women of MEC. These women were not merely objects of my research, but active subjects who did exert quite a bit of control over me as an ethnographer and over my relationship with the organization. To complete this project I needed access to MEC activities, participants, and organizers, as MEC leaders were well aware. And I witnessed MEC leaders send one cooperante packing when they did not feel that she was sufficiently committed to their Movement.

On the other hand, I cannot claim that this book escapes the politics of representation and its accompanying contradictions. In this text, as I have noted, the women of MEC speak only through the filter of my interpretations. I can only offer the reader this one account, acknowledging that it is one story of many that could be told about this organization and these women. Indeed, like Nancy Scheper-Hughes (1992), as an ethnographer with close personal relationships with her "respondents," I have come to believe that not every story *should* be recounted, so this text inevitably generates new silences even as it dispels others. Using these women's words has been both an uncomfortable impropriety and a weighty responsibility. Before returning to the United States, I presented my preliminary findings to the organizers of MEC and left a copy of this document with the organization's Center for Documentation. I have worked to incorporate the comments and reactions of the women and when possible have consulted with organizers about my ideas.

The experience of working with and, indeed, becoming a member of MEC's *equipo de trabajo*, or working team, dramatically affected not only my perspective as a researcher, but as a feminist. I came to consciousness during the third wave of feminism in the United States when the movement was plagued by identity crises. And most of my engagement with the feminist movement had been in connection with academe. For me a movement in which feminists openly talked or wrote about "sisterhood" existed only in books and in what I perceived as the much outdated memories of activists from the 1970s. In my own experiences with the feminist movement in the United States (particularly the feminist movement within the academy), diversity was generally attributed all-important status, while unity was practically a taboo subject.

This is not to "flip over the tortilla," as they say in Nicaragua. I do not mean to call for a return to some notion of the "good old days" when we could all invoke an unreflective and naive idea of sisterhood. And yet, for white academic feminists in the United States who came to political consciousness in the mid- to late 1980s, the experience of the feminist movement has been a bit like being a film critic without ever having seen the movie (see Whittier 1995). As an activist and feminist used to the angst and hyperreflexive paralysis stemming from all things "post," it was powerful to be part of a collective that valued principles of "organized autonomy" and "unity in diversity." I also came to appreciate the power of the idea of unity and (dare I admit?) of sisterhood (organizers would often refer to each other and to me as either "sister" or "compañera"), or at least *compañerismo*—perhaps the single most important inheritance that the Sandinista revolution left to Nicaraguan oppositional movements.

I am not the first feminist from the North to appreciate the vitality of the feminist and women's movement(s) in Latin America (Chinchilla 1994; Sternbach et al. 1992; Miller 1991). There is an energy and creativity in these movements in Nicaragua that might seem surprising given the paucity of material resources available to such groups. For example, the level of discussion, the amount of time, and the degree of resourcefulness that accompanied decisions within the autonomous women's movement to create organizational forms that would reflect and coincide with principles of autonomy and diversity were impressive. And MEC's continual engagement with and incorporation of a base of poor working and unemployed women would put many feminist initiatives in any geographical context to shame.

The experience of working with MEC reoriented my thinking away from postmodernist concerns toward more materialist ones, from questions of identity to ones of political economy. And despite continued evidence that some forms of Marxist ideology and class-based oppositional practice exclude race and gender, constantly reinforced by the testimonies of the women of MEC, I gained a new appreciation for socialist ideals.

2 Oppositional Politics in Nicaragua and the Formation of MEC

The Front [FSLN] taught me to be very much in solidarity, very critical and responsible. . . . It taught us [all] to be revolutionaries in the integral sense of the word, not only like from our mouth outwards, but, let's say, revolutionary on the inside, right? . . . Look. [D]uring the revolution it didn't matter to us if we were men or women. But history taught us something very different. . . . Practice has taught us that the ones who have taken part in action are women. And the men have shone with a light that is not their own. . . . Before we used to say that in order to be a "revolutionary," one's sex didn't matter. Later, they told us the opposite. So, our consciousness was formed from the blows and the abuse and the battle that we suffered.—LOLA, regional MEC organizer, 1996

Nicaragua's is a long history of foreign occupation and invasion, class polarization, civil war, and social upheaval. In contrast to Honduras to the north and Costa Rica to the south, when the Spanish conquistadors arrived in what is now western Nicaragua, they encountered a substantial indigenous population, which they subdued and which became an exploited underclass.[1] This peasantry suffered under a cruel agro-export system that developed in the late 1800s and continued until the 1979 triumph of the Sandinista revolution. The rural poor often rose up in opposition to this exploitative system, and the history of Nicaragua is punctuated with peasant rebellions, among them the 1881 War of the Comuneros and the immortalized nationalist guerrilla struggle led by Augusto César Sandino in the 1920s and early 1930s (Walker 1997).

Foreign interference and national imperialism are recurrent themes in Nicaraguan history. After its independence from Spain, the United States and Great Britain struggled over control of the region. In the mid-1850s a filibusterer from the United States, William Walker, assisted the local Liberals in gaining power, but then quickly declared himself president. After his overthrow the United States became an increasingly formidable force, repeatedly involving itself in Nicaraguan affairs. In the early twentieth century the Taft administration, frustrated with the refusal of the Liberal dictator José Santos Zelaya to yield canal-building rights within the country's borders, orchestrated an uprising by the Conservative Party and then sent a military force to the Atlantic coast to support the rebels. In 1912 U.S. marines occupied the country to ensure that a rebellion against the Conservative Party, led by Benjamín Zeledón, would not succeed. This occupation continued more or less uninterrupted until the end of 1932, when Sandino's prolonged guerilla war forced the marines to withdraw from Nicaraguan shores. Two years later, Sandino was assassinated by the National Guard commanded by Anastasio (Tacho) Somoza García, who seized control of the state in 1936.

The Somoza dynasty lasted more than forty years. "Tacho" Somoza would rule until his assassination in 1956, at which point his eldest son, Luis Somoza Debayle, took control of the country. Next, Luis's younger brother, Anastasio (Tachito) Somoza Debayle, came to power in 1967 and ruled until the revolutionary Triumph of 1979. The Somozas' regimes were characterized by corruption, stemming from their control of the hated National Guard, which operated like a kind of mafia, taking bribes and demanding kickbacks. Co-optation of the national elites and kowtowing to the United States were also key elements of the dictatorships. The regime of the last Somoza, "Tachito," was the most brutal, and he used the National Guard to silence all opposition through disappearances and torture.

In 1979 Somoza was ousted in a revolution described by its vanguard as "popular, democratic, anti-imperialist, based on a political project of national unity and a mixed economy" (Harris and Vilas 1995). The Nicaraguan revolution captured the imagination and the dreams for a true democracy of internationally recognized activists, intellectuals, writers, and even celebrities.[2] It was the culmination of a long and tumultuous history of resistance to colonialism, imperialism, and dictatorship and was supported by a diverse blend of oppositional forces. These included various groups of the bourgeois opposition, trade unions and popular groups of peasants, students and urban barrio dwellers, unified only in their opposition to Somoza.

This chapter will explore the processes within Nicaraguan revolutionary politics that gave rise to the formation of the autonomous women's movement and to MEC. The rocky and contradictory relationship between the FSLN and women's "gender politics" (Dore 1997) goes back to the revolution and continues today. A majority of organizers of the autonomous women's movement came of political age within the FSLN, and many remain firm believers in the principles of the revolution. At the same time, however, the birth of the autonomous women's movement— of which MEC is an example—came about through a highly painful process of division, betrayal, and disillusionment. These complex processes reveal what is a fundamental paradox in Nicaraguan oppositional politics: for many participants in the revolution, particularly women, the FSLN was a source of self-determination and political empowerment, but ultimately also a constraining and even oppressive force in their lives as political actors.

THE SANDINISTA PERIOD

Founded in Honduras in 1961, the Frente de Liberación Nacional, later to adopt the name Frente Sandinista de Liberación Nacional in honor of Sandino, waged a rural guerrilla war throughout the interior in the 1960s. By the 1970s the Frente had begun to turn its attention to the Pacific region, particularly the departments of Carazo, Chinandega, León, and Managua, where they began to organize agricultural workers, as well as the urban masses, around a revolutionary, anti-dictatorial, and anti-imperialist agenda (Vilas 1986: 90–91). It was characterized by a Guevarist variant of Marxist-Leninist ideology, tinged with a radical Christian element (Lancaster 1992; Gonzalez 1990; Booth 1985). By 1978 when a series of popular uprisings occurred in the wake of the assassination of Pedro Joaquín Chamorro, a well-known member of the bourgeois opposition to Somoza and the editor of the national newspaper *La Prensa*, the FSLN assumed a vanguard role. On July 19, 1979, revolutionary forces overthrew Somoza, and a junta, dominated by the FSLN, took power. Ultimately, the FSLN gained full control over the state.

The new Sandinista government faced enormous challenges. It inherited a war-torn country and an economy in shambles. The insurrection had cost some five hundred thousand lives or about 2 percent of the population (Walker 1997: 7). Only $3.5 million remained in the government's coffers; its foreign debt of $1,600 per capita was the highest in all of Latin America (Sagall 1995: 119).

During the 1980s and 1990s Washington continued its policy of foreign intervention in Nicaraguan domestic affairs, ranging from the drastic full-scale assault of the Reagan years to the "low intensity" warfare of the first Bush administration. Viewing the 1979 Sandinista revolution as a victory of Soviet-backed communism, the newly elected Reagan administration imposed an economic blockade, which placed a stranglehold on the country's attempts at economic recovery. The administration also sponsored the contra war, supporting exiled military in a prolonged campaign to harass and destabilize the regime, causing further economic devastation as badly needed resources were funneled into military defense. Reagan's administration also mounted a massive anti-Sandinista propaganda campaign to discredit the government.

Under these conditions, with severe shortages of basic goods and food products, inflation soared. In response to U.S. pressure, the World Bank and the Inter-American Development Bank (IDB) cut off loans (Walker 1997: 9). Eventually, the Sandinista government was forced to discontinue many of its innovative social programs, such as its internationally recognized literacy campaign and public health and education programs (Spalding 1987). In a desperate effort to bring the country out of this deep crisis, the floundering Sandinista government imposed austerity measures, eliminating many consumer subsidies and laying off thousands from the public sector.

By the late 1980s, the impact of the trade embargo, the contra war, and the suspension of World Bank and IDB funding was staggering. The country's infrastructure sustained between $1.5 billion and $4 billion in losses (Conroy 1990). Skyrocketing inflation had caused wages to fall to 1950s levels, and a massive emigration of professionals and those merely seeking economic survival ensued (Economist Intelligence Unit 1989: 17). With casualties estimated at thirty thousand, the contra war left an emotionally scarred population whose faith in the revolutionary promise of the Sandinistas was shaken, not only by the economic crisis, but by indicators of FSLN corruption and by the obligatory military draft of young males (Isbester 2001: 97).

Some have attributed the "failure" of the FSLN to the corruption of its leaders, a rigid and hierarchical connection between the vanguard and its social base, or the lack of a true vision of socialist transition, as well as the party's ineptitude at addressing women's issues (see Hale 1994; Gonzalez 1990; and on women's issues, see Chinchilla 1990: 291). Other observers blame the trade embargo and U.S. aggression (see Hale 1994; Lancaster 1992). The Sandinistas ultimately lost at the polls in 1990, but this electoral failure defies the simplistic explanations often put forth in polarized political debates.

The Sandinista government faced enormous obstacles in its revolutionary project, to destroy "the ruling political system" and carry out socioeconomic transformation in favor of the interests of the majority (Nuñez 1986: 240). The party called on its supporters to defer immediate interests for the sake of the revolutionary project. In return "the people," who shaped this project and stood to benefit in the long term, were to be represented by mass organizations, which were structured to represent the interests of each sector of society. In the early years the six major organizations included the Sandinista Defense Committees (CDS), the July 19th Sandinista Youth (JS-19), the National Union of Farmers and Ranchers (UNAG), the Association of Rural Workers (ATC), the Association of Nicaraguan Women, "Luisa Amanda Espinoza" (AMNLAE), and the CST (Luciak 1995: 25).

These organizations were intended to serve as the primary mechanisms of popular empowerment and as the direct communication link between the Sandinista party and its social and political base (Vanden and Prevost 1993: 51). Representatives from these organizations were appointed to the Council of State, a national assembly that exercised legislative and policy-making power within the evolving governmental structure. Despite the participatory democratic aspects of the mass organizations, Leninist "vanguardism" was also discernable. Thus, when disagreements between the Sandinista party and popular sectors broke out, the vanguard, represented in the FSLN's National Directorate had the final word.[3]

In addition, participatory democracy within these mass organizations themselves was often limited, and in many cases there were conflicts between the base and leadership. In the case of the trade unions and AMNLAE, the Sandinista women's organization, many leaders took a hard line when faced with criticism or dissent in part because of the close ties between the leaders of these organizations and the party vanguard (Chinchilla 1994). Compliance with party demands often took precedence over democratic process (Polakoff and La Ramée 1997).

THE POST-SANDINISTA PERIOD

The Chamorro Administration. In 1990, in the second national elections since the revolution in 1979, voters rejected the Sandinistas and elected Violeta Chamorro, the widow of the assassinated Joaquín Chamorro and head of the opposition coalition UNO. The first Bush administration threw its weight behind this umbrella party and the subsequent government, which was made up of factions from almost all non-Sandinista political forces with the common agenda and objective to remove the Sandinistas from power. After the elections the U.S. government provided Nicaragua with a two-year $541 million package to support neoliberal reforms, including $25 million in political assistance that was channeled through the Agency for International Development (USAID) and the National Endowment for Democracy (NED) (Walker 1997: 31). USAID sent a team of advisers to the Chamorro transition team, and the U.S. government pumped money into programs to train National Assembly legislators, the electoral commission, judicial institutions, and the controller general. After 1992, bilateral U.S. aid was phased out, as Washington adopted a "trade not aid" policy. It was largely replaced by funding from international financial institutions (Robinson 2003: 78).

After the Chamorro government came to power, the country once again began receiving large amounts of foreign aid, amounting to 40 percent of the GDP between 1991 and 1992 and inserting Nicaragua ever more firmly within the global economy (Evans 1995: 192–93). In 1991 the government signed its first contingency agreement with the IMF and in 1994 signed a comprehensive three-year Enhanced Structural Adjustment Facility (ESAF), a special structural adjustment program (SAP), available to low-income countries. Designed on neoliberal lines by representatives of the World Bank and IMF, along with USAID officials, this program made all credits, disbursements, and debt restructuring contingent on compliance with strict conditions for the government's social and economic policies.

By 1992 structural adjustment lending made up some 30 percent of the country's loan portfolio, and the country's foreign debt stood at nearly $11 billion, one of the highest per capita debts in the world (Robinson 2003: 79; Metoyer 2000). Of the $1.2 billion in foreign aid (both bilateral and multilateral) to the country in 1991, over $500 million—or 43 percent—went for debt servicing. In 1992 Nicaragua paid $495 million in interest alone on its debt (Robinson 2003: 79). The country could, however, barely comply with the conditions of this aid and by 1995 was no longer receiving aid or "soft loans" due to noncompliance (Evans 1995: 192–93). The "global economic straitjacket" imposed on Nicaragua by foreign debt ensured the country's continued adherence to the neoliberal agenda of privatizing the national economy, restructuring the economy around exports, and promoting property ownership as determined by free market forces (Robinson 2003: 79).[4]

In order to meet SAP conditions and stabilize the economy, the Chamorro regime moved quickly to implement economic reforms and drastically cut public services, including health and education (Metoyer 2000; Evans 1995; Renzi and Agurto 1993). In 1991 the Chamorro administration implemented a "maxi-devaluation" of the córdoba in an attempt to bring down inflation. The regime eliminated remaining consumer subsidies and privatized 80 percent of state-owned enterprises (Babb 1996; Renzi and Agurto 1993: 38). Public spending dropped 37 percent, from an average of $70 per person in the last half of the 1980s to $44 in 1992 (Renzi and Agurto 1993: 34). Real wages in the country dropped 50 percent in the first year of the new government (Robinson 2003: 85).

To reduce state spending, the government laid off thousands of workers from the public sector. Between March of 1991 and March of 1992 a total of 22,561 workers left public employment (including positions in state-owned enterprises), entering the government's Plan of Occupational Conversion, funded by USAID. Through this program workers received at least one year's salary and in some cases small business loans in exchange for vacating their positions (Babb 1997; Evans 1995). For those remaining in state employment salaries were incrementally reduced. By 1993 the average salary of those employed by the state was 60 percent of its value in 1980 (Evans 1995: 221).

As expected, after the Chamorro administration implemented stabilization and adjustment measures, the contra war and U.S. trade embargo came to an end. The government's efforts to control inflation resulted in its dropping from levels of 1,300 percent to 12 percent. In the years from 1994 to 1996 the economy showed positive growth, reaching a level of 5.5 percent in 1996 with exports growing 10.1 percent between 1990 and 1996 (Neira 1997: 15).

Notwithstanding, as the Chamorro years progressed, conditions in Nicaragua remained grim. Inflation was brought under control, but unemployment was rampant. The end of the trade embargo meant that more goods were available, but the prices of the imports and the newly devalued national currency meant that they were unattainable except to the most elite sector of society. In 1996 the Ministry of Labor estimated open unemployment at 16.2 percent, and 51.4 percent if underemployment was taken into account (quoted in Economist Intelligence Unit 1997: 62). Reductions of the public sector meant that former state workers swelled the ranks of the informal workforce. And the microenterprises encouraged by the government's Occupation Conversion program faced a market flooded with small businesses. Nicaraguans would wryly compare their lives before and after the 1990 elections, "Before we all had money in our pockets, but there was nothing in the stores to buy; now the stores are filled, but no one has *un chelín* [twenty-five cent piece] to spend."

Although social conditions had deteriorated somewhat in the late 1980s because of the contra war, remaining social gains achieved during that decade suffered a dramatic reversal in the 1990s (Robinson 2003: 85–86). Infant mortality rose from 50 per 1,000 births in the 1980s to 83 per 1,000 in 1992. Diseases like cholera, malaria, and measles that had been nearly eradicated in the 1980s reappeared in the early 1990s and reached epidemic proportions (Andersson 1993: 12–13). The crime rate more than doubled between 1985 and 1995 (Close 1999: 94). Illiteracy rates, which over the course of the 1980 national literacy campaign had dropped from 50 percent to 13 percent (Ruchwarger 1987: 111), returned to original levels. In absolute numbers, in 1993 there were approximately half a million more illiterate Nicaraguans than in 1980 (cited in Prevost 1997b: 25). In 1996, the year of the country's first "free" and democratic elections, Nicaragua was the second poorest country in Latin America with 50.4 percent of its population living under conditions of poverty and able to meet only one half or less of the cost of the basic food basket (Neira 1997: 15).

The 1996 Elections and the Liberal Alliance under Alemán. The 1996 elections gave voters the opportunity to select the president, deputies for the National Assembly, mayors, vice-mayors, and municipal council members. For the first time, mayors would be elected directly, while deputies to the national and departmental assemblies and council members would be elected on a partisan ticket. The Supreme Electoral Council registered thirty-four political parties for the elections. Despite the existence of multiple parties with distinct platforms, the two majority candidates, Daniel Ortega for the FSLN and Arnoldo Alemán, the former mayor of Managua and the candidate for the Liberal Alliance Party, represented the same political polarization that had characterized the 1990 elections. Analysts argued that in the 1996 elections voters cast their ballot not so much *for*, but rather *against* a political party, as Ortega and Alemán ran on platforms of anti-somocismo and anti-sandinismo, "Nicaraguans' familiar demons" (Gorostiaga 1997).

Neither of them proposed a detailed plan for economic recovery. Alemán garnered popular appeal through an anti-Sandinista campaign. Though the campaign virtually ignored the fact that the FSLN had been out of power for seven years, it nevertheless tapped into popular fear and resentment surrounding the war-torn years under the Sandinistas. The Liberal Alliance flooded the television with images of Ortega, dressed in fatigues, reminding voters of the imposed military service of the 1980s. Both the Catholic Church and the United States threw their weight behind Alemán. The church hierarchy's support was so blatant that on the eve of the elections Alemán served as a lector at mass at the National Cathedral. Above all, Alemán promised employment, promising to create one hundred thousand jobs per year during his term (Barrios 1997: 10). His platform lacked a clear plan for bringing this about, although the images of women diligently working in the factories in the free trade zone, which appeared in his campaign television ads, provided a clue.

At the same time, former president Daniel Ortega reworked his political image to appear as the reborn father of the "people." Shedding his military fatigues and his kerchief of black and red (the colors of the revolutionary FSLN), he made public appearances sporting a white button-down shirt. Sandinista television and radio spots did their best to construct Alemán's Liberal Party as "Somocistas without Somoza," even juxtaposing images of the two men side by side. Despite Ortega's campaign slogan of "el gobierno de todos," (everyone's government), serious questions arose regarding his democratic legitimacy. The FSLN held a "popular consultation" in which Sandinistas and all other sympathizers were invited to vote in a primary election for presidential nominees to be submitted to the party's National Congress to be elected. Unfortunately, the primary elections were poorly organized and funded, with an overburdened electoral commission coordinating the efforts of inexperienced volunteers. And this effort to get back in touch with the social base was unsuccessful. For many in the party the primary election did little to dispel concerns about "an inertia in the national directorate" and the need for "a profound transformation in the [party's] leadership" (Vilma Núñez, quoted in Ampié 1996: 15).

The Sandinistas boasted more female candidates than any other party. After a heated debate at its National Congress, the party instituted a quota system, dubbed "the braid," for candidates to the national and departmental assemblies as well as the municipal elections. Separate lists of male and female candidates were compiled so that, depending on the number of votes received by the party, candidates would be alternately appointed from each list. Theoretically, this would ensure that equal numbers of men and women would be appointed to positions won by the party. Unfortunately, the party won few positions with sufficient votes for many women to gain office, and, despite the many female candidates, the number of women in the assemblies dropped slightly in 1996 (*Boletina* 1997c; Luciak 1997: 13).

Ortega's nomination by the party reflected long-standing questions about women's access to positions of power within the FSLN. His victory over Vilma Núñez, a woman with a long history of involvement in the revolution and the FSLN, was reminiscent of the 1991 rejection of the candidacy of former commander Dora María Téllez for election as the first female member of the party's National Directorate (Chinchilla 1994;

Randall 1994). In fact, a woman was not elected to the National Directorate until 1994, well after the FSLN's loss at the polls. By 1995 tensions were so strong within the FSLN, and divisiveness had reached such a degree, that several key figures, including Téllez, left the party (Prevost 1997a). In 1996 Téllez and former Vice President Sergio Ramírez ran for (and lost) seats on the National Assembly on the ticket of the Sandinista Reformist Party (MRS).

The election results were much contested, with accusations of fraud, destroyed ballots, and nonexistent voters. (Many candidates demanded a recount, which did produce some changes from the first results.) Alemán won the presidency with 904, 908 out of 1,865,833 votes, and the conservative Liberal Alliance gained the majority of seats in the National Assembly (Canales and Candia 1996: 1). The FSLN was the next largest political bloc in the Assembly. Daniel Ortega garnered approximately 38 percent of the valid votes cast (*La Prensa* 1996), and a scattering of seats were held by other parties. After one hundred days in office Alemán's promise of jobs, "change without violence" and respect for *el estado derecho* (a government that is accountable and abides by the law) were far from being realized. In a "sweep" of various state institutions, Alemán replaced, among others, the Controller of the National Budget, as well as the Minister of Education with his supporters. In addition, he proposed legislation that would virtually cripple municipalities' independent access to state funds as well as measures that would impose close state monitoring of all international NGO donors. In keeping with his party's right-wing orientation and close alliance with the hierarchy of the Catholic Church, his office dismantled the Nicaraguan Women's Institute (INIM), combining it with the Nicaraguan Fund for Children and the Family (FONIF) to form a Ministry of the Family (MIFAMILIA). Finally, the straw that broke the camel's back, in the continued effort to resolve the property disputes that involved 12 percent of the country's territory, the government began mass displacements of peasants, small farmers, and urban dwellers (Nitlapán-Envío Team 1997b).

In April of 1997 a mass uprising of peasants and small and medium producers resulted in a national strike. As the major opposition force, Daniel Ortega and the FSLN once again became the vanguard of this popular discontent. Protesters sealed off all highways connecting Managua to the rest of the country. Soon other sectors joined the work stoppage, finally prompting the government to cease plans for further dislocations and to negotiate with Ortega and a group of peasants and small producers.

This was only the beginning of Alemán's rocky term as president. Though the promotion of "estado derecho" was a major component of Alemán's political campaign, the president's popularity flagged in the late 1990s as accusations of rampant and flagrant corruption emerged. Reminiscent for many Nicaraguans of the last Somoza's regime, these accusations came on the heels of a natural disaster—not an earthquake, as had hit in 1972, but rather Hurricane Mitch in late October of 1998, which left not only physical ruin in its wake but also a heavily damaged economy, especially in the already impoverished Northern region.

During Alemán's presidency, the comptroller, Agustin Jarquín, uncovered financial irregularities in the Central Bank amounting to $500 million. More serious accusations focused on Alemán himself. In 1999 the office of the comptroller exposed rampant misuse of funds, suggesting that Alemán personally skimmed money from state services and then used the capital to purchase property from farmers impoverished by Hurricane Mitch. In 1999 Alemán's annual budget included $130 million (20 percent of the total budget) that was allocated to the Central Bank and the president for discretionary use. Jarquín also disclosed major irregularities surrounding the sale of the state-owned Nicaraguan Bank of Industry and Commerce (BANIC). The Alemán family had received what amounted to kickbacks from a Florida-based bank for the sale of 51 percent of the state-owned bank's shares (Isbester 2001: 200–201).

After the 2001 election of former Vice President Enrique Bolaños, further and even more outrageous examples of Alemán's corruption came to public light. The president had traveled to India, Egypt, and Paris and paid thousands of dollars for "entertainment" using a government-paid American Express card. The bill for this lavish personal spending amounted to $1.8 million (Sullivan 2002). Because he still served as the president of the National Assembly, Alemán enjoyed immunity from legal prosecution. In 2002 after the continuing demands of President Bolaños and a national and international outcry, Alemán was eventually put under house arrest. Later, he was tried and convicted of having stolen $100

million and was sentenced to prison, though the sentence was later soft-
ened into house arrest after pressure from Liberal party loyalists (Kampwirth 2003: 14).

Gender and Privatization. Many studies have shown how neoliberalism
and structural adjustment programs have a particularly adverse effect on
women, especially poor and working-class women, given their traditional and, indeed, cross-cultural role as primary caregivers for family
and household (see Bose and Acosta-Belen 1995; Safa 1994; Benería and
Feldman 1992). Nicaraguan women have borne the brunt of the dramatic
reduction in public spending, and with the erosion of social safety nets
like food subsidies and public healthcare the burden of household survival shifts to women. Poorly funded public services like sanitation and
potable water have meant that women must walk long distances to dis-
pose of waste, wash clothes, and carry drinking water (Metoyer 2000;
Babb 1997; Pérez-Alemàn 1992). Since saps have been implemented in
Nicaragua, poor women increasingly have had to engage in the cash
(often informal) economy, while still meeting their daily household and
caretaker responsibilities (Metoyer 2000).

Privatization has further had harsh consequences for Nicaraguan
women, as reductions in the public sector launched many female government employees into the informal sector (Babb 2001: 115). Between 1993
and 1994 64 percent of women who made up part of the urban economically active population were engaged in activities in the informal sector,
such as paid domestic work and street vending (Banco Central de Nicaragua 1995: 5).

The entrance of women into the formal labor force has also increased
dramatically in Nicaragua, jumping from 25 percent of the economically
active population in 1990 to 47 percent in 2000 (Robinson 2003: 290).
This increase is part of a global phenomenon of the feminization of the
labor force. In Nicaragua, as elsewhere in Latin America, women's continuing entrance into the formal labor market occurs in the context of a
decline in male employment and real wages, increasing women's relative
importance as wage earners. Increased labor market activity for women is
especially prominent in maquila production, where the drive to keep

labor costs low fuels transnational capital's predilection for hiring supposedly "docile" young women.

The Free Trade Zone. In the 1980s women made up 70 percent of the textile workers employed in state-owned factories, mainly in the areas of sewing machine operators and maintenance (Pérez Alemán et al., 1987: 5–7).[5] After the electoral defeat of the Sandinistas in 1990, the state-owned textile industry was liquidated as part of the Chamorro regime's political and economic development strategy. (See below for a discussion of this process.) The closure of these textile factories eliminated 85 percent of the jobs in the sector, launching some ten thousand workers, the majority of whom were women, into unemployment (CENIDH 1996: 53; Renzi and Agurto 1993: 41). This once unionized, largely female workforce was dislocated when these plants closed, providing a trained and desperate labor pool when transnational assembly factories set up production in the newly opened and nationally owned Free Trade Zone (Renzi 1996).

As noted above, factory owners also targeted young women for hiring, and in the 1990s one frequently saw newspaper advertisements seeking women workers between the ages of sixteen and twenty. Though the composition of the free trade zones' labor force shifts rapidly, statistics put the percentage of women workers as fluctuating between 80 and 90 percent (ILO 1996; MEC 1996). A study by the International Labor Organization indicates that in 1995, 57 percent of the workers in the zone were between fifteen and twenty-five years of age, and 66 percent of the persons interviewed for this study indicated that they had more than three dependents (ILO 1996: 283, 284).

As in export-processing industries all over the developing world, conditions in Nicaragua's FTZS are harsh, and workers face injustices on a daily basis. Sexual harassment and shop-floor violence have also been major concerns. MEC organizers have encountered several reported cases of women workers being fired for refusing to grant sexual favors to their supervisors. Pregnancy and child care also pose difficulties for women workers, who are often fired if they become pregnant or if they miss work in order to care for children who have fallen ill.

For example, at the time of my research, Isabel, a twenty-four year-old single mother of two and a MEC promotora (a worker who receives extra training and serves as a liaison within her factory between workers and MEC) lived in a barrio along with her mother and her grandmother in the northern part of the city along the Carretera Norte (Northern Highway) and was the sole breadwinner in the household. Isabel's toddler son had a neurological disorder. In order to take her son to see a specialist, she had to ask for permission to miss work and lose a day of pay. Her employer deducted a total of C$170 (US$20.14) for the day for estimated lost production (even though Isabel would make less than this amount on a typical workday). Social security did not cover medical care from specialists, so Isabel had to pay for the appointment as well as transportation to and from the doctor's office.

Workers complained of long days (10–15 hours) and few breaks (MEC 1997c: 8). For example, Isabel worked from 7:00 A.M. until 5:15 P.M. with a forty minute break for the midday meal. Her job entailed numbering pieces of material that were then sent to the sewing lines to be assembled. She also attached tickets to each piece of fabric with the size and model number of the garment. Isabel's wages were calculated according to the number of pieces of fabric that she and her co-workers at her work station cut and numbered. For this reason, she often rushed through her lunch in the "green cafeterias" (the workers' name for the yard which was the only space available to many of them to sit and eat their meal) in order to get back to her station and continue work.

Some workers stored homemade food in lockers, but many made purchases from street vendors who gathered at midday outside the chain-link fence and passed banana leaves full of rice and beans or other typical Nicaraguan dishes like *baho* (steamed meat, plantains, and yucca), and plastic bags full of juices or soft drinks through the holes in the fence. Workers complained of the meager quantity and poor quality of this food, as street vendors took advantage of their hold on the market. In some rare instances workers reported that during times of mandatory (often unpaid) overtime, management might provide food for the evening meal. The portions of these meals were small and often consisted of merely a *pico* (sweet roll) and a bag of cola or *tajadas con queso* (fried plantains and cheese).[6] Though a few factories had dining areas for worker use, the majority did not. Thus, for their midday breaks, Isabel and her co-workers had to sit under the blazing Managua sun in the summer or gather under the edges of rooftops during torrential downpours in the rainy season.

Workers contended with unfair pay practices and often experienced forced or unpaid overtime. In fact, they found it very difficult to determine if they were being paid fairly. Overtime hours as well as production quotas and incentives were often calculated incorrectly, leaving workers short-changed. In addition, pay stubs were often printed in English or Chinese, the languages of the factory owners, making them nearly impossible for workers to decipher.

Workers experienced health problems ranging from arthritis to respiratory disorders from the abundance of dust. If they took ill at work, workers at the nationally owned FTZ could visit the small, poorly staffed clinic. However, visits to this tiny facility came at a cost, a considerable deduction (in some reported cases C$50 or US$5.92) from workers' wages. Workers also complained bitterly about the poor service in this clinic. Bertha, a worker and active participant in MEC, noted angrily: "They give the same pills to everyone. It seems like we all must have the same illness. They give everyone acetaminophen . . . and send them back to work!"

Although pay in the maquilas was higher than most of the few available employment options, there was still a disparity between the basic cost of living and the average wage for a worker in the Free Trade Zone (Renzi 1996).[7] In 1997 the estimated cost to meet basic needs for a family of six was calculated as US$162 a month(Witness for Peace 1997), while a 1999 diagnostic study completed by MEC found most workers' basic monthly wage (before bonuses or production-based wages) to range between C$251 and C$750 (US$30–89) per month (MEC 1999).

Facing this disparity, in addition to the "second shift" that women workers complete in their home, maquila employees often worked a "triple shift," supplementing their wages with economic activity in the informal sector (Ward and Pyle 1995). Some sold homemade fruit juices and other drinks and food items from their homes in the evenings and on weekends. One rather ingenious entrepreneur used a loan from MEC's microcredit program to travel north to Honduras and purchase cheap household goods and clothing which she then sold at the teeming outdoor market that appears outside the FTZ every evening at quitting time and is especially busy on payday.

The complex history of relations between the FSLN and organized labor helps explain MEC's formation as well as the rise of an autonomous women's movement. Women gained important organizing experience from the Sandinista women's mass organization, AMNLAE, and from other Sandinista organizations, such as the union federations of the CST. At the same time internal contradictions within AMNLAE and divisions and disagreements between union federations and the FSLN party leadership created conditions that prompted women to establish autonomous organizations (Quandt 1993; see also Ewig 1999: 81).

During the revolution, the FSLN mobilized the mainly rural sectors of peasants through the ATC and the urban poor through the Sandinista Defense Committees (CDS) and Christian base communities. When the Sandinistas took power, the working-class movement was dominated by the Communist Party, which had its own organizing traditions and social base. Unionization was limited: according to the Ministry of Labor, when the Sandinistas came to power in 1979, only 12–13 percent of the wage-earning population belonged to unions (cited in Vilas 1986). The first years of the Sandinista era then saw dramatic increases in unionization. By 1983, Carlos Vilas (1986) estimated that between 41 and 43 percent of the economically active population was unionized.

Although the Sandinistas were influenced by Marxist-Leninism, their ideology was also strongly nationalistic and anti-imperialist. And, despite the class-based rhetoric of many of the speeches of Sandinista leaders, the FSLN did not advocate a completely nationalized economy. Rather, their objectives were to establish a mixed economy and maintain national unity. The patriotic bourgeoisie and middle classes who supported the revolution would have a role to play in this "new society," cooperating with workers and peasants to reactivate the economy after the defeat of the dictatorship. And, although all of Somoza's properties and enterprises were nationalized, including the banking system, passing on a production potential of about one quarter of the GDP to the Sandinista-controlled state, the new government needed the support of the broad coalition that had brought down Somoza in order to rebuild the economy. Thus, after the triumph some sectors of the economy remained largely private—in fact, nearly 60 percent of the GDP in 1980 was generated by private businesses. For example, in 1980 although 99 percent of the mining sector's share in the GDP was publicly owned, 75 percent of the industrial sector's share in the GDP was in private hands, as was 81 percent of the agricultural sector (Dijkstra 1992: 72–77).

Shortly after taking power the Sandinista government reorganized the urban trade unions by founding the mass organization, the Sandinista Workers' Central (CST). This confederation, whose leadership was appointed by the FSLN, was charged with organizing and supervising production and quickly dominated the labor movement, squeezing out other unions. In 1980, 369 of the 457 urban unions were affiliated with the CST (Pérez-Stable 1982). Close relationships between the CST and the Sandinista Front and the appointment of CST leaders by the state meant that the union's and party's directives were virtually one and the same. In the context of the contra war and trade embargo called by the United States in 1985, union federation leaders were charged with ensuring worker support for austerity measures adopted by the FSLN (measures that even Daniel Ortega called "an IMF program without the IMF"), which translated into the sharp decline of wages as well as layoffs of close to thirty thousand workers from the public sector (O'Kane 1995; quotation on 185).

As the production arm of the state, the CST's role was to support the state and, later, to support the civil side of the war against the Contras. This brought national defense to the workplace, as the union federations formed militias to defend the centers of production against enemy attack. Though wages continued to drop throughout the 1980s (indeed, by the late 1980s many textile workers were not even receiving wages in the form of cash but were being paid with provisions), the government's plan was to compensate workers through the development of social services and increased participation in production decisions (see Gonzalez 1990).

The FSLN showed little tolerance for nonparty unions, frequently jailing their leaders. The CST openly engaged in confrontations with competing unions on the left and right, particularly when strikes occurred. And CST members were known to ransack the offices of other unions in an effort to maintain Sandinista hegemony in the labor movement. Indeed, the Sandinista government approved legislation that allowed legal status for only one majority union per workplace (O'Kane 1995).

With the election of the neoliberal Chamorro regime, the CST was forced to change dramatically. Most significantly, financial support from the state was cut. During the Sandinista regime, unions had received money from a tax administered by the Ministry of Finance which was deducted automatically from workers' wages. The Chamorro government was openly anti-labor, and one of its first moves was to eliminate this quota. Suddenly, the federations had to finance themselves independently. The gap that had developed between CST leadership and its social base was reflected in the wave of workers who left the Sandinista federations.

Shortly after the Chamorro government came to power, the Sandinista labor movement consolidated its federations into an umbrella organization called the National Workers Front (FNT). The general secretary of the CST, Lucio Jiménez, was elected as the coordinator of this new organization, the membership of which included all Sandinista labor organizations. In July of 1990, in reaction to the government's austerity measures, the union federations of the FNT, led by the CST and backed by the Sandinista party, launched a nationwide general strike. Violence broke out throughout the country as police and workers clashed. Transportation of goods and people came to a halt, and water and electricity services were disrupted. Managua was paralyzed, as workers barricaded all major highways leading to the city.

Finally the government announced it would negotiate with the unions, although in fact secret negotiations had already begun between the FSLN and the UNO coalition. Tripartite negotiations began between unions, the government, and the business sector over how to resolve such issues as property rights and wages (O'Kane 1995). These negotiations represented just a part of what would become an ongoing dialogue about the state's social contract, known as *concertación*. Talks would continue through the 1990s as the government, members of the private sector, and different representatives of the FSLN (including key members of the CST leadership) battled to hammer out the conditions of privatization as well as other issues.

In the negotiations, FNT members (including those representing the

CST) slowly began to assert autonomy from the Sandinista party and to negotiate according to their own interests. As negotiations continued, the CST reluctantly agreed to the privatization of certain industrial factories, retaining 25 percent of the shares for workers' ownership in each business. By the middle of 1992, however, the CST leaders changed their strategy, concentrating on obtaining majority worker ownership of shares in sixty-six factories, rather than pursuing minority ownership in all businesses that were to be privatized. Workers in some factories ended up with no shares, and in some factories (such as a number of the sugar refineries) a group of CST leaders acquired a controlling number of shares. This change in strategy was made without consulting the union's base, and sections of the rank and file accused leaders of taking advantage of the negotiations to benefit personally by acquiring private shares in various businesses (Evans, 1995:248; *Barricada,* 1994a, 1994b). In the words of one former federation member, during the course of the privatization negotiations "everyone began to reveal his own 'me.'"

The personal appropriation by Sandinista leaders of state property was known as *la Piñata*, and it contributed to the emergence of a new Sandinista elite who began to merge with the bourgeoisie as landlords and business owners (Robinson 2003: 84). Many of the federations that made up the CST publicly opposed the leadership's personal acquisitions in the scramble to gain ownership of what had been state-owned and worker-controlled enterprises. Certain federation leaders and the national leadership of the CST came under scrutiny and were accused of selling out by many dissident federations. Lola, a former leader of the women's secretariat of Granada, expresses the feelings of betrayal of many federation members at that time: "We hadn't put them there to become businessmen. We brought them as leaders. . . . What happened? One poor leader of workers becomes a businessman—a capitalist. Now they don't think like poor people or like a leader. They are thinking like a businessman. But, for us, this leader is useless, because he is gaining for his own interests, not for the interests of the workers. . . . And for this reason, we as a regional federation decided that we weren't in agreement with the national CST and that we were behind other people."

FNT and CST leaders became the object of further accusations when negotiators conceded the liquidation of the entire state-owned textile industry as well as the approval of legislation to create the state-owned

Free Trade Zone. Though one cannot discount the vulnerable position of the negotiators as well as the pressure from the Sandinista party to reach an agreement, to many members of the labor movement's social base, this was yet another instance of betrayal by the CST.

Between 1991 and 1992 the Chamorro government passed a series of laws establishing the creation of free trade zones. Further legislation offered substantial benefits to attract foreign investments, exempting businesses from import and export duties as well as income, city, and county taxes.[8] The Free Trade Zone "Las Mercedes," which is located on Managua's Northern Highway and constitutes an area of 80,652 square meters, was first established by the Somoza government in 1976. At that time eleven U.S. plants (mostly textile producing) set up operations within it, producing exclusively for a U.S. market. These factories' presence was, however, short-lived; as the country's political unrest increased, the producers relocated (ILO 1996).

When the Chamorro regime took over, the free trade zone was opened once more to foreign investors. Reflecting changes in international production schemes, Asian investors as well as U.S.-owned factories set up production in the zone. By 1997 U.S. companies owned five of the eighteen factories in operation; Taiwanese companies owned five; one was Italian, one was Hong Kong–owned, three were Nicaraguan, and three were South Korean–owned (*Barricada* 1997a). The state-owned zone is administered by the Corporation of Free Trade Zones, which is run by a directing council made up of the Minister of Economy and Development, the Minister of Finance, the president of the Central Bank of Nicaragua, the Minister of Construction and Transport and his/her delegates (ILO 1996: 288). In 1995, 80 percent of the products from the zone were destined for the U.S. market (Zuñiga 1995). By 2000 this percentage had increased to 87 percent (*Observador Económico* 2002: 3). Production in the zone grew at a rapid rate, from $2.9 million (1.3 percent of national exports) in 1992 to $124.2 million (or 20.6 percent of national exports) in 1996 (*Barricada* 1997a; Renzi 1996: 39).[9]

In 1997, five years after the zone's creation, the CST began organizational efforts with the workers of the free trade zone. The Textile and Apparel Workers Federation of the CST was able to establish legal union presence in two factories. The Confederation of Syndical Action and Unity (CAUS) was also able to establish a presence in one factory, and the independent Central de Trabajadores Nicaragüenses formed unions in three other factories during 1997 and 1998. By 1999 seven CST-affiliated unions were registered with the ministry of labor (MITRAB). Though its base was extremely small within the zone (it had no more than 286 registered affiliates in any factory), the CST used its long-standing relations of international solidarity to launch an international campaign denouncing labor conditions in the FTZ. Despite these efforts, unions in maquila factories have faced a tentative existence, and unionization remains relatively low, with only seven unions registered with MITRAB between 2001 and 2002 (Bellman 2003: 2, 13).

THE WOMEN'S MOVEMENT IN NICARAGUA

The history of gender-based oppositional politics in Nicaragua is closely tied to the FSLN party and to its mass organizations. During the revolution the FSLN organized women to form the Association of Women Confronting the National Problem (AMPRONAC). This organization's revolutionary origins were hidden. Women organized as wives and mothers to protest human rights abuses by the dictatorship (Isbester 2001: 30–38; Criquillon 1995; Murguialday 1990). AMPRONAC represented a first step in articulating demands based on women's issues, "giving a revolutionary perspective to the organized struggle of women" (Criquillon 1995: 211). Many AMPRONAC members also served as FSLN collaborators and lost their lives supporting the revolution. In the early 1970s increasing numbers of poor and bourgeois women became *guerrilleras*, combatants in the armed struggle. Following the triumph AMPRONAC was renamed the Association of Nicaraguan Women, "Luisa Amanda Espinoza"(AMNLAE), after the first female member to die in combat. Its early members were urban women, many of whom were professionals and the mothers of combatants. During the first years of the revolutionary government, AMNLAE gradually incorporated more and more working-class and peasant women into its ranks.

In its early years AMNLAE experimented with different organizational models. In 1981 organizers adopted a strategy whereby, instead of operating solely as a separate organization, members would work within other mass organizations in order to facilitate women's overcoming obstacles that prevented their full participation in the revolution (Criquillón 1995: 213). By 1982, however, as the contra war escalated and the trade embargo took hold, the FSLN assigned AMNLAE specific roles according to national priorities. Under a directive from the party leadership AMNLAE worked particularly to mobilize material and moral support for the mothers of combatants (Randall 1992: 46).

As time wore on, the leaders of AMNLAE were no longer willing to passively accept the priorities defined by the male party leadership. At times, individual female leaders made valiant efforts to articulate needs and demands based on the particularities of women's experiences. In addition, as the organization matured, its members began a slow process of establishing their own democratically determined political agenda. One of the first instances of disagreement between AMNLAE and the FSLN came after the Sandinistas, in response to the escalated contra war, instituted a compulsory military draft. AMNLAE representatives argued for the inclusion of women in the draft, but the FSLN refused, stating that, because of the lack of social services, women were needed to stay at home and care for their children (Randall 1992: 46).

This instance was the first in a series of disagreements. AMNLAE gradually began formulating its own agenda based on the needs and interests of grassroots women. By the mid-1980s efforts aimed at articulating "gender claims" (Alvarez 1990) within the mass organizations of the FSLN began to bear fruit. In 1986 the first women's secretariat formed in the Association of Rural Workers (ATC) to facilitate women's participation in a democratic union. As the former ATC leader Ana Criquillón explains, "It was not a question of women gaining a place within a union, nor of incorporating the demands of women into the list of things the union sought. Rather, it was a question of transforming how the union operated, of developing a different concept of union work" (1995: 217). Subsequently, women's secretariats or sections formed within other mass organizations, such as the National Confederation of Professionals (CONAPRO), UNAG, and in 1989 the CST (Saakes 1991: 170).

Inspired by the success of the women's secretariats, AMNLAE renewed its effort to return to its grassroots. It held a series of town meetings to hear women's concerns and demands and held forums as part of the preparation for negotiations for the creation of Nicaragua's constitution and for AMNLAE's second national assembly (Isbester 2001: 76–77). At these meetings, in which forty thousand women took part, the lack of contact between AMNLAE leaders and women at the base came sharply into focus, as women expressed their demands and critiques, highlighting a gap between women's expectations of AMNLAE (and the FSLN) and the organization's offerings. Participants raised important issues that needed to be addressed beyond work in support of the war. Among these were discrimination in the workplace, access to birth control, women's unpaid labor, and domestic violence (Isbester 2001: 77; Criquillón 1995: 218; Randall 1992: 47). AMNLAE's renewed contact with the grassroots prompted the organization to seek a new identity based more squarely on women's demands and perspectives.

In 1987 at AMNLAE's second national assembly, the organization launched an internal political process for the democratic election of a new national assembly and leadership committee. This process marked a sharp contrast with the organization's history, in which the FSLN had always appointed the national leadership. Women from the various sectors within AMNLAE once again came together in a heated discussion about their needs and how they should be reflected in the organization's agenda.

AMNLAE's increasingly independent activities drew attention and at times at least verbal support from the FSLN leadership. For example, in 1986 and 1987 Daniel Ortega and Bayardo Arce both made specific mention of sexism and discrimination against women in public speeches. Even as early as 1982 Commander Tomás Borge delivered a famous address to a national assembly of AMNLAE, declaring, "We must guarantee in daily practice full equality between the sexes" (quoted in Criquillón 1995: 217).

Nevertheless, efforts by the leaders of AMNLAE to implement a more feminist agenda were frequently met with blatant opposition from leaders of the mass organizations and the FSLN's national directorate. Many male leaders considered such demands to be secondary to the party's immediate priorities of production, the contra war, and, later, the electoral campaign of 1990. One former AMNLAE leader remembers her efforts to "sensitize the men [within the mass organizations] so that they would understand our work. And what we encountered there were ramparts of contention, walls of contention. . . . We brought the great work plans with the concerns and suggestions of the women, and when we arrived at the committee, . . . they would say: 'This cannot be! You are crazy! When are you going to do this?! . . . This is not a priority. We'll do this after the war ends.' "

To the surprise of many members, in 1989 the FSLN abruptly put an end to AMNLAE's democratic process and removed the organization's national leadership. The party appointed Commander Doris Tijerino, previously the national chief of police, to be the next secretary general of AMNLAE and Commander Mónica Baltodano and three other party members to leadership roles. Tijerino and Baltodano had long histories in the FSLN and were well-known combatants in the revolution, but they also held more traditional views regarding AMNLAE's relationship to the party and were known to be quite critical of feminism (Randall 1994). At the same time, the FSLN canceled the Latin American and Caribbean Feminist Meeting, which had been planned for later that year. This coup on the part of the FSLN leadership, which occurred just before the electoral defeat of the Sandinistas in 1990, set the stage for the emergence of an independent women's movement in Nicaragua (Criquillón 1995: 224; Randall 1992: 52).

In 1992 a number of women's collectives and centers, NGOs, theater and arts groups, and independent feminists gathered together to hold a landmark event, signaling the first public expression of an autonomous women's movement. Organized as an alternative to AMNLAE's national congress, the "Festival of 52 Percent" was held in Managua's central fairgrounds on International Women's Day. The groups in attendance, the majority of which had emerged from Sandinista organizations, asserted their independence from all political parties and other "mixed" organizations. In this manner, participants in the emerging autonomous women's movement "clearly staked their ground and claimed a new social space in which to build a movement" (Babb 1997: 59), insisting that "internal democracy and autonomy vis-à-vis the FSLN were essential" (Criquillon 1995: 228).

The 1992 gathering created a momentum that led to organizational plans for a national conference to be held the following January in Managua. Eight hundred women took part in the Nicaraguan Women's Conference "Diverse but United." Initially, the organizing committee for the conference consisted of a number of autonomous groups, centers, and organizations, but the committee made itself open to participation by individual women who later joined its ranks. Indeed, any woman could attend the conference as an individual, and participants did not have to be representatives from any particular group or organization. Diversity marked the participation in the conference and its workshops, with urban activists working alongside *campesina* women (Babb 1997; Criquillon 1995).

The event was also marked by controversy and heated debate. One of the main issues discussed was the meaning of autonomy. Many at the conference rejected all proposals to form a coordinating organization for the new movement. Those holding this position were wary of going down the road taken by AMNLAE (and, some even maintained, that taken by the women's secretariats) of assuming the role of a vanguard organization. Others recognized the legitimacy of the fear of reproducing the vanguard, but were concerned that without a coordinating organization the new movement would flounder (Kampwirth 2000; Criquillón 1995).

The conference had far-reaching implications. In addition to collectively generated assessments of the situation facing women in the country and concrete proposals for action, a series of networks were formed to address specific issues. Two of these networks, the Network of Women Against Violence (which became the Network of Women Against Violence Against Women and Children in the mid-1990s) and the Women's Health Network are still in existence and have taken an active role in waging widespread media and public-awareness campaigns.

Thus, in the early 1990s, a triangle of women's groups emerged from a complex tangle of political alliances, cleavages, and disagreements— autonomous women's organizations (many of which identified as feminist), the women's secretariats of the mass organizations (including trade union federations), and AMNLAE (Kampwirth 2000).[10] AMNLAE was particularly resistant to moving toward autonomy from the FSLN. The women's secretariats of the mass organizations were stuck in the middle, not willing to ally completely either with AMNLAE or with the autonomous organizations, which increasingly rejected political ties to the Sandinista party.[11]

Characterized by one scholar as a hybrid result of "internal party insurgency and identity-based social movement organization," the women's secretariats also differed from the autonomous women's organizations in their priorities (Isbester 2001: 101). As the economic crisis progressed, the women's secretariats addressed issues arising from privatization and structural adjustment and were less aligned with many of the concerns of the autonomous organizations, such as reproductive rights and access to abortion (Criquillon 1995).

As the autonomous women's movement grew, it became largely dominated by independent feminist NGOs, run by urban professional women. International agencies, foreign governments, foundations, and Northern-based NGOs provided crucial financial resources and seed money for the creation of women's centers and independent organizations that offered services to women in grassroots communities. As globalization intensified, transnational feminist networks increasingly played an important role in strengthening the Nicaraguan autonomous women's movement (Ewig 1999).

THE WOMEN'S SECRETARIATS

The creation of women's secretariats in the CST and trade union federations opened a space for women to articulate gender-based demands within the labor movement. But as Sara Rodríguez, who in 1989 was named the first director of the CST's National Women's Secretariat, noted in a 1994 interview: "The machismo inside our union structures isn't any different from that in the rest of our society. It is no different. They [male leaders] are immersed in a world in which power is concentrated in the hands of men, and they are accustomed to making all of the decisions." Despite the formation of this space, then, women leaders in the labor movement met with great resistance within both the party and labor movement. As a former union federation leader and regional MEC organizer recalls, "either they would strip us of our militancy or they would call us political 'deviants' or 'counter-revolutionaries.' "

This "power struggle," as MEC organizers often refer to it, had its roots in a long-term effort on the part of women union members to promote and strengthen women's leadership within the labor movement and specifically in the CST. Before 1990, not a single woman had been elected to the CST's national executive. In 1992, after a concerted effort by the women of the Secretariat, five women delegates from the various regional federations were elected to the seventeen-member national executive. This new leadership worked to promote and develop projects and programs that reflected women's experiences as workers. Regional women's secretariats were established in various departments in the country, and each union federation within the CST elected its own representative to each regional secretariat.

The Secretariat's articulation of "gender claims" or interests—what the women of MEC would later term a "gender perspective"—did not arise a priori from the fact that those who held leadership positions were women.[12] Looking back, former Secretariat leaders describe a process of developing their own approaches. Sara reflects:

> I am one of the founders of the Sandinista Workers' Central. I came out of a local with the idea of contributing to this organization. I have always been in the Central. And we didn't understand the work of the women [of AMNLAE] either—we were like any other male union leader, emphasizing the strike, moving the people to the military organizations, the production of brigades, mobilizing women, mobilizing men. . . . Women leaders have always existed in the Central . . . women who worked for the organization but without any gender consciousness. We were motivated only by class consciousness. . . . We began to work to incorporate gender into the class struggle. . . . We began to discuss gender with some fear and often clandestinely. Perhaps . . . with fear that the space that we had opened would be closed.

MEC leaders attribute the development of this gender consciousness to their conscientious listening to the women at the grassroots, a connection that former Secretariat leaders recall with pride:

> We began with a discussion with the women from the base to hear what they had to say, hear their demands, know what they wanted, and from there we began. . . . After being a leader like any other man, in order to have a consciousness of what we were going to do, we had to first appropriate the suggestions of the women, make

them ours, revise them as women, wake up our own consciousness too, because we did not have it. . . . So we worked with the base for three years—constant communication with the women at this level.

Out of these discussions with women at the base, at national and regional meetings, the CST's National Women's Secretariat developed projects that its leaders believed reflected the needs of their women constituencies in the political and economic context of Nicaragua in the early 1990's.

The Secretariat quickly saw the need to address the impact of structural adjustment and neoliberal policies on women, who were struggling to meet the survival needs of their families. In response to the privatization of state-owned enterprises and the health system that the neoliberal Chamorro regime set into motion, the national and regional women's secretariats established women's clinics that were open to those who could not afford the services at private clinics and hospitals. Privatization also involved the systematic dismantling of public child care or CDIS (Child Development Centers). These government cutbacks profoundly affected women workers, and the Secretariat established several free or subsidized child-care centers.

Not surprisingly, women in poor communities also wanted to find ways to earn more money for their households. The women's secretariats developed projects to provide women with job training in nontraditional areas such as welding, masonry, and auto mechanics. European NGOs, like the OXFAM family, and Canadian organizations, like CoDevelopment Canada, as well as labor groups in both Canada and Europe, funded these initiatives and a program to provide women with loans for women's collectives that would establish microenterprises in their communities.[13]

Finally, the secretariats initiated efforts to organize two growing sectors of labor in the post-Sandinista context—domestic workers and maquila workers. The domestic workers succeeded in forming a legally recognized union named the Domestic Workers' Union, "Rigoberta Menchú," which had a desk in the National Women's Secretariat's office in Managua.[14] They were also successful in achieving legal recognition of December 10 as the National Day of the Domestic Workers, a holiday when all domestic workers were to be given the day off.[15] The National Women's Secretariat also began to organize workshops for women workers in the Free Trade Zone. By 1994 the women's secretariats within the CST had established several active and successful programs in Managua as well as in several other departments in the country, including Chinandega, Chontales, Matagalpa, Estelí, Granada, and León.

The National Women's Secretariat had been critical of the CST's failure to oppose the legislation for the establishment of the Free Trade Zone and the concessions made during negotiations with the state, which Secretariat leaders saw as a betrayal with bitter results for women workers. As one former regional secretariat leader says: "Now they [federation leaders] are businessmen, so they are looking out for their business. . . . It is said that it is incompatible to be a businessman and to be from the working class. They say, no, it isn't. . . . So, [to them] what does not generate any kind of benefit has to be thrown out and doesn't matter. . . . And never mind that they [workers] are women, it is beside the point that they committed the great sin of being born women!"

Many of the women who were formerly employed in state-owned textile and garment factories found jobs in the Free Trade Zone, but for several years the CST made no effort to organize this sector. Their apparent disinterest in the plight of the maquila workers further delegitimized the CST in the eyes of the leadership of the secretariats. A MEC publication contends: "For women workers, the traditional mechanisms of syndicalism seem to be worn out, since they are not able to fit together demands of gender and class. The traditional conception of the application of the methods of syndical struggle such as violence, 'negotiation' in which the big losers are the workers, as well as demagogic processes of concertación [social contract talks with the government], in which the claims of the sector in power within the union are negotiated, are not sufficient . . . to convince the women of the free trade zone to rise up in the struggle to form unions" (MEC 1996: 26).

Despite the lack of union representation in the zone, the Women's Secretariat continued to support women workers in the garment factories. In 1993 a group of workers in the Taiwanese-operated factory FOR-TEX Group called a strike and took over the factory for a period of ten days. The workers were protesting management's having eliminated the base wage, substituting a piece-rate system which included production norms that workers found impossible to meet (MEC 1996; Beteta 1993). In addition, workers had suffered from physical and psychological abuse at the hands of shop-floor supervisors. The Women's Secretariat was the only labor organization that responded to the workers' call for support in forming a union, and despite some 590 signatures collected and submitted to the Ministry of Labor, the union was not recognized or legalized (Valverde 1993b).

Although a commission of workers negotiated with the factory administrators and reached a series of agreements, including lowering some piecework quotas to their original level, management subsequently fired ten members of the commission (MEC 1996). When they arrived at the scene of the strike, Sara and three workers were beaten, pistol-whipped, and kicked by Taiwanese managers (*El Nuevo Diario* 1993; Valverde 1993a). The CST refused to publicly denounce this action or to support the criminal charges that Sara lodged against the managers.

The unresponsiveness of the CST national leadership reflected the ongoing conflicts and disputes between the CST administration and the Women's Secretariat. The male leaders of the CST consistently questioned the Secretariat's priorities and activities (such as separate congresses for women constituents) and attempted to administer the funding that the National Secretariat independently acquired from international NGOs. In addition, the CST leadership discouraged Secretariat members from joining with other women's organizations for fear of "dividing the union" (Jubb 1995: 15). CST administrators used the organization's hierarchy to undermine the Secretariat's authority and impose an agenda based on priorities that they defined. In the words of one Secretariat leader: "We had to consult with the men, even in projects relating to our own specific gender needs" (quoted in Jubb 1995: 15).

Although five women belonged to the National Executive in 1992, their minority status (five of seventeen) made it difficult for them to be heard. In an interview one of them remembers: "I was there and I lived that experience. I saw how they mistreated them, . . . how the decisions and comments of the women were not taken into account at the meetings of the National Executive."

The Women's Secretariat and its members were extremely active in implementing projects and programs aimed at women and in participating in the actions promoted by the national CST organization but felt that they received little recognition for their work. One former leader of a regional women's secretariat testified: "When there were mobilizations and marches, who mobilized those groups of men and women? It was we women of the women's secretariat. And the ones who got up on the platform to show their faces were the men. They fought to be in front and to appear on television, in the media." In MEC organizers' view the conflicts that gave rise to their organization's formation were a result of both gender-based conflicts and what they saw as corruption on the part of CST leadership, who were "selling out" the true principles of unionism and Sandinismo. Eloisa, a former Secretariat member explains:

> They [CST leaders] saw that these compañeras in their own women's movement . . . [were] organizing and how the women were gaining more and more ground, organizing space in the struggle for the demands, not only of women, because we women are not only in the women's struggle but also supporting the male compañeros in the struggle for their demands. So, practically, they were fearful that they could be displaced by the women, who were the ones who were truly representing the workers' problems, the struggle of the workers. . . . So, they had an adversary. . . . These women now had four secretariats and so they were gaining space, and every space that the women gained was a space that they [male CST leaders] felt that they lost.

As mentioned in chapter 1, these tensions came to a head at the CST's national congress in 1994. Sara had announced her retirement at a national assembly of the CST's women's secretariats. Seven hundred women from the various union federations elected seven candidates for the national executive as well as a candidate to replace Sara as the director of the National Women's Secretariat. The national CST leadership, fearing loss of power, made enormous efforts to *planchar* (iron out or prevent) the attendance of their political adversaries, including members of dissident federations and the leaders of the National Women's Secretariat. Less than a week before the congress, the CST leadership changed the location from Managua to Estelí, a city in the far north of the country about four hours from Managua. Several federation representatives, including supporters of Sara and representatives from seven federations were not even invited to the congress. Those not invited who managed to reach Estelí met with a large force of armed security and were not granted access to the building in which the congress was to be held. In typical and ingenious *Nica* style, many still managed to enter, shouting and disrupting the proceedings and later breaking open the doors from inside the building to allow others access.

Even given these obvious efforts to prevent political opponents of the national CST leadership from attending, the women were shocked when not one of their candidates, not even their candidate for the director of the National Women's Secretariat, was elected to a leadership position. Instead, a political ally of the general secretary (and the rumored lover of a member of the National Executive) was appointed to that position. Whether or not the elections were fair, the women of the Secretariat saw this as a final blow. Lola from Granada explains: "We as founders of the CST . . . What happened? We saw this as not only the personal, political interests [of the CST national leaders] . . . but also as the corruption of the national directors of the CST. . . . So, if . . . the Front taught us to be honest, hyper-pensive, analytical, critical, we are not going to allow this. We're not going to wash anyone's face" (whitewash these "dirty" politics).

In the month following the congress a group of over four hundred women met in Managua to form a separate and autonomous women's organization. They voted to name the organization the Working and Unemployed Women's Movement, "María Elena Cuadra," after an organizer of the domestic workers who had been killed in a car accident by a drunk driver. Many of the women who attended this meeting had not anticipated giving up their work or affiliation with the CST. Shortly after the meeting, however, the CST national leadership began a defamatory campaign against Sara and her supporters. Those who had worked on projects and programs under Sara in the Secretariat found the doors of the office locked to them, and some were thrown into the street. Formal complaints were launched against Sara and five other former Secretariat leaders, accusing them of embezzling funds, stealing office equipment, and ransacking the National Secretariat's office (*Barricada* 1994a, 1994b; *El Nuevo Diario* 1994). A warrant was issued for their arrest.

In August of 1994 when I met Sara and some of her supporters, the newly formed movement was in crisis. Sara and two others still faced charges, and meetings were taking place in the home of Evelyn, another former Secretariat leader. MEC did not have legal status as an organization, and relations with funding organizations were tenuous, as some international funders were disconcerted by the scandal and not sure whom to believe. In addition, the Sandinista media had published the claim that Sara and her supporters had ransacked the Women's Secretariat office, though some sympathetic radio stations invited Sara and the others to tell their side of the story. Worse still, women who went to the CST office to seek the programs offered under the former Secretariat were told that the former leaders were criminals—another blow to the reputation of the group. With no office space or legalized status, the group's members faced huge uncertainties regarding their future as organizers.

3 Gendering Power and Resistance in an Era of Globalization

Although it is a relatively small organization, MEC simultaneously occupies multiple positions, defying simplistic categorizations or the application of a single framework for generating a theoretical understanding of its many dimensions. MEC's positions include being (1) a social movement organization that engages with global and nationalist discourses and sometimes enacts transnational political strategies; (2) a working women's organization that seeks to address the negative effects of globalization; (3) a member of the Latin American women's movement that provides services to women workers and unemployed women. In order to lay out a framework for this case study, this chapter considers these simultaneous positions and explores their theoretical implications by discussing how MEC fits within the wider phenomena of women's resistances and accommodations to global restructuring and of women's movements in Latin America.

MEC's complex dimensions require an innovative approach that complicates binary categories such as NGO versus social movement, women's versus labor organization, strategic versus practical gender interests (Molyneux 1985) and globalization from "above" and "below" (Brecher et al. 2000). This book situates MEC where the global and local meet (Guidry et al. 2000a) and applies to the study of social movements in an era of globalization a gender perspective that foregrounds power relations. Rather than seeing power as emanating from "above" and so focusing exclusively on MEC's encounters with the state and its political strategies vis-à-vis the transnational corporations that locate production in Nicaragua, a conceptualization of power as more dispersed, multi-sited, and pervasive shifts analytical attention to how power based on gender, race, class, and nationality shapes relations between MEC and other organizations "from below," such as Northern NGOs, traditional labor movements, and even feminist groups. Indeed, taking into consideration the multiple sites and forms of power also allows us to examine the way these many forces affect the relationships among MEC participants and their subjectivities and identities.

This study endeavors to bridge the structural/cultural divide in social movement theory by analyzing the constraints and opportunities that MEC encounters at conjoining local, national, and global levels, but also the meanings that organizers ascribe to structural conditions and movement practices which emerge from locally formed political identities. Thus, the ways in which local identities articulate with globally circulating discourses is another important focus.

OPPOSITIONAL POLITICS IN THE GLOBAL SYSTEM

Globalization has transformed many different aspects of people's daily lives and the practices of "local" organizations. It also poses challenges to social science methods of inquiry by calling into question the units of analysis of social relations, destabilizing embedded notions of "place" and "community," and disrupting underlying assumptions about what constitutes a society (Gille and Ó Riain 2002; Albrow 1997). Thus, attempts to study global processes have also generated some rethinking of how social scientists should approach their objects of inquiry (Seidman 2000).

The study of migration was perhaps the first field to analyze systematically how everyday lives are shaped by globalization and how people on the ground enact transnational processes. Social anthropologists established the field of transnational studies and introduced the term *transnationalism* because of their interest in how immigrant communities have been transformed under conditions of globalization (Glick Schiller 1999; Mahler 1999; Guarnizo and Smith 1998).[1] Calling attention to how global processes are localized in historically specific ways, the concept of *transnational* refers to the ways in which people "on the ground" in particular local settings react to, engage with, and even re-create and influence global processes.

It is often said that political action is always local. Like the experiences of "transmigrants," the politics of social movements requires analytical focus on the local setting, and calls critical attention to the issue of mobility—what is mobile and what is not (e.g., discourses, bodies, capital, goods, information) at specific conjunctures within a global system (Mahler 1998). Although the movement of discourses (e.g., human rights discourse) and information may approximate truly *global* flows (Appadurai 1990), the ways in which local subjects appropriate and deploy globalized discourses are shaped by local conditions and identities.

Scholars of social movements have increasingly directed attention to how global processes shape both domestic and transnational movement practices (Smith and Johnston 2002a, 2002b; Burawoy et al. 2000). Transnational social movements have adopted political strategies that establish and engage with cross-national networks of organizations and individuals in order to achieve greater access to resources and to state and global institutions (Keck and Sikkink 1998a; Smith 1997). The UN summits of the last three decades have been particularly important for stimulating transnational advocacy efforts. Political actors use global communications technologies, such as the Internet, to mobilize, establish, and maintain such transnational networks.

The study of transnational social movements (often abbreviated as TSMs) has also transcended the borders between disciplines, resulting in a cross-fertilization of work by political scientists, international relations specialists, and social movement scholars (Tarrow 2001). Much of this literature, however, has drawn heavily from North American social movement theory and uses core concepts from the political process approach, such as opportunity and mobilizing structures, repertoires of contention, and strategic framing to explain how already constituted transnational social movements develop and seek to accomplish their goals (McCarthy 1997).[2]

Considerably less analytical attention has been directed at processes *within* or *among* the organizations that engage in transnational practices—such as the negotiation and constitution of collective identities, the subjective meanings that social movement participants assign to collective practices, and the relations of power within transnational coalitions or networks.[3] The theoretical framework of this book draws on scholarship that has focused critical inquiry on the "internationalization" of *cultural* politics (Alvarez et al. 1998b; Lowe and Lloyd 1997b; Lowe 1996).[4] Analysts of cultural politics see social movements, particularly in Latin America, as being engaged not only in political struggles in terms of access to institutional power but also in cultural struggles for different identities. Latin Americanist scholars who analyze cultural politics and resistance in the region seek to transcend narrowly defined liberal concepts of politics, political culture, citizenship, and democracy (Alvarez et al. 1998b; Escobar and Alvarez 1992; Slater 1985).[5]

It is no coincidence that studies of Latin American resistance have foregrounded culture and identity. After the class-based movements that dominated the oppositional landscape from the 1960s into the 1980s, the rise of what has been termed identity politics in Latin America in the last two decades has captured the attention of scholars. The emergence of new social movements in Latin America—indigenous, women's, gay, and ecological movements—exhibit important parallels with what European scholars had been observing on the other side of the Atlantic, where newly emerged movements had centered on issues related to identity and lifestyle (Melucci 1985). For groups of marginalized people in Latin America, however, struggles over cultural meanings are inextricably linked to material demands for inclusion, economic rights, and changes in governmental policy.[6]

Central to the study of cultural politics is the idea that to understand social movements, we must consider not only *how* they do what they do, but *why* they do what they do. According to this more culturally informed approach, social movement participants continually construct and negotiate the "we" of social movements through collective activity (Melucci 1995; Taylor and Whittier 1992). Such negotiations involve contestation and disagreement, as much if not more so than consensus, as different actors bring with them diverse experiences and perspectives. Thus, this approach centers analysis on the cultural practices of oppositional actors, how they *interpret* and *understand* external conditions and struggle to unsettle dominant cultural meanings in an effort to redefine social power (Alvarez et al. 1998a). This case study of MEC attempts to bridge the cultural/structural division in social movement theories by analyzing the opportunities and constraints that MEC faces and the strategies and practices in which the organization engages but also by exploring the subjective meaning that external conditions and movement practices have for MEC organizers (cf. McAdam et al. 1996; Johnston and Klandermans 1995; Morris and Mueller 1992).[7]

Although some have turned away from the term, citing a lack of conceptual specificity, I find the concept of *resistance* useful for generating a deeper understanding of the multiple forms and pervasiveness of power, including power based on gender, under globalization.[8] Resistance implies power that is not just an externality, but is dispersed within and through oppositional movements.[9] Social movements are not merely *nested* in power structures, as Smith and Johnston (2002a) employ the metaphor. Power stemming from race, class, gender, and other forces shapes the internal dynamics of social movement organizations, the social relations between movement participants, and the relations between groups within domestic and transnational movements. That is, "movements can never be entirely 'innocent,' power-free forces of resistance" (Eschle 2001: 129). This adds complexity to the binary conceptualization of power "from above" and "from below" found in recent characterizations of globalization (Brecher et al. 2000), leading us away from a view of power as operating along discrete and demarcated levels.

Theorizing power in this way leads to a fuller recognition of the complexities of social movements under globalization. By calling analytical attention to multiple sites and forms of resistance, such a conceptualization can integrate missing dimensions of gender. Such an approach goes beyond an interpretation of resistance that considers only "a contemporary variation of the international working-class struggle as worthy of attention" (Marchand and Runyan 2000a: 19). A broader, gender-aware conceptualization of resistance in turn contributes to a more nuanced understanding of women's politics, as will be seen when we evaluate MEC's "self-limiting" strategic orientation in its political work with FTZ workers and its rejection of many direct action tactics such as boycotts and picketing of retailers. Although the final goal of the program for FTZ workers—to empower female maquila workers and enable them to improve their lives—ultimately involves transforming dominating social structures, the political strategies of MEC organizers also reveal a complex dialectic of resistance and accommodation.

Structural approaches to social movements are also important for the analysis of MEC under global conditions. Globalization offers social movements new ways to mobilize resources, new communication networks, and transnational linkages that can enable them to access governing (state and multilateral) institutions in unprecedented ways. Global political processes and shifting relations between state actors and global capital have reconfigured a transnational field of power relations, creating spaces for resistance as national and transnational interests line up differently at different points in time. Operating at what Lisa Lowe and David Lloyd (1997a) term "sites of contradiction" between national, local, and transnational political spaces, MEC organizers negotiate the opportunities opened within a system characterized by global processes, and they continually evaluate the national and international political landscape to determine what they believe to be the location of these openings and how best to exploit them. Thus, structural approaches and a gendered reconceptualization of resistance open "the possibility to identify multiple forms of resistance and sites of intervention" (Marchand and Runyan 2000a: 18).

NGO OR SOCIAL MOVEMENT?

The last two decades have witnessed the virtual explosion of nongovernmental organizations onto the international political scene. Extremely diverse in their functions, activities, funding sources, size, and orientations, NGOs have undertaken a wide variety of activities, including the promotion of human rights and social justice, the protest of environmental degradation, the implementation of local development projects, and the provision of social services to disadvantaged groups (Fisher 1997; Edwards and Hulme 1996; Princen and Finger 1994; Sikkink 1993). NGOs have stepped in to fill the vacuum left by the declining welfare state, taking up public service functions that have been eschewed by the state as part of the current dominant neoliberal political and economic trend. They have also engaged at the transnational level, forming transnational advocacy networks (or TANs), and some have reached an international scale in their practices and organizational capacities (O'Brien et al. 2000).

What then distinguishes an NGO from a social movement organization, or a transnational network of NGOs from a transnational social movement? In particular, how should we categorize MEC? MEC's emergence and institutionalization can only be understood within the context of broad trends associated with civil society in Nicaragua, Latin America, and even more globally: the rise of NGOs as new political actors in Nicaragua, as well throughout the world; the "NGO-ization" of Latin American women's movements that characterized the 1990s; the emergence of the autonomous women's movement in Nicaragua in the early 1990s; and the growing predominance of service-providing organizations within this movement. Thus, in many ways MEC fits the description of a service-providing NGO.

But MEC could also be categorized as a social movement organization. Analysts have struggled to define social movements and more recently to create analytical categories that effectively capture the range of transnational and national actors in civil societies. Those who use cultural approaches to explore issues of power point to shared oppositional narratives, systems of meaning, collective identities, and oppositional consciousness as defining aspects of social movements.[10] Resource mobilization and political process theorists have emphasized the groups, formal organizations, and networks, or "mobilizing structures," that social movements use to mobilize and engage in collective action (McAdam et al. 1996).

In their book on transnational social movements, Jackie Smith and her collaborators (1997) have defined social movements in terms of their goals, as "collective, cooperative efforts at social change" (see McCarthy 1997: 250). Sidney Tarrow disagrees with this approach and instead defines social movements by their actions, that is, by their "sustained, contentious interactions with powerholders" (2001: 12).[11] He, as do Margaret Keck and Kathryn Sikkink, distinguishes transnational advocacy networks of NGOs from social movements, based on the former's primary focus on the exchange of information and the latter's contentious politics (Tarrow 2002; Keck and Sikkink 1998b).

In my view the diverse theories on social movements demonstrate that these movements cannot be reduced to their organizations, goals, and practices. A structural yet culturally informed approach to social movements reveals other cultural, subjective, and identity-based dimensions. And reducing social movement organizations to an objective view of "contentious" politics and NGOs to their "information politics" runs the risk of reifying the revolutionary versus reformist dichotomy, the limits of which are exemplified in the case of MEC. Viewing MEC as merely a service-provider (and hence an NGO) ignores its political history (for example, its origins in the mass organizations of the FSLN), its social change agenda, its engagement with the state, and the practices and shifting political identities of its organizers.

To take issue with Tarrow, a more culturally informed conceptualization of resistance (or, in his word, "contention") reminds us of the importance of avoiding narrow definitions of what is political or transformative. Historically, politicians, social movement theorists, and Marxists have categorically dismissed women's political activities as being everyday, "practical," or "merely" reformist. If, however, we take an approach that legitimates the subjectivities and perspectives of participants in social movements, then we cannot ignore how these participants interpret their own actions. This means that the exchange of information is not de facto apolitical or somehow not contentious. My analysis takes seriously how the women of MEC see their collective actions—including their information *politics* (Keck and Sikkink 1998a). MEC's goals, its practices as an organization, the politicized identities of its participants and their coming to political consciousness during the revolution, and participants' interpretations of their collective actions suggest that the most accurate and theoretically useful way to categorize MEC is as a social movement organization belonging to the wider women's movement(s) in Nicaragua, Latin America, and the world, and to the transnational anti-sweatshop movement.

GENDER, RACE, AND RESISTANCE
UNDER GLOBALIZATION

Gender is an integral part of globalization, and gendered and racialized assumptions about work and workers form a foundation upon which the global economy rests (Grewal and Kaplan 1994b). Examples that point to the importance of gender in the growth and intensification of global capitalism include the rise of the global sex industry (Enloe 1989); the justification of below-subsistence wages for women by transnational capitalists, who celebrate female workers' "nimble fingers," "docile" orientations, and "naturally" high turnover rates (Wright 2001; Wolf 1992; Elson and Pearson 1981); and the international division of reproductive labor in which the world's care work is undertaken by poor women of color and which is made possible by transnational migration and necessary by declining public services (Hondagneu-Sotelo 2002; Parreñas 2001).

The extensive scholarship on gender and the restructuring of the global economy goes back to the early 1980s, when Falker Fröbel and his colleagues (1980) first identified the "new international division of labor" and women's overwhelming representation in export-processing zones. Since that time, researchers have explored the feminization of industrial labor and the targeting of female labor markets (Bergeron 2001).[12]

Further, women's class experience as workers in the global economy cannot be understood as separate from their race position (Nash 1988). As Lowe notes, the "new" workforce in the global economy is not only feminized, but racialized, and "capitalism has emerged in conjunction with, and is made efficient by, other systems of . . . subordination: patriarchy, racism, and colonialism" (1996: 362).

The trope of women as "cheap" and "docile" labor—naturally nimble-fingered and culturally predisposed to be patient with tedious work, submissive to male authority, and prone to high turnover—is both a gendered and a racially based construction. For example, Carla Freeman (2000) illustrates this point in the case of Barbadian data-entry workers, where the notion of women as "ideal" workers incorporates contradictory images of the "docile girl" and the "strong black matriarch." Karen J. Hossfeld (1990) examines the case of assembly plants in Silicon Valley and shows how labor control on the shop floor is governed by both gender and racial logics. Management draws from racial assumptions about worker abilities (e.g., Asian workers are superior to Mexican; Asian women are obedient) in assigning work tasks, organizing production, and seeking to increase output. What is revealed, then, is a new social formation that emerges under global capitalism in which preexisting race and gender inequalities are incorporated into flexible accumulation strategies to target a racialized female workforce, and gender and race ideologies become the basis for worker control.

On the other hand, globalization can produce new possibilities for marginalized people to create new hybrid identities and spaces for resistance (Marchand and Runyan 2000a; Castells 1997; Lowe 1996; Dirlik 1994). Beyond simply demonstrating how firms incorporate gender into their global strategies for reducing labor costs to create a new female industrial workforce, scholars have documented worker resistance within FTZS and off-shore production sites. Women in Asia, Central America, and Mexico as well as immigrant women in the First World are seen, not as mere victims of global capitalism, but as actors who engage in struggles over cultural meanings and values and create alternative survival and social change strategies (Flora 1998: 247; Ong 1997).

This view of globalization centers analysis on women's agency and how women's resistance to old and new oppressions connects the global and the local, renegotiating the various boundaries between the state and civil society, the public and the private, and the global economy and national spheres of political struggle (Marchand and Runyan 2000a). Feminist theories and women's activism have challenged Marxist privileging of class and class relations as central axes of oppression and of the idea that the transformation of the capitalist system would make gender and race oppression things of the past (Dore 1997); this has forced, not the abandonment, but "a reconceptualization of the traditional terrain of class struggle and its privileged subjects" (Camacho 1999: 79).

Studies in the 1980s and early 1990s focused on workers' resistance defined broadly to include cultural struggles, "oppositional tactics, embodied desires, and alternative interpretations and images," and not limited to terms of labor-capital confrontations (Ong 1997: 78). Workers in different geographical and cultural contexts have used a range of tactics, such as engaging in slowdowns when pressured to meet higher quotas (Peña 1987) or to help a worker who is slow to meet her quota (Rosa 1994: 86); using managers' racist assumptions about workers to their advantage in order to slow the work pace or avoid undesirable tasks (Hossfeld 1990); frequently leaving the shop floor to attend to "female" problems (Ong 1987); or, in the case of Malay workers, actually experiencing spiritual possession and disrupting production to the point of factory shutdowns (Ong 1988). Such cultural resistance and covert tactics rely on the social regulation of women, especially young women, in public spaces.

A few studies have documented cases of more organized forms of female resistance in and around maquila factories. In South Korea women workers in textile factories have organized militant unions, rejecting male leadership to cultivate their own organizations (Kim 1992). They have drawn on religious traditions to struggle as workers to protest working conditions and have waged hunger strikes.

In Sri Lanka, Malaysia, and the Philippines women workers have found ways to organize even under the strictest conditions of labor control. Sometimes resistance takes the form of spontaneous wildcat strikes, but other, more organized forms also prevail. In Malaysia, for example, the government permitted electronic assembly workers to organize in-house unions. This, as Kumudhini Rosa (1994: 88–89) points out, curtailed workers' ability to mobilize, as they could not form national unions. But these smaller unions by necessity revolve around rank-and-file workers on the shop floor and so may provide greater opportunities for women's participation. In addition, women's committees linked to trade unions emerged, offering women a semi-autonomous space for worker mobilization. Community organizations outside the factories are also an important site for women's organization. In Sri Lanka religious organizations established food co-ops, boarding houses, and legal centers, which became important spaces for women workers to build solidarity and to educate themselves about their rights (Rosa 1994: 92–93).

Finally, women's activism along the U.S.-Mexican border around issues related to the maquilas has been widespread and extensive, incorporating a wide array of strategies. Networks of community-based women's organizations have promoted economic justice and human rights using legislative and legal tactics to direct action and even unionization (Bandy 2004). In these unions the majority of leaders are women, who determine the priorities and strategies for action. Shortly after the 1985 earthquake, in which many garment workers were killed, the Nineteenth of September National Union of Garment Workers emerged as an independent union made up solely of women. Their demands included respect for women's rights, such as the right to free maternity leave and freedom from sexual harassment, as well as demands that reflected the economic situation of the country as a whole, such as suspension of payment to the external debt. The union was successful in obtaining compensation for eight thousand women workers who had lost their employment during the earthquake (Tirado 1994: 108).

As capital has become increasingly global and free trade agreements like NAFTA have allowed transnational corporations to cross national borders, so too women's movements have mobilized in response to the gender inequalities upon which the global economy relies for its growth and expansion. Women workers on both sides of the U.S.-Mexican border and in Canada have formed coalitions to struggle for social justice in the face of NAFTA (Bandy 2004; Dominguez 2002; MacDonald 2002; Gabriel and MacDonald 1994). And women in Central America, Mexico, and Asia have come together to hold dialogues and compare strategies for fighting sweatshop abuses against women workers.[13] As we shall see in the case of MEC, some of these initiatives have been built on a feminist worker or popular feminist perspective (Bandy and Mendez 2003; Dominguez 2002).

Despite the creativity and resilience of these cross-border initiatives to resist global restructuring, scholars have noted that these networks have made few inroads in injecting gender into debates on NAFTA or on international public policy related to free trade (MacDonald 2002; Jaquette 2001: 123). Nonetheless, these initiatives and the coalitional politics that they embody represent innovative forms of resistance. They challenge the view that identity politics and workers' class-based movements are mutually exclusive and the idea that feminism is a movement of middle-class white women in the West, characterized by single-issue and particularistic demands (Molyneux 1998: 81).

FEMINISM AND WOMEN'S ACTIVISM IN LATIN AMERICA

The emergence of women's movements in Latin America and throughout the developing world has challenged the perception of Third World women as apolitical agencyless victims, and Latin American women's increasingly visible participation in social movements has created a new conception of what is political.[14] Those familiar with the feminist movement in the United States will find that Latin American feminist organizing and debates have followed a slightly different trajectory, a reminder that there is no one single feminism, but many forms of feminist practice and organizations and many kinds of feminists.[15]

The first wave of Latin American feminism was largely middle-class in character and devoted to social reform and women's suffrage. Second-wave feminism in Latin America arose from what has been termed the "new left." In Latin America this was largely composed of class-based and—in the case of Central America—Marxist-inspired movements that struggled against authoritarian regimes (Miller 1991; Sternbach et al. 1992).

By the 1980s women were engaged in political life in Latin America in unprecedented ways. In Central America and Cuba women were active participants in the guerilla movements of the mid–twentieth century. In the case of Nicaragua analysts estimate that 30 percent of the combatants in the revolution were women (see Kampwirth 2002: 2). In South America women played major roles in the struggles against military dictatorships in Brazil, Argentina, and Chile (Alvarez 1990; Feijoo and Nari 1994). And throughout Latin America women were active in peasant organizations, neighborhood protest movements, and Christian base communities (Jaquette 1994b; Jelin 1994c).

In the 1970s and 1980s the left-wing organizations in which many women had mobilized to struggle against authoritarian governments in Central and South America were often openly hostile to issues related to gender inequality. Feminism was portrayed as "counterrevolutionary," bourgeois, or a "Yankee imperialist" creation. And feminists were dismissed as upper-class women who had lost touch with their national identity. Marxists argued that sexism could only disappear with the overthrow of the capitalist system, and the industrial class (overwhelmingly male) was seen as embodying the greatest revolutionary potential. Finally, the vanguard model predominant within many of these organizations made internal debate difficult (Chinchilla 1992; Randall 1992).

A new wave of feminist and women's political organizing thus occurred in those same decades, as Latin American women began to form feminist and nonfeminist and often autonomous organizations in order to choose their own leaders and political agenda. Researchers have maintained that this process and the discussions that occurred in these spaces played a major role in Latin American feminists' turning to theoretical discussions about the intersections and interconnections of different struggles and forms of oppression (Chinchilla 1992).

Given the emergence of many Latin American women's movements from the progressive organizations of the Left, the issue of autonomy from class-based movements has been a pivotal point of debate. Scholars and activists alike have hotly argued the meaning of autonomy as well as whether autonomy is always advantageous for women's organizations or a prerequisite for meeting goals based on women's gender interests (Molyneux 1998: 71–72; Chinchilla 1994; Jaquette 1994b; Hellman 1992; Sternbach et al. 1992). Indeed, some feminists contend that feminism and autonomy are inseparable and that women's real gender issues can only be achieved in an autonomous organization (González and Kampwirth 2001a: 17–21; and see Molyneux 1998: 71; Chinchilla 1994: 191).

We can find examples of this debated issue in the case of MEC. For organizers, internal discussions in the autonomous space that they had created opened up new issues that led them to explore understandings of gender-based oppression. For example, they began to identify connections between political violence and domestic violence as they compared their experiences with their respective compañeros who had returned from the front of the civil war with new, more violent tendencies toward their partners and children. On the other hand, autonomy from a male-dominated movement has not guaranteed that MEC organizers can define their own interests. Autonomy from the labor movement has meant that MEC must seek its own funding from international donors, and as we shall see in the next chapter, reliance on northern NGOs brings with it a whole new set of issues, compromising to some degree MEC's ability to establish independently its own agenda.

Thus, for feminists in Latin America feminist consciousness and debates were fueled by multiple contradictions experienced in the movements of the Left. At the same time, "although feminism in many countries broke with the Left organizationally, it did not fully do so ideologically" (Sternbach et al. 1992: 211). The struggle for class equality has been an integral component of Latin American feminist theory and practice. And strong tensions continue to exist in the Latin American feminist movement regarding the relationship between struggles for gender and class equality (Chinchilla 1992). For example, in South America that movement has been unable to systematically confront the issue of domestic labor. Furthermore, as the second wave of Latin American feminism has progressed, women have continually bridged the dichotomies of practical versus strategic gender interests or feminist versus feminine organizations, instead articulating identities based on *feminismo popular*, or a feminism grounded in the experiences and perspectives of grassroots women (Stephen 1997: 12; Sternbach et al. 1992).

Issues of race and racial and ethnic differences have not been absent from feminist and women's movements in Latin America. From the mid-1980s through the 1990s black and indigenous women have organized all over the region. And black women have been important actors at regional Latin American feminist forums, calling for the women's movement to take up issues of racism and for the particularities of the experiences of black women to be included in feminist struggles (Alvarez 1998: 301). Nonetheless, because of the historical relationship between women's movements and the revolutionary movements of the Left, class identity and issues have played a more visible role in women's organizing (González and Kampwirth 2001a).

It is also important to situate the creation of autonomous women's and feminist organizations in Latin America within the transition to electoral democracies that occurred in the 1980s and 1990s in much of the region. Democratization and women's mobilization have been mutually reinforcing in Latin America and other regions of the world (Jaquette 2001). Of course, as William Robinson (1997) insightfully points out, the electorally appointed regimes of countries in the Central American region are better characterized as "polyarchies" than democracies. In such a regime a small group actually rules, and participation by the majority is confined to choosing among elites in a tightly controlled electoral process (Robinson 2003: 53, 71). Regardless, the transition of political regimes and the accompanying explosion of "new social movements" that occurred in the 1990s has also meant that a vocabulary of democracy has became increasingly predominant, not only in elite political circles but within oppositional movements and political parties as well.

Women's Movements Go Transnational. Women's organizing around gender issues has not been limited to national politics. International activism has played a major role in both first- and second-wave feminisms in Latin America and most of the world's regions (Keck and Sikkink 2000; Miller 1991). And from the 1990s into the 2000s feminism has become increasingly global. Thus, we should view MEC's practices within a context of increasingly transnational women's activism in the last decades of the twentieth century.

The influence of women's rights advocates' and global feminist discourses within international and national policy arenas has received considerable scholarly attention (Meyer and Prügl 1999; Clark et al. 1998; Staudt 1997; Peters and Wolper 1995). The UN and its world summits have been especially significant in creating spaces for transnational political organizing. Preparatory processes for international conferences such as the women's world conferences in Mexico City in 1975, Nairobi in 1985, and Beijing in 1995 have reinforced global coalition-building among women's organizations (Desai 2002; Basu 2000, 1995; Stienstra 2000; Vargas and Mauleón 1998). National, regional, and transnational networks have intensified and linked women's organizations working on a wide range of issues, facilitating the transnational circulation of feminist demands, practices, and discourses (Alvarez 1998).

In particular, beginning in the 1980s, Latin American feminisms have "gone global" through the "transnationalization" of feminist discourses: "Local movement actors' deployment of discursive frames and organizational and political practices . . . [have been] inspired, (re)affirmed, or reinforced—though not necessarily caused—by their engagement with other actors beyond national borders through a wide range of transnational contacts, discussions, transactions, and networks, both virtual and 'real' " (Alvarez 2000: 30).[16]

The globalized discourse of human rights has offered women's groups a powerful tool that lends international legitimacy to political demands. The challenge facing women's groups, however, has been to transform the human rights agenda to include women—that is, to make women's rights truly human rights. This is an especially difficult task. Despite the globalized aspects of human rights discourse, human rights and international laws that codify them are based on the sovereign nation-state, and patriarchal nation-states are the only true enforcers of human rights laws. Women's voices and/or a "gender perspective" are often absent within state institutions to define human rights and decide when the state should intervene in response to violations. Indeed, some would argue that the contractual foundations of the modern nation-state are based on the patriarchal dominance of men over women (Pateman 1988). The struggle for feminists and women's movements is to transform the human rights agenda while conserving the power and legitimacy of this discourse as a political tool (Cook 1994; Peters and Wolper 1995).[17]

But global discourses do not seamlessly influence local politics in a unidirectional, top-down manner (Basu 2000; Thayer 2000). Rather, globally circulating feminist discourses "are dispersed into varied local sites where they are picked up and refashioned as they resonate in contextualized ways" (Desai 2002: 15). Latin American feminists have built transborder connections from the bottom up, and the transnational linkages that they have formed are intimately connected to local political goals and politics (Alvarez 2000). In the case of MEC, then, I examine how organizers make global discourses like feminism and human rights their own by deploying them within specific situations in their struggle.

Strategic or Practical Gender Interests? Latin American women's activism has raised questions about how, when, and in what form women's organizing can bring about changes in gendered power structures. These questions resonate in new ways under conditions of globalization. An oft-cited example of Latin American women's politicization is the case in Argentina of Las Madres de la Plaza de Mayo, who mobilized around the disappearances of their loved ones during the military dictatorship (Feijoó and Gogna 1994). Observers have attributed the dictatorship's relative tolerance of the Madres' weekly appearances at the plaza and their organized protest against the disappearances to the cultural reverence for the sanctity of motherhood and gendered cultural constructions of women as naturally altruistic and apolitical (Jelin 1994a). On the other hand, the very presence of the Madres in the public space of *la plaza* (traditionally designated as a male realm) as well as the group's development of new forms of protest and mobilization and the *political* content of their agenda resulted in a transformation of politics and ultimately the creation of a new political culture and redefinition of the "traditional female role" of passivity and subordination (Feijoó and Gogna 1994).

The example of the Madres calls attention to the varied interests around which women have mobilized. Debates over Maxine Molyneux's (1985) influential heuristic distinction between "practical gender interests" and "strategic gender interests" have extended to the discussion of women's organizing and structural change. The former concept refers to those interests derived from women's position in the sexual division of labor, including their role as caregivers in the household. For example, women may organize around an issue that affects their ability to meet the basic, immediate needs of their families (Blondet 1995). "Strategic interests" involve "claims to transform social relations in order to . . . secure a . . . lasting repositioning of women within the gender order and within society at large" (Molyneux 1998:75; see Molyneux 1985). These interests form around strategic goals that challenge the existing gender order, including such issues as violence against women, discrimination, and political inequality.

One contested issue in the debates about women's interests is whether or not the concept undervalues "practical" interests, suggesting a hierarchical relationship and a linear progression from less sophisticated "practical" to more advanced "strategic" interests (see Molyneux 1998;

Radcliffe and Westwood 1993: 20). Others have suggested that the distinction describes feminist versus nonfeminist demand-making and that the concept privileges feminist organizing over other forms, suggesting that only "strategic" interests can have transformative consequences, while "practical" interests result merely in reform (Peterson and Runyan 1999: 178; Stephen 1997: 12; Wieringa 1994; and see Alvarez 1990: 24).

Some theorists have taken issue with what they see as a structurally determined conceptualization and object to a notion of discernable, objective women's interests (Kabeer 1992). What is contested is a notion of "true" women's interests, the existence of which would open up the possibility for outside agencies or organizations to impose their version of interests on women (Molyneux 1998: 76). But others are wary of purely subjective and culturally relativistic constructions, fearing that such a view would compromise both the explanatory power and the political relevance of the concept of interests (Jackson and Pearson 1998: 7; Molyneux 1998: 77).

Like other women's organizations that have articulated a class-based or populist version of feminism, MEC demonstrates a bridging of the strategic/practical binary. Its programs for women are developed in close consultation with poor unemployed women and women workers and are oriented toward pragmatic concerns, centering on the realities of women's daily struggle for survival—what might be categorized as "practical gender interests." Thus, the organization provides microcredit for the purpose of home improvement for women whose homes may have only dirt floors. The job-training program has the goal of enhancing women's ability to generate income by inserting them into nontraditional economic activities, and another credit fund supports women's microenterprises like street vending, small grocery stores, or market booths to sell vegetables or cheese. At regional offices teenage girls may receive training in beauty care and learn to cut hair or to knit in order to help them earn money in the informal economy—hardly "radical" activities.

As we shall see, however, the content of MEC's workshops and organizers' understandings of their strategies and their autonomous organization reveal both perception and acknowledgment of gender as a structure of power. And through its programs, publications, and activities the organization articulates a vision of social transformation that would extend democracy to the "domestic sphere" and empower women to claim their human, labor, and civil rights. All MEC programs include workshops and training on gender issues, such as domestic violence, reproductive health (from a gender perspective), gender roles, and gender and self-esteem, as well as human and labor rights. MEC's feminist curriculum emphasizes gender and power and connects women's domination in the home with subordination that occurs in the workplace, community, and, indeed, within organizations like unions. Many organizers identify as feminists, and they articulate an understanding of MEC's split from the labor movement as the result of gender discrimination and oppression. MEC organizers regularly participate in activities organized by feminist groups and have close relationships with feminists. The organization belongs to different networks of women's organizations that include feminist groups that wage national campaigns on issues such as violence against women.

One of the complexities that MEC illustrates with regard to the practical/strategic distinction is not only the complicated overlap of types of interests, but also the subjective aspects of how interests are perceived. V. Spike Peterson and Anne Sisson Runyan (1999: 178) suggest that it is best to conceptualize women's interests as existing in a continuum of struggle rather than as a dichotomy. And MEC's case shows that the meaning of interests shifts, depending on the given situation and interpretation at that moment, and can vary for different individuals involved. Thus, women's interests do not exist a priori; they arise out of a context of struggle (Alvarez 1990). This observation is in line with Molyneux's contention that "The formulation of interests . . . is always linked to identity formation" (1998: 76).

IN SUM, MY theoretical framework situates MEC where the global and local meet and arises from MEC's simultaneously being ascribed membership in different categories. But understanding the theoretical implications of these multiple positions requires an approach that foregrounds power relations, especially those based on gender. I seek to show how multiple forms of power operate to shape the political landscape upon which MEC acts as well as the relations among organizations and individuals that are actively resisting but also sometimes accommodating global processes.

This analysis attempts to bridge the structural/cultural divide in studies of social movements that engage in transnational practices. I devote attention to the role that external, structural factors have played in MEC's strategies but also to the subjective perspectives and identities of MEC organizers. My ethnographic method allows me to examine internal processes of identity negotiation within MEC and how they articulate with globally circulating discourses and meanings. Although, as I have said, I am not naïve enough to suggest that the women "speak for themselves" in this book, I do strive to offer a window into these women's perspectives— framed as it is by my own interpretation. Thus, I take very seriously the perspectives of MEC participants and how they interpret their organization's strategies and practices. I believe that this view of the practices of MEC has much to teach us about movements for social justice in the South under globalization.

4 "Autonomous but Organized": MEC's Search for an Organizational Structure

They [men] continue to believe that it is they who make the transcendental decisions in this country. The women are always relegated to a secondary level, as if we couldn't think or as if we had no great ideas. . . . Now we would like to be subjects of our own transformation. They want us to sing about unity . . . a unity conceded by men and seen from their point of view. We have proposed a real unity in our organization. And a real unity means recognizing the existence of women, recognizing that women are substantial actors in the development of an organization.—SARA RODRÍGUEZ, MEC's coordinator, 1994

After MEC's formation following the 1994 CST national congress, the organization's founders devoted all of their efforts to the immediate crises before them: the trial of two of the five women facing criminal charges, the costly and complicated process of licensing MEC as a nonprofit association with the state, the construction of an office in Managua, and the reestablishment of contact with international NGO donors. It was at this difficult time that I first met some of the founding members of MEC and began my interviews with them. By the time I returned to Nicaragua in 1995 for my second research stint, organizers had made enormous strides in surmounting these immediate crises.

The most important victory was the reversal of the guilty verdict rendered in the CST's case against the two former leaders of the Women's Secretariat. After the women's lawyer publicly raised questions about the possible corruption of the judge, CST representatives offered to drop the charges. Sara and the other five women who were charged (though only she and Patricia were being tried at this point) decided to hold their ground in order to clear their names. They won the appeal, and a new judge found them not guilty of charges of destruction of property and embezzlement. This official recognition of their innocence was extremely important for the organization's future relations with NGO funders.

By the organization's first anniversary in May 1995, MEC leaders had also successfully navigated the complicated bureaucratic process for obtaining legal status as a nonprofit association. In addition, MEC founders from Managua obtained a loan to purchase land and build a tiny office. With the support of friends from two Canadian NGOs Sara had also reactivated ties with other international NGO donors. Funding for a job-training program was pending, and Sara had secured financial support from a Canadian labor union for the publication of workshop materials to be used in educational programs.

When I returned to Nicaragua in July 1995, it was evident that MEC had come a long way in its institutionalization. MEC's Managua-based team was made up of former leaders of the National Women's Secretariat, the Managua women's secretariat, and the secretariats of various union federations based in Managua, such as the Textile and Apparel Workers Federation. Evelyn, Sara, and Reyna greeted me warmly in the newly constructed national office, a small house located a block away from the National Assembly building and just around the corner from the Intercontinental Hotel. The one-room office had several conference tables, two or three old desks, and a few dilapidated file cabinets and bookshelves. There was no air conditioning, but a broken fan in the middle of the room brought at least a degree of relief from the tropical heat and humidity.

One desk stood apart in the corner to create a small consultation space for Alicia, a labor lawyer whom I had met in 1994, when MEC's offices were still in Evelyn's home. Eloisa served as the receptionist for this make-shift *bufete* (legal office). And when I arrived, Alicia was meeting with two aggrieved workers who had been fired from a factory in the Free Trade Zone. Eloisa had access to the only computer in the office—an outdated DOS-based PC. The office had no phone, and every day Evelyn would walk several blocks to the central TELCOR (the state-owned telephone company and postal service) office in Managua to check the post office box, then stop at her house on the way back to make phone calls from her private phone. Sometimes Sara's husband, who owned one of the few vehicles to which the organization had access, would pick up Sara at midday and drive her to their home so she could make calls. None of the other women who worked in the office had telephones.

Brightening the somewhat stark surroundings were a number of large potted plants, gifts from other women's organizations sent to MEC on the organization's first anniversary. Sara and Evelyn showed me with pride the building's exterior. The front of the office was painted pink, and in the center was MEC's name and logo, painted large so that it was visible from the street. The image was of the face of a woman with the hair forming a multicolored outline of the map of Nicaragua. Tamara explained how they had decided upon this logo. In anticipation of the upcoming anniversary they had asked women from the different communities in which the Women's Secretariat of the CST had launched programs to submit drawings; MEC organizers and women from the communities then voted on the image that would become MEC's logo. Eloisa showed me with pride the new letterhead and envelopes, bearing MEC's name and the new, colorful logo.

The presence of international cooperantes was an important sign of MEC's continued connection with networks of NGOs from the North. Shortly after the establishment of the national office, Jill, who worked for the NGO CoDevelopment Canada, began working with MEC as a cooperante. Filling a role that was part volunteer and part consultant, she helped draft project proposals, participated in Managua team meetings, and offered workshops on such topics as gender roles and self-esteem to groups of program participants.

Despite these advances, in late 1994 and early 1995 MEC had entered a period of rather dramatic transition, even crisis, stemming this time, not from external, but from internal forces. With autonomy from the CST came the opportunity but also the responsibility for devising a new organizational structure for this new "women-only" space that MEC founders were creating. How would the organization be structured? How would decisions be made? Who would develop work plans and how would they be implemented? After the dust settled from overcoming the immediate and urgent obstacles, it became apparent that there were dramatically different perspectives among MEC participants regarding these questions.

In this chapter I trace MEC's rocky search for an organizational structure that accurately reflected the organization's objectives, its founding principles, and the constructed collective identity(ies) of its participants. Underlying MEC's internal organizational processes are a series of layered local, regional, and global stories. First, to understand shifts in MEC's organizational structure one must turn to its roots within the CST, a mass organization of the FSLN. MEC gradually underwent a process of institutionalization that involved shifting away from a vertically structured national federation with centralized decision-making and toward a horizontal network of loosely coordinated regional offices, each with its own working team or collective. At the same time (somewhat contradictorily), MEC became more professionalized, and the Managua office began to look more and more like an NGO, though organizers continually articulated a collective identity of being "women from the base." And notably, MEC maintained a strong connection to grassroots communities, with its founders and new organizers' alike residing in working class and poor barrios.

Within Nicaragua this dual process is not unique to MEC—the autonomous women's movement and even the popular and mass organizations have undergone a similar process—what has been called "NGO-ization" (see Alvarez 1998: 306–15). And if we look outside of the country, we see that these same transitions "correspond with general changes in the potential for national sovereignty, in the relationship between the state and civil society, and in the very nature of social movements throughout the Americas" (Polakoff and LaRamée 1997: 188). Thus, the shifts involved in MEC's changing organizational structure run parallel to and reflect a wider regional historical process in social movement practice—the rise of the NGO as a social movement organizational form.[1]

The emergence of NGOs onto the political scene reaches global as well as regional proportions. The proliferation of NGOs must be understood in the context of wider global phenomena—the hegemony of the neoliberal development model, the dismantling of the welfare state, and the debt crisis in the developing world. Further, the web of connections among NGOs, social movements, government agencies, and cross-national networks of grassroots organizations involves transnational processes, as ideas, funding, knowledge, and people move through various local, national, and international sites (Alvarez 1998; Fisher 1997; Lebon 1996; Safa 1996; Appadurai 1991).

MEC's very local organizational processes were infused with transnational ones. Participation in both the internationally connected Nicaraguan autonomous women's movement and the wider transnational feminist movement, as well as connections with NGOs and labor organizations in the United States, Canada, and Europe, also played an important role in the constitution of MEC's organizational practices. By disseminating different models for organizational practices and different ideas about autonomy and personal empowerment, transnationally circulating discourses, including feminist ones, influenced MEC's organizational strategies.

The construction of the MEC organization has involved the localization of transnationally flowing ideas and discourses. The "indigenization" of imported discourses, however, is by no means a passive or evolutionary process (Thayer 2000; Grewal and Kaplan 1994). Indeed, MEC actors not only adopted certain elements of a feminist conceptual framework but also reformulated feminist notions to coincide with the specific "multiple, overlapping and discrete oppressions" that they faced (Grewal and Kaplan 1994: 17). Furthermore, depending upon their own particular experiences, as well as the specific ways in which they viewed themselves as political actors, MEC participants actively adapted and drew upon feminist discourses and language, often in diverging ways.

AUTONOMY VERSUS UNITY:
MEC'S INSTITUTIONALIZATION

Following the 1994 exoneration of Sara and the other Secretariat leaders, MEC's next struggle was to obtain its legal status as a nonprofit association—in Nicaragua known as its *personería jurídica*. In order to apply for this status, organizers had to clearly define MEC's organizational structures and the positions within them. At the founding congress in 1994, 400 women elected Sara as the organization's coordinator, and the original group of 14 MEC founders met to devise a structure and appoint women to various leadership positions. The resulting structure was strikingly similar to that of the women's secretariats of the CST. A national headquarters based in Managua was to coordinate and plan a group of regional offices. Sara and a core group that had formed the leadership of the National Women's Secretariat as well as leaders from the women's secretariats of Managua-based union federations ran this national office, though two of the regional leaders also held national positions in addition to managing regional offices. Regional offices were established in the departments of Granada, Matagalpa, Chontales, Estelí, Chinandega, and León.[2] Each regional office elected its own coordinator. At national meetings all MEC leaders would come together to establish an agenda and a set of programs for the entire MEC federation.

Despite what appeared to be a relatively representational decision-making structure, in practice the organization functioned in nearly exactly the same way that it had when the women of MEC worked within the CST. Sara and to a lesser extent Evelyn, Tamara, and Laura of the national office continued to be the only participants who had experience in writing project proposals and searching for funding from international organizations. The fact that they would be the ones who would write up and present all of MEC's projects to international donors meant that they largely determined which projects would be implemented. If a proposed regional project did not seem fundable to them, it would not be written up. International cooperantes like Jill and later Andrea, who joined the Managua team in 1996, were also important resources in that they reviewed project proposals and gave suggestions as to where to submit them. Still, as the national coordinator, it fell upon Sara to decide which projects would be developed into proposals.

In fact, because the regional coordinators were not accustomed to independently seeking funding for their own programs, they expected Sara, as the national coordinator, to dole out materials and funding for the daily operations of the departmental offices. Most of them did not possess the necessary connections with international agencies and NGOs to seek funding, nor were they sure how to go about establishing ties or writing proposals. Although some of the regional coordinators had attended occasional workshops or seminars on how to write project proposals, for the most part these women lacked the professional skills and educational background necessary to successfully formulate and complete a plan for long- and short-term projects. In addition, they lacked Sara's years of experience spent establishing networks and ties with international organizations.

The differences between regional-level leaders and the MEC organizers who were more successful project developers can be traced to MEC's roots in the CST and the democratic-centralism practiced within the mass organizations of the FSLN. Their organizational structure involved a national-level headquarters, regional offices, municipal-level branches, and local-level committees. Once the women's secretariats in the CST were established, a parallel organizational structure was also put in place—again with a national headquarters in Managua, regional women's secretariats, and so forth.

National leadership of the mass organizations (in the case of the CST, the National Executive) was appointed by the FSLN, and in most cases the directorate of the mass organization appointed regional leaders as well (Polakoff and LaRamée 1997: 153). And interlocking membership between the FSLN party and the mass organizations meant that top-level leaders of the mass organizations were also militants of the FSLN. Democratic practice within the mass organizations, then, was compromised by a verticalism between the party and the organizations. Local and regional leaders primarily carried out party directives from above with little decision-making power about work plans or the development of projects.

María Luisa and Lola, the regional leaders of MEC's Granada office, came from poor backgrounds, but they had been active in the insurrection that brought the Sandinistas to power as well as in the militant trade union federations of the CST's region of Granada. María Luisa grew up on Ometepe Island. In an interview she told me, "I never wore shoes until I was twelve"—the age at which she migrated to Granada to begin work as a live-in domestic in order to send home money to her impoverished family. Neither she nor Lola had received any schooling beyond primary school—in fact, María Luisa was illiterate until well into adulthood. As was typical for many, these women received their education later in life as part of their training as *both* cadres in the FSLN and regional leaders within the CST. In 1982 María Luisa, who had been working as a CST union leader in a textile factory in Granada, was selected to travel to Cuba to study. Later, the CST leadership in Granada sent her and four other cadres to Estelí for schooling. There they spent eighteen months living, growing their own food, and studying. María Luisa remembers: "In those eighteen months I went through first, second, third, fourth, fifth, and sixth grade. That's how I completed my primary school education. We studied from seven in the morning until ten o'clock at night." Similarly, Lola had completed the sixth grade, and the FSLN sent her to Germany to finish her secondary education.

Although regional leaders like Lola and María Luisa were able to receive their education through their involvement in the CST, they did not have the same kind of leadership opportunities as did those who achieved higher positions within the mass organizations of the FSLN. As noted, Sara had been a national leader in the CST. Another important leader in MEC was Julieta, who though she technically served as MEC's regional leader for León, had been a high-level regional leader in both AMNLAE and the mining federation of the CST. Sara and Julieta's high-ranking positions contributed to their receiving more education and training, which in turn led to more contact with international solidarity organizations that supported many of the Sandinistas' initiatives. They were also trained to take part in the development of projects and engaged in decision-making about the development of work plans at the national or regional level.

Thus, Sara and Julieta's positions within the FSLN afforded them more social and cultural capital that could later be put to use in their efforts within MEC. After the formation of MEC, both went on to pursue college and graduate degrees. Sara's previously established relations with solidarity organizations that funded programs during her tenure as the national director of the Women's Secretariat of the CST meant that she was known within networks of international solidarity organizations—especially Canadian organizations and the Canadian and European OX-FAM family. In the internal politics of transnational funding, personal relationships and reputation count for a great deal, and NGO representatives relied on their personal knowledge of Sara as a responsible and honest "counterpart."

Julieta had been elected by the women's constituency of the CST to be the next director of the National Women's Secretariat after Sara announced her resignation, but of course was not appointed after the coup at the CST congress that prompted MEC's formation. She too had cultivated relations with international donors and was the only regional leader of MEC who was able to obtain fairly quickly funding for projects in her region of León.

International donor agencies and NGOs generally require that one person be named as the principal administrator of a project to be funded. Because many individuals within international organizations knew Sara well and had worked with her over the years, she was usually the preferred person named. As the national coordinator of MEC, if Sara applied for funding for projects that were to be implemented in the regional offices, she felt (and rightly so) that her reputation was on the line. Future funding of MEC projects depended on the continued responsible management of funds and accountability to donors. For this reason, Sara felt compelled to be directly involved in the supervision of regionally implemented projects. Decision-making, then, on program and project implementation tended to be centralized in the national office, just as it had been within the women's secretariats of the CST. In effect, the national office took charge of distributing and administrating program funding for the entire MEC federation.

It is not surprising that the women opted to adopt this centralized organizational structure. Though their separation from the CST was in part to flee the hierarchy of the traditional labor movement, the women of MEC remained strongly influenced by over a decade of political upbringing in the FSLN. As Norma Chinchilla observes: "The political movement that served as the framework for Nicaraguan women's political coming of age was heavily influenced by the tradition of clandestine armed struggle, which emphasized military hierarchy and discipline, centralization of leadership, compartmentalization of information, the subordination of individual needs to the collective, and the public (productive) sphere as the force behind all change" (1994: 193).

Soon, however, it became apparent (especially to the women of the Managua collective) that this top-heavy and centralized organizational form was neither viable nor appropriate. In purely pragmatic terms, the old model of the CST hierarchy, in which a national coordinating office distributed project funding and other support to regional subsidiaries, presupposed a larger institutional support base and human resources that the MEC simply did not possess. Meanwhile, Sara, Evelyn, Laura, and the others were exhausted, working superhuman hours with little or no income. As the national coordinator, Sara was simply unable to single-handedly secure funding for individual projects for each region of a national organization.

Regional organizers from places like Juigalpa (in Chontales) and Matagalpa that did not have funded projects were angered by what they saw as the lack of support offered to them by the Managua office—support that many felt was due them for having loyally followed the leaders of the National Women's Secretariat in leaving the CST. On the other hand, Sara and the other organizers of the national office felt that this was like "charging for solidarity" (*cobrando la solidaridad*). The expectations of the regional offices as well as their own need for funds were overwhelming. During my months of fieldwork Sara would often complain, "I'm tired of being the mother hen with the little chicks. . . . In this Movement there are no mothers, or aunts, or godmothers, and this Movement is going to need qualified women. Whoever doesn't want to work should get out of the way to make room for one who is interested in doing so!"

THE ISSUE OF AUTONOMY

The centralized organizational structure of MEC was undeniably reminiscent of the verticalism for which the women had criticized the CST. Some of MEC's members felt that it did not coincide with the overall political vision and the founding principles of the organization. As early as 1994 Sara worried to other MEC founders about "reproducing the same methods that we criticize the men for." In a group interview Alicia, Evelyn, and Eloisa nodded in agreement as Sara remarked, "We hope not to repeat the same patriarchal vices. We are going to be very careful about avoiding *caudillismo*" (political bossism).

The challenge before the women as they continued the process of constituting MEC was to balance practical funding demands with the founding principles of personal and organizational autonomy and to devise an organizational form that would reflect "unity in diversity." The words of one organizer from the Managua team became the theme of a 1995 strategy-planning session: "We want to be autonomous and diverse, *but* organized."

As part of this process, MEC organizers secured funds from a Canadian NGO to gather their constituency together for a national congress and commemoration of MEC's first anniversary. Entitled "United and Strong Against Discrimination Against Women," the event was to begin the next phase of the organization's constitution by formulating MEC's objectives and a plan for achieving them. MEC organizers were overwhelmed by the level of participation in this event—eight hundred women attended the celebration and discussion sessions. MEC's Managua team organized eleven workshop and discussion sessions, which were facilitated by movement organizers as well as leaders from autonomous women's movements, who in a show of solidarity offered to help. Topics of the sessions included women and violence, women and human rights, gender and self-esteem, the labor code, gender and labor relations in the Free Trade Zone, and women and the economic crisis. At the end of the work sessions the groups summarized points from their discussion to the larger gathering, which could then discuss and prioritize them to compose a collectively generated set of recommendations.

An entire discussion session was devoted to "Women and Organization," and it was from this session and the larger discussion that it sparked that MEC founders drew plans for the organization's reconstitution. MEC organizers facilitated the discussion and compiled a list of the women's responses to the question "What should the Movement [MEC] be like?" (*¿Cómo debe ser el movimiento?*) Some of the women's comments: "The Movement should defend our interests . . . and struggle for a more just society for women." "The Movement should be broad-based [*amplio*] and contribute to the unity of women." "It should stimulate work of grassroots women to strengthen the work of our Movement." "It should create commissions to look for employment opportunities for unemployed women." "It should create mechanisms that will permit us to be active within our organization." "It should organize women, but respect our diversity." "There should be no political [party], religious, or other affiliations, and it should continue to be autonomous." "It should be an alternative that integrates women . . . into society." (See MEC 1995.)

MEC organizers concluded from the session that "the women emphasized the autonomy of the Movement, imparting the principle of a broadbased, pluralist, and strong movement that brings together [*aglutina*] women from diverse social sectors, without distinction of race, political [party], or religious orientation and with a multiplicity of demands" (MEC 1995).

MEC's statement seems in line with the orientation of the so-called new social movements, which in the view of some have signaled a significant shift in the nature and scope of collective action by embracing principles of democracy, creating a politics based on identities other than class, and rejecting the idea of a master narrative of social transformation (Mouffe 1995; Jelin 1994b). This new politics has made autonomy a key issue for the diverse popular organizations that have emerged in the Latin American context under contemporary conditions of global capitalism, including Latin American women's movements (Jaquette 1994b; Chinchilla 1992; Hellman 1992; Alvarez 1990). For women's movements in Latin America autonomy "entails a recognition of the diversity of social interests, the refusal of class reductionism, and, above all, of economism" (Chinchilla 1992: 47).

It is important not to gloss the complexity involved in the construction of collective definitions of autonomy within the organizations that make up this movement. Shared understandings of the meaning of autonomy do not exist a priori, but rather emerge from the articulations of members' identities as political actors with the specific political and social conditions. Contemporary meanings of autonomy draw from particular interactions between global and local processes and social movement participants' understandings of them. In MEC autonomy came to hold varied meanings for the different women of the organization, in part due to their positions within MEC as well as to their experiences in the CST. The organizers' positions on the issue of autonomy also reflected contrasting definitions and understandings of feminism, linked to debates within a transnational feminist movement.

At the moment of MEC's formation there was strong agreement among the founders regarding the need for the creation of a separate organizational space. María Luisa, the Grenada office coordinator, explains: "Our Movement was born out of women's very own necessity, . . . a women's movement with its own identity. . . . The principles with which it was born . . . were organic unity, autonomy, pluralism, without political or religious distinction—that it suffice that a woman be willing to be in the Movement to open the doors to her without having to say: 'Well, since you are with such and such a party, you can't come.' These are the principles: unity, solidarity among us—gender solidarity among other things."

In such an organization, as María Luisa says, participants would not have to "be submissive and lower our heads like an ostrich . . . asking for permission for everything and doing what they order us to do." Julieta, the coordinator of the León office, comments, "Autonomy allows me to use my creativity. It is the right to say 'yes' or 'no.' " Auxiliadora, from the regional office in El Viejo, reflects: "Before they limited [us] . . . in making our own decisions . . . as women before the collective, because the ones who always gave the directions were the men. They always oriented us to what they said, what they decided. . . . That is the big difference that I feel, that we formed this group of women of the Movement, that we are the ones who decide according to the different places where we are, and we do what we think is appropriate and what is good for us, the women. . . . We are not limited by anyone."

An emphasis on autonomy for the organization and for the individuals within it reflects another important departure from traditional leftist ways of organizing, which were epitomized by the FSLN during the 1980s. Individuals within the revolutionary collective were conceived of as "militant[s] committed to a collective ideal to which individuals themselves could legitimately be sacrificed. Self sacrifice was elevated to the highest moral status, to an ethical value sanctioned by superior significance of the collectivity" (Melucci 1996: 184). The leftist activist Margaret Randall (1994, 1981) has documented the rich testimonies of women who grew up politically in the FSLN and whose commitment to the revolutionary cause often involved deep personal sacrifices—for example, the abandonment of young children and family members, undesired abortions, and the loss of sons, husbands, and lovers to war.

The women of MEC were no strangers to these kinds of sacrifices. At a workshop on feminism facilitated by the well-known Nicaraguan feminist María Teresa Blandón, a group of MEC founders spent time discussing how gender played an important role in their experiences within the FSLN. The women spoke of being forced to leave small children in the care of mothers and grandmothers and being separated from them for months at a time. Sara recalled her fury when a member of the FSLN party told her that she owed the FSLN a huge debt. She replied: "I left my oldest son from the age of one year to the age of nine—that is the debt I have with the Frente. . . . I am what I am because of the mother who gave birth to me and sent me to school and my compañero who supported me in my studies." Others remembered being accused of being *burguesa* (bourgeois) for requesting time to care for a sick child. In the words of one workshop participant, " *la patria* was above all else: a mother's love, love of ourselves." Julieta remembered: "I felt the load here [motions to her back]. . . . We had to give two hundred percent. . . . There was never a Sunday or a Saturday with all the tasks of the revolution."

In contrast to the demands of the militant organizations of the revolution, the women of MEC envisioned their organization as a space in which participants could achieve personal autonomy. Sara puts it this way: "That everyone shine with her own light and search for her own identity. . . . Shoemakers, to your shoes!!" Julieta spoke of her pride in finally being able to pursue a degree in psychology. Others also had personal and educational goals, such as returning to high school. Thus, the organization sought a type of collective that was strengthened by individuality and difference, and involved a transformed relationship between the individual and the collectivity. Sara contends, "This Marxism-Leninism—this kind of collectivism—ya no me va [I no longer hold with it]. . . . [Instead], the collective oppresses the individuals within it. . . . Each of us has to defend herself within her own space, . . . assuming her own role within this space. . . . There is the collective, but there is also individualism within the collective. . . . We never speak of these things—of the individual processes within groups."

Feminist ideas offered the women of MEC a new conceptual understanding of their experiences within the Sandinista party as well as organizational principles that coincided with their rejection of class-reductionism. Many MEC organizers, particularly those from the Managua team, but also individual regional leaders, came to openly articulate a feminist identity.

FEMINISTAS DE BASE OR TRANSNATIONAL
FEMINISTS?: FEMINIST IDENTITIES AND MEC'S
RELATIONSHIP WITH THE AUTONOMOUS
WOMEN'S MOVEMENT

Sonia Alvarez (1998) has observed that Latin American feminisms have "gone global" through the transnationalization of feminist discourses and practices. The preparatory processes for international conferences, like UN conferences, have reinforced global coalition building among feminist NGOs and women's movement organizations (Basu 1995). National, regional, and transnational networks have linked women's organizations working on a wide range of issues (Alvarez 1998). These networks have facilitated the transnational circulation of feminist demands, practices, and discourses. More direct participation in the Nicaragua autonomous women's movement and participants' closer association with self-identified feminists led to MEC organizers' becoming more exposed to and gradually appropriating discourses from the transnational feminist movement.

Feminism provided the women of MEC a new framework for understanding their experiences within the mass organizations of the FSLN. MEC organizers often drew a comparison between their own experiences in the CST and those of a battered woman in an abusive relationship. In a 1995 interview Sara remembered: "So we said, 'Hey, this is like masochism,' like staying in a masochistic relationship . . . when you are adoring, idolizing the man, while the man beats you, beats you, beats you. . . . One day we woke up and we said, 'Enough!' And *I* was the first to wake up. I said, 'Enough already! How long?!' "

Making the link between gender oppression in the home, such as in the case of domestic violence, and gendered power differentials that occurred within the mass organizations like the CST was an important consciousness-raising process for many MEC organizers—especially those from the Managua team. This process was bolstered by MEC organizers' participation in events, workshops, and seminars organized by the feminist movement in Nicaragua and abroad.

At the national level when MEC was newly formed, with virtually no financial base, and still had not established an office of its own, the feminist organization Puntos de Encuentro (Points of Encounter) offered MEC its conference room to hold a retreat for organizers to discuss and collectively process the emotional trauma that they had suffered from their break from the FSLN. A leader from Puntos, whose organizational work included years with AMNLAE and the ATC, facilitated the event, which supported MEC organizers' developing a vision for their new organization's future trajectory. Puntos assumed the cost of recording the sessions of discussions and personal testimonies to be used as a tool for reflection by MEC organizers. For the MEC leaders, this process was an extremely important step in the organization's constitution.

In addition, transnationally circulating feminist discourses—particularly the language of rights and discrimination—became effective frames for articulating MEC's demands and objectives. The language of human rights gave a name to MEC organizers' experiences within the CST (Keck and Sikkink 1998a). Phrases like "gender discrimination," "gender equality," and "rights" resonated with their experiences. Founders would speak of how "el odio machista" (masculine male hatred) of the CST leaders "violated our human rights."

The language of rights, based on the individual as the bearer of rights, also jibed well with the value that MEC participants placed on personal autonomy within the collective. Rights discourse and feminist concepts like "the personal is political" became important idiomatic tools for developing and articulating MEC's organizational principles, mission, and collective identity(ies). In this manner globalized discourses gave participants the words to articulate their grievances in the CST as well as to describe what they sought in the local, autonomous, "women only" space which they were in the process of creating.

The use of such language also was intimately connected with participants' construction of feminist collective identities. Jill, the cooperante from Canada, who had worked for twelve years with the women who became the MEC organizers observed: "They became used to talking about defending their rights as workers. Soon they started talking about defending their rights as women. . . . They started to see that being a feminist isn't being more than what they are, . . . that it wasn't just an intellectual term." Indeed, many MEC organizers would define feminism as "the struggle to defend women's rights" and described MEC's principal objective as being: "to organize women to defend their rights." Thus, a language and concepts shared with the transnational women's movement played a key role, not only in framing MEC's demands, but in constructing a vision of how the women of MEC saw themselves and the history and objectives of their organization. At a 1995 national meeting in which national and regional leaders developed the work plan and organizational strategy for the coming year, Sara, who in the past had been known to be publicly critical of feminism, declared: "We need feminism. We have to get to know it better." And, indeed, the organization pursued this deeper understanding of feminism by sponsoring a national leadership training on the topic and later incorporating workshops on gender and feminism into leadership training offered to women in all of MEC's various programs.

In expressing their feminism, however, MEC organizers emphasize and clarify that they adhere to a particular interpretation of feminism, calling themselves *feministas de base* (grassroots feminists). In this manner, MEC participants who identify with feminist principles do not merely *adopt* feminist principles, but actively construct and reconfigure them, making them their own. In other words, because of suspicions about the place that class issues hold within feminism, participants are reluctant to identify themselves or their organization with a predefined notion of *feminist*. Their articulation of a "popular feminism" echoes that of working class and grassroots women's organizations throughout Latin America, who are claiming feminism as their own in order to cope with poverty, inequality, and austerity brought about by globalization (Safa 1996). Just as Alvarez (1998, 1994) describes in the case of Brazil, MEC organizers' expression of a class-based, feminist identity involves a criticism of *las institucionalizadas* (the institutionalized ones) who in the post-1990 context have increasingly focused efforts at political lobbying and public opinion campaigns, turning away from work centered in grassroots communities. The women of the Managua collective would frequently lament: "No one wants to do work with the base anymore."

MEC participants' continued identification with and as *mujeres de base* represents one component of an articulated collective identity of movement members. All leaders come from poor or working-class backgrounds, and the great majority of them continued to reside in poor barrios. As the Managua collective and regional coordinators secured funding for programs, they continually recruited women from the grassroots communities to work in administering those programs. This system of using grassroots promotoras to run programs in the communities served as a mechanism to promote leadership among women from poor or working-class backgrounds, and these women were gradually incorporated into the Managua team.

This practice, which reflects MEC members' identification as grassroots women, is consistent with the Leninist strategy of creating cadres. As former cadres of the revolution, MEC founders were well acquainted with the idea of gradually incorporating members of the base who showed special potential. This practice, left over from their days in the FSLN, maintains and reinforces an important aspect of MEC's collective class-oriented identity, differentiating the group from many other autonomous women's organizations.

Just as gender-based contradictions led to the creation of the autonomous MEC, MEC organizers' identities, not only as women, but as women workers, caused their organization to hold a particular position within the autonomous women's movement. Their "humble" or working-class backgrounds set organizers apart from feminist collectives, such as Las Malinches,[3] Cenzontle (the name of a bird), and Mujer y Cambio (Women and Change), or professional service organizations, such as S. I. Mujer (Women's Integral Services) and IXCHEN (named after a Mayan goddess), that provided reproductive health education and training to women. Although some members of the MEC collective completed college degrees after MEC's formation, they were not educated abroad, did not speak English—a particularly acute limitation given some of the transnational strategies in which they engaged—and had not received expensive private educations like many well-known feminists active in the autonomous women's movement.

These differences would be clear at coalition or network meetings of the larger Nicaraguan women's movement that MEC members—usually members of the Managua office—attended. Sara, Evelyn, and Laura would often speak of feeling "out of their environment" at events like the 1996 meeting organized by the Nicaraguan Women's Institute (INIM), at that time a government office. The purpose of the meeting was to "consolidate the coordination and cooperation between INIM and the Nicaraguan Women's Movement" (INIM 1996b: 2). Participants formed working groups to draft a document specifying how INIM and the various organizations that made up the autonomous women's movement would cooperate "to accomplish greater levels of influence within the Nicaraguan state in solving the problems that affect women" (INIM 1996a: 2).

Representatives from twenty-nine women's organizations attended this event, held in the Intercontinental Hotel in Managua. The luxurious surroundings of the conference area gave it a professional and business-like atmosphere. A catered lunch was served in the hotel's dining room, and the event closed with a cocktail hour. Many well-dressed professional women active in organizations such as International Foundation for the Global Challenge (FIDEG), Cenzontle, and Colectivo Itza were present and were among the most vocal in the discussion. Despite efforts by organizers to include all participants in the forum and the election of Sara as the moderator in one of the working groups, it was in spaces such as these that MEC leaders often felt confronted with their own class origins and in many cases comparatively limited educational backgrounds and cultural capital.

The process of simply getting to such meetings reflected what MEC members perceived as class biases. MEC organizers expressed frustration at the assumption that everyone owned her own car for transportation to and from such activities, especially at night, when travel on public buses was dangerous. Often I would attend meetings with Laura, Sara, or Evelyn. As the meetings would begin to draw to a close, we would scurry to the parking lot to *pedir ray* (hitch a ride), hoping we would not have to make the long walk in the hot sun to get to the bus. One night, after an activity sponsored by INIM, Evelyn and I were too embarrassed to ask anyone for a ride. In a rather symbolic incident, as we waited for the bus in the rain, we were drenched when the car of one of the other feminists splashed us with mud.

Some of the Managua team members often commented that the parking lots in front of certain well-known feminist organizations gave a clear indication of the class position of the women who worked there. In contrast, at MEC only the two international cooperantes owned their own cars—a luxury in a country where the price of gasoline is high even for those earning U.S. dollars. Members most often relied on public buses to visit local communities or the FTZ. Or, they would hitch a ride from the international cooperantes or the coordinator's spouse, who had a pickup truck.

MEC's vision to address both class and gender issues—in fact, to transcend this dichotomy—also led to instances of tension and alienation within the broader women's movement. For example, as the director of MEC's Documentation Center, Evelyn participated in the Network of Documentation Centers Concerning Women and Children. This network of centers from various autonomous women's organizations that collected documents and information pertaining to their organizations' specialties on women and children's issues met to exchange information and sources. (Like many networks, clear criteria for membership were only loosely established.)

Evelyn had recently met the director of the Documentation Center in the government's Ministry of Labor. This woman had a personal interest in learning more about work issues relating to women and in extending the center's collection to include more information pertaining to gender. Evelyn told her about the Network of Centers of Documentation and invited her to come. At the next meeting, however, the other participants received her very poorly, indicating that only members of "women's" groups could participate. The representative from the Ministry of Labor never returned, and Evelyn was embarrassed and frustrated by the other women's refusal to welcome her. Again, the dichotomy of woman/worker that MEC organizers wished to transcend in their objectives and practices was reinforced at the level of practice by other political forces.

MEC's close connection to poor communities was recognized within the autonomous women's movement and was a source of pride for organizers. When a group of women's organizations organized a preparatory meeting for the 1995 Beijing conference, a leader from Puntos de Encuentro called Sara at home in a desperate plea to mobilize women from grassroots communities. MEC's mobilizing influence in these communities was clear when Sara and the other women from Managua immediately sent word to MEC's regional offices and filled several buses of women to participate in the event. Sara proudly sat outside the conference hall greeting the women personally, as bus after bus pulled up to the entrance.

In another crystallizing event, at a 1997 celebration of International Women's Day, Josefina, who later became an important leader in the Managua office, working with maquila workers, and the others expressed dismay when we arrived at the assembly hall to find it only a quarter full. MEC had been told that there were only limited spaces available. When we arrived, however, it was apparent that the women that MEC had invited represented about one fifth of those in attendance. "Had we known, we could have filled this place with women from the base," remarked Sara. Josefina confided to me: "I'm not just saying this, Jennifer, but it's as if there has been a failure of the work at the grassroots. . . . There is no social base." The problem, according to the women of MEC, was that the women's movement–feminist movement is made up of mostly NGOs that provide services to grassroots women. Fewer and fewer groups continued work at the grassroots to organize the women or to operate directly within the barrios themselves. Again the lament, "No one wants to do work at the base anymore."

And yet in an ironic way, MEC's connection with its social base was also something of a liability, given the pressure to professionalize that women's organizations in Nicaragua and elsewhere faced in the 1990s. Thus, when organizers from a well-known professional feminist organization received funding to create a revolving credit fund, they contacted the women of MEC and proposed that the graduates from the job-training program be recipients of the loans in order to establish microenterprises. Sara, Laura, and Evelyn were indignant at the suggestion. "Why would women who have just undergone six months of training in a trade want to set up *fritangas* [popular food stands] like every other woman in Nicaragua?" asked Sara in disbelief. But what was even more insulting to these organizers was the division of labor that was presupposed by the offer: "They want us to bring the women together while they manage the fund! And at 5 percent interest!" Their interpretation of the proposal was that MEC was left with the "dirty" grassroots work of producing worthy candidates from local communities, while the feminist organization would conduct the "professional" work of managing the program and controlling the funds. "Relations of power between women's organizations that are like this [holds one hand over the other to indicate a hierarchy] aren't appropriate. Egalitarian relations are the ones that we agree with," Sara declared.

DIVERSITY AND DIVERGENCES WITHIN THE MEC ORGANIZATION

As we have seen, at the time of MEC's formation, participants collectively placed a high value on organizational autonomy and articulated an identity of "women of the base"—sometimes even "feminists of the base." Beneath the surface of these collectively voiced ideas, however, were differing views about the appropriate course that MEC should take in its development as an organization, representing diverging orientations among organizers regarding the deeper meanings of autonomy and feminism and participants' own identities as political actors.

By early 1996, these sometimes conflicting ideas came to a head in a crisis that nearly brought about MEC's dissolution. A number of MEC's founders did end up leaving the organization, several of them returning to "mixed" (gender) organizations affiliated with the FSLN. Ana María, the regional coordinator of the Chinandega office, returned to the CST to become the new director of the National Women's Secretariat. Other leaders and former leaders ran for offices under the FSLN banner in the 1996 elections. A leader from El Viejo won a seat in the city government, though she opted to continue her work with MEC. The most conflictive separation came when Tamara, who had been in charge of the Managua-based programs, and Reyna, who had led the domestic worker union in Managua and was originally in line to run the Documentation Center (Evelyn eventually took on this responsibility), left MEC to return to the CST metal-workers' federation.

These departures caused great upheaval and deep emotional wounds among the women who remained with MEC, who saw them as an almost unspeakable betrayal. More than simply a product of personal disagreements (though certainly there were personal tensions and a degree of competition between Tamara and other members of the Managua collective), these internal conflicts reflected participants' differing notions of what the goals and organizational practices of an autonomous women's organization should be. A common refrain among MEC's organizers was to say that MEC was an autonomous organization with its "own identity" (una identidad propia) and a "gender vision." However, a clear consensus about the definition of these ideas and what they meant for MEC's organizational practices did not exist.

As participants collectively grappled with how to structure their organization in a manner that would reflect MEC's founding principles, disagreements arose over the tension between notions of autonomy versus unity, which in turn reflected differing ideas about feminism. Simplifying complex relationships and debates, it is possible to identify three camps: the Managua collective (some of whom had worked in the National Women's Secretariat office); the regional leaders (most of whom were founders of MEC); and a group of founders who continued to maintain close relations with organizations of the labor movement and/or the FSLN (some of whom eventually left MEC to return to mixed organizations).

The Managua Collective. The Managua group gradually began to put less weight on an idea of unity and more on "local autonomy." They called for the abandonment of a centralized national structure and proposed that each regional office work independently, coordinating efforts with the other offices, but not hierarchically linked to Managua as a national office. In this model, regional "teams" or "collectives" at each office would form their own local strategy and plans of action; the regional offices would be horizontally linked in a network-like structure and would implement few national programs.

The regional leaders embraced this idea in differing degrees. Some were in favor of the idea of regional autonomy but were apprehensive at the prospect of having to independently plan and seek funding for local programs and projects. In the words of one coordinator: "Autonomy has its pro's and con's." Others were extremely reluctant to let go of a national structure, and some regional coordinators felt abandoned by Managua—formerly the national office. Referring to the idea of the financial autonomy of the regional offices, a coordinator from Granada contended: "That's fine for her [referring to Julieta, who had secured funding for her office's operation], but what am I going to do? I don't have anything." At a national meeting regional coordinators expressed doubts: "We're not entirely convinced of this autonomy and separation." "It would be a loss if only Managua were able to come out well."

In turn, Sara and the Managua collective felt tired of having to "carry the big load of the departments on our backs. . . . They only want autonomy when it is convenient to them." Evelyn, Sara, and Laura were frustrated by what they perceived as the regional coordinators' counterproductive fear of autonomy. Sara pointed out that "the international organizations are not interested in the Movement's national plan; they are interested in local plans and 'local power.' "

At a national meeting Sara suggested that the coordinators' real desire was to replicate the hierarchical structure as used by the leaders of the CST: "I hope that my compañeras do not fall into this same error. . . . We should eliminate this fear of *desmembraño* [loss of membership] and eradicate the concept of 'separatism' from our vocabulary." "We must manage [*manejar*] this concept [autonomy] without using the word 'separation,' " said Laura, a Managua leader. "No one is separating," reassured Sara; "what is happening is the development of structural autonomy." Indeed, Sara, Laura, and the others from the Managua team saw the decentralization of MEC as an "internal process of democratization."

The Managua collective and the regional leaders also differed in their orientations toward the autonomous women's movement in Nicaragua as well as concepts and ideas connected with the larger transnational feminist movement. After MEC's formation, the women of the Managua collective began to engage in more active participation in the activities, networks, coalitions, and meetings of the autonomous women's movement, but regional leaders did not join to the same extent. Some of the regional offices took part in isolated activities of the women's movement, but most of them maintained their alliances and organizational relations with local Sandinista organizations.

The Managua collective's more active entrée into the world of the internationally connected autonomous women's movement was due in part to the fact that most of the movement's activities were held in Managua. Increased affiliation also resulted from the fact that the organizers' from the Managua collective had been the national leadership of the CST's Women's Secretariat and were accustomed to networking with other organizations. Within the CST, the responsibilities of regional coordinators like María Luisa were limited to local coordination with few interorganizational contacts—especially outside of their regions. After MEC's formation groups from the autonomous women's movement, like Puntos de Encuentro, supported the fledgling organization by offering training workshops at the Managua office and assistance with the first anniversary commemoration event.

Within the Nicaraguan women's movement(s), divisions among "las feministas," AMNLAE, and the women's secretariats of the CST, ATC, and the National Union of Farmers and Ranchers (UNAG) had a long-standing history. Class-based tensions stemmed from the upper-class backgrounds of many of the feminists. Women who continued to work in the mass organizations, such as the leaders of the women's secretariats, often complained that feminists from the autonomous women's movement looked down on their work in the mixed organizations and were not supportive of the "popular demands" of grassroots women (Criquillon 1995; Chinchilla 1994). In many cases, distrust went back even further, resulting from individuals' differing positions within the hierarchy of the FSLN. And some MEC organizers could not forget the treatment they had received when they had served as the subordinates to high-ranking women in the FSLN who were now prominent members of feminist organizations.

Coalitions and cooperation with organizations from the autonomous women's movement soothed some of these tensions, bringing women from the Managua collective together with self-identified feminists, such as members of the feminist collective Las Malinches. In many cases the women of the Managua office discovered that they shared similar experiences with organizers from these feminist groups, including those of sexual harassment and discrimination within the FSLN. For example, Evelyn and Sara attended meetings with well-known feminists like María Teresa Blandón, whose upper-class origins and feminist orientations had earned her the labels of "bourgeois" and "lesbian separatist" on the part of some leaders within the FSLN. As described above, the Managua team invited Blandón to conduct a national workshop in Managua on the topic of feminism, and organizers from the Managua office as well as most of the regional offices attended the activity. Participants were riveted by Blandón's testimonies, and despite her clearly different class origins, they nodded in empathy, sometimes tearfully, when she described her experiences within the FSLN: "When I was in the Front I learned that we women have to do three times as much to receive the same recognition. . . . Men who didn't do half what we did are now among the high-ranking leaders." A leader from the Managua office agreed emphatically: "In the world of the trade union movement we had to demonstrate that we were just as capable as they. It was a huge survival struggle. The male militants always saw us as hardly capable. . . . For us women the only thing missing was to slit our wrists to prove our commitment—that was the only thing that the revolution didn't ask of us."

María Luisa from Granada reflected on MEC's break from the CST: "We, the women, don't believe that a 'godfather' is going to come along and solve everything for us. I feel that they [FSLN] opened a space for us. It's as if there were a fence, and on the other side is a lagoon or a mountain. And they said, 'I'm going to open the door for you, but if you get yourself killed, you get yourself killed.' What we have no one has given to us as a gift. Our Movement was born in a storm. If we hadn't been capable, we would have died of a heart attack by now. We have come to prove that we women *can* do it."

Organizers from the Managua collective participated in national networks of women's organizations like the Network of Women Against Violence Against Women and Children and the Network of Documentation Centers Concerning Women and Children. Sara became involved with the National Coalition of Women, "March 8th," a coalition of women's organizations dedicated to increasing women's political representation and women's issues in the 1996 elections and named after International Women's Day (see Blandón 2001). These loosely coordinated networks formed as the result of the 1992 *encuentro* of autonomous women's organizations held in Managua (Babb 1997) and represented the movement's search to overcome divisions resulting from differing orientations and histories—particularly in regard to relations with the FSLN. In a pattern similar to what the women of MEC were now experiencing, the issue of autonomy had been at the center of the discussions at this 1992 meeting.

As was the case for many class-based movements of the Latin American left, in the organizations of the FSLN, the common orthodox view was to see feminism as "foreign," divisive, and even counterrevolutionary (Randall 1994, 1992; Sternbach et al. 1992). In the words of one MEC organizer, "The word *feminist* was like the devil." Other women spoke of how Sandinista leaders would ostracize feminists by labeling them as lesbians. Though some MEC founders had been exposed to feminism before the Movement's formation, and even identified as feminists, for most, feminism was a murky or new area. María Luisa commented, "I began to get to know the word *feminism* in 1990. I didn't know this word—I didn't know if it was something you eat with a fork or with a spoon."

For the Managua collective, especially, the dramatic split from the CST as well as changed orientations, contacts, and experiences in the broader women's movement led them to identify themselves and their work as "feminist." By 1996, after the crisis and resignation of several dissenting MEC founders, the Managua team revised its statement of purpose to describe their collective as a "feminist, environmentalist, autonomous, pluralist movement that promotes solidarity among women . . . and contributes to the improvement of the socioeconomic situation of women."

Thus, the Managua collective's process of identification with feminist principles coincided with its view that autonomy was more than just independence from male-dominated organizations and political parties. For them autonomy had become closely meshed with feminist organizational principles of participative democracy, gender solidarity, and the personal as political. Rather than just working in a separate organizational space from the men and the Sandinista party in order to improve the situation of women workers, the women of the Managua collective began to envision the aim of their struggle as the transformation of gendered systems of power.

Workshops offered at the Managua office showed clear evidence of the collective's greater integration of a conceptual framework of gender and power into their work. All programs—job training and microcredit as well as those directed at maquila workers—included educational workshops on discrimination, gender roles, gender and reproductive health, self-esteem (from a gender perspective), and domestic violence. Job-training programs offered technical training in nontraditional areas such as auto mechanics, masonry, and electrical work.

MEC's Managua team published materials to be used in workshops with program participants, and here the use of feminist language from various feminist traditions is especially evident. A handbook for use in workshops with maquiladora workers quotes the radical feminist Adrienne Rich (MEC 1997b: 4) and incorporates both a liberal feminist challenge to the public/private dichotomy and the Marxist-feminist notion that patriarchy works hand-in-hand with a class-based system of domination. The publication "Gender and Discrimination in the Free Trade Zone" begins with a dedication that states: "With this booklet we wish to . . . provide you with the necessary tools for deepening your understanding about *gender and discrimination*, and how gender relations affect our *family and work lives*" (MEC 1997c; second emphasis added).

The booklet cites free trade zones as an example of "patriarchy at the global level." One page features an illustration with the kneeling figure of a woman bearing the crushing weight of an enormous globe on her back. On the globe appear the words, "Free Trade Zones," and labels hang from it bearing the English words "Made in Korea," "Made in Nicaragua," and "Made in Mexico."

Another cartoon image is of a maquila worker sitting at a sewing machine with piles of clothes behind her. Her mouth is gagged, and the words "Free Trade Zone" are printed on her covered mouth. In the next frame the same woman is stirring a pot of food with one hand and holding a baby with the other, while another child is clinging to her leg and crying. Two other children sit nearby, and a bucket and mop in the foreground and laundry in the background evoke the idea of endless household tasks. A man sits in the background of the illustration, idly reading a newspaper (see figure 13).

These images reflect the kinds of concepts used and discussed in MEC's workshops. All program participants take part in workshops which are organized around themes such as gender and reproductive health, self-esteem, human rights, and domestic violence and which involve discussions about concepts such as "discrimination," "gender roles," and "patriarchy." Small group exercises facilitate participants' reflecting on relations of power within their own lives. Participants were encouraged to share their experiences of domestic violence, sexual discrimination at work, and how they felt that gender roles had shaped their lives.

Many workshops and program activities had the feel of consciousness-raising groups. Indeed, participants often described a transformative process that accompanied their participation in these programs. The testimony of a woman who used a MEC scholarship to complete a job-training program in auto mechanics is revealing:

> When we started perhaps it was with a lot of fear because we didn't know what we would be capable of. . . . In the course they looked at me like a strange animal, because they were all men, and I was the only woman. But, later my compañeros congratulated me, because I started and I finished. . . . At first I knew absolutely nothing about mechanics, but in the course I began to realize that *yes*, I could do it, that we can learn anything—even nontraditional work. The training makes us feel that we can continue to move ahead. On a personal level the training about violence has helped me to be different. I hadn't realized that at times we women also use violence. Now I think before I hit my son. On the other hand I have also come to realize that I, too, can [financially] support my children.[4]

This participant's comments demonstrate the connections between women's personal lives and their work that the program is designed to facilitate, bridging the public/private gap. Organizers' experiences of sexism and discrimination within the CST lent an organic quality to their feminist orientations. The influence of the Nicaraguan autonomous women's movement, however, as well as a transnational feminist movement, also played a role in the formation of the Managua collective's feminism. This is reflected in the organizational structure of the collective as well as its grassroots works with program beneficiaries.

Regional Leaders. With some notable exceptions, regional coordinators were less inclined to define autonomy in this way or to bring feminist language and ideals into their work. For most of the regional coordinators and leaders who made up this second camp of MEC organizers, autonomy meant little more than access to decision-making power without "un hombre que anda atrás jodiendo" (a man going along behind screwing around). Regional organizers viewed autonomy as the freedom to independently pursue the very same kinds of projects and programs as they had within the CST organization. Activities launched by the regional offices tended to be focused on creating income-generating activities and job training for women and girls. Most of the offices offered training in very traditional skills such as sewing, knitting, and cutting hair. Others offered credit programs for women to start microenterprises. Health programs and small clinics were also common in the regional offices. Such programs included little emphasis on gender as a system of power. In some cases regional coordinators professed little familiarity with feminist concepts, viewing feminism as, in the words of an organizer from Chichigalpa (a regional office established in 1997), "men and women pitted against one another."

Although in other cases particular regional leaders did identify as feminist, there was a qualitative difference to the way that they expressed their feminism. As for the women of the Managua collective, the break from the CST played an important role in their identities. Yet there was a militancy about the way that they talked about their feminism that echoed the revolutionary discourse of the Sandinistas. The first time that I asked Lola, an organizer from the Granada office, if she saw herself as a feminist, she nodded her head definitively. "Until death!" she declared. The comments of María Luisa, the former revolutionary from extremely poor origins and the coordinator of the Granada office, challenge notions of feminism as solely holding relevance for upper-class women and demonstrate how the experiences within the CST contributed to her developing a feminist consciousness:

> Yes, I have identified as a feminist from the moment in which our supreme leader, . . . when we saw that after this woman had offered so much to the labor movement and in the most cynical and brutal manner this woman is injured by the leadership of the CST. . . . So,

this is the transcendental moment for me to reaffirm and ratify one more time my feminist principles. . . . Because feminism is born out of the great injustices that women suffer. It's not like . . . it occurs to someone, "Well, I am going to be a feminist." No. It is [born of] the very same struggles and hard experiences that life has given us—these experiences and a will and decision to fight for feminism . . . and to struggle against all those injustices that are committed.

María Luisa's testimony illustrates the almost militaristic feminism of many of the regional leaders. Along with their sandinismo and class consciousness, these women see their feminism as embodying principles of struggle—something to live and die for. A typical meeting or event at the Granada office, for example, would often begin with María Luisa leading participants in populist cheers reminiscent of the Sandinista years. The only difference was that instead of "Viva Carlos Fonseca!" (Long live Carlos Fonseca) or "Viva la revolución!" María Luisa would shout: "Que viva el Movimiento de Mujeres, María Elena Cuadra!" Those in attendance would respond with a rousing: "Viva!"

The "Doble Militantes." The third camp that emerged within MEC comprised leaders who maintained relations with (and in many cases continued to participate in) organizations of the FSLN. Some of these women took on an orientation of what has been termed "doble militantes" (double militants), doing their "gender work" in MEC, but continuing to participate in regional FSLN union federations or other Sandinista organizations (see Sternbach et al. 1992). For example, Auxiliadora, the coordinator of the El Viejo office, continued her work with MEC while simultaneously holding an office in a municipal post under the FSLN party banner. Many women of this group were not willing to concede the spaces that they had fought for within these "mixed" organizations. For example, Tamara refused to give up her spot within the metal-workers' federation: "We have fought for this space in the union and . . . it's not going to be easy to get rid of us" (quoted in Jubb 1995: 20).

Some members of this camp eventually left MEC to return to the mixed organizational spaces of the Sandinista party and mass organizations. These resignations resulted from personal conflicts and disagreements regarding organizational strategy, depending upon the individuals involved. For example, differences arose regarding how best to serve the needs of women workers. Ana María, the regional coordinator for Chinandega who returned to the CST to serve as the director of the National Women's Secretariat, reflected to me that truly "integral" work could only be completed within the mixed *instancias* (spaces): "It's always easier to talk about gender among women. . . . If we really want to transform society, then we have to make the men conscious of the importance of women's participation."[5] To varying degrees, the women of this camp continued to see the labor movement and the FSLN party as the most appropriate place for working to improve the conditions facing women workers and unemployed women.

MEC's increasingly close affiliation with the autonomous women's movement, especially the activities and orientations of the Managua office, became another source of disagreement among organizers. Members of this third camp never completely cut ties with Sandinista organizations, including trade union federations, and they tended to see the problem for women in the unions as particular corrupt leaders—leaders who forgot that "revolution is made starting at the base, not the 'cupola'"—rather than intractable sexism. Women from this faction, like Ana María and Auxiliadora, left their federations (though in some cases they never officially resigned) only after they were told in no uncertain terms they "should decide, either . . . stay with Sara or . . . stay with the federation." Despite being forced out of the union federations, they continued to see their place as squarely within the labor movement, even if the oppressive actions of certain individual leaders had prompted them to form the autonomous MEC.

The three camps of MEC organizers thus espoused contrasting definitions of feminism and feminist practice. For example, Ana María, from the doble militante camp, is critical of the feminist movement for "not taking women workers into account" and for belittling the organizational efforts of women within the labor movement: "They see us as if we were submitting to the men, when in actuality we are struggling in the other spaces where the women are. . . . We are a women's movement within the labor movement." Nonetheless, like many of the women of this group, Ana María sees herself as a feminist—albeit a particular kind of feminist. "Feminism is very broad," she contends.

Organizers who maintained close relations with the FSLN also emphasized the importance of autonomy and connected it to feminist ideas. But for them feminist autonomy meant primarily the freedom to work with women only. Auxiliadora, who continued her work with MEC while holding a municipal position as an elected official of the Sandinista party, explained her views: "Before I saw it [feminism] as work that was too narrow in focus. . . . [But now] . . . Work with women only, for me that's it; that's feminism . . . Work with women and always with women."

The divisions among these three camps did not stem solely from differing views of feminism and degrees of contact with the autonomous women's movement. Organizers' individual experiences of the gender-based conflicts within the organizations of the FSLN were also a source of these divisions. The founders who remained with MEC had directly experienced harsh treatment at the hands of the national leaders and were more convinced of the need for complete separation. They were joined by unemployed women whom they recruited from the grassroots communities; these women had not directly experienced the break from the CST, having lost their union affiliation when they lost their jobs. Those who returned to the "mixed" organizations tended to be women who had maintained ties with their former organization even after MEC's formation. In fact, several of the regional federations of the CST did not support the orientations and decisions of their national leadership, and many male regional leaders remained supportive and sympathetic to the women's plight.

Some members of this camp straddled the line between the women's movement and the labor movement, and others returned to the labor movement but maintained friendly contact with MEC. A few members of this third camp, however, became the centers of great upheaval within the organization. After a series of heated conflicts between Tamara, Laura, and Reyna and the rest of the Managua collective over the use of funds and equipment purchased with NGO money and over the three women's continued involvement with the CST federations, Tamara and Reyna stormed out of MEC's office. Subsequently, at a national meeting the regional coordinators voted that they not be permitted to return.

At a national meeting several months later, participants voted to implement the more "network-like" organizational structure proposed by Sara and the Managua collective. Regional coordinators agreed (some very reluctantly) that the task of funding regional programs should be the responsibility of regional offices. In practice, however, this change in organizational structure could not be implemented immediately. Many regional offices simply were not able to operate autonomously from the former national office and still remain in existence.

For example, one of my responsibilities as a cooperante was to assist the Granada office in devising a plan of action for the coming year. Sara and some of the members of the Managua team became concerned when I described the Granada team's progress. It was apparent that the group needed more in-depth *asesoría* (guidance or support) to establish a year-long plan that included fundable projects. Sara and Andrea, one of the Canadian cooperantes, agreed to spend the day working with the group from Granada to come up with such a plan. At first, however, Sara insisted that the Managua team should actually charge the group from Granada or at least ask them to sign a document to acknowledge that it was a donation of time worth a certain amount of money. Sara argued that the Managua team's work—and her work specifically as the person in charge of writing and submitting funding proposals—had become invisible, like domestic work. Asking that the Granada group acknowledge the value of this work would make the Managua team's support visible again. Sara also insisted that the women from Granada find their own way to pay for transportation to and from Managua and to pay for their own lunch.

In the end, however, Sara relented, and used money from Managua's administrative budget to pay for the women's transportation and food costs. The women from Granada arrived and spent the day with Sara and Andrea. They left with a detailed yearlong plan that included a list of proposed programs with concrete objectives. In addition, a group from the Managua collective eventually wrote a proposal for a credit and home-improvement project and included Granada as one of the communities in which the program would be implemented. Though Managua organizers did not wish to be responsible for developing and seeking funding for national level programs, they felt that there was no alternative if particular regional offices were to survive. Sara also worked to facilitate relations between the Estelí office and a Spanish NGO in which she had contacts and to work with the Juigalpa office to submit a project proposal. Sara's hope was that after receiving funding for one or two projects the women of the regional offices would become more independent.

Indeed, in the case of the León office, these hopes were realized, as Julieta developed ties with German solidarity groups and received funding to implement local programs. When I left Nicaragua in 1997 the fate of the other regional offices after the conclusion of the current programs remained tenuous.

Internal divisions and diverging orientations among MEC organizers reveal that although the Movement's "official" narrative regarding the group's formation relates a story of an unequivocal break from the labor movement, in fact it was a complex process that varied depending on each participant's personal history as a political actor. The complexity that lies below the surface of collective action and the formation of collective identity(ies) serves as a reminder that organizations do not simply possess lives of their own and that it is artificial to separate an organizational analysis from that of the experiences of the individuals that comprise it. Organizations are not homogeneous; they embody an array of orientations, identities, and perspectives. In the case of MEC each participant's view of herself as a member of the movement arises from a distinct set of experiences framed by the specifics of place and local history. For example, María Luisa explains what the formation of MEC meant to her: "So on the personal level, very personal . . . the Movement for me was a space that came to fill an aspiration that I had. . . . I considered that it was my space."

NGO OR SOCIAL MOVEMENT REVISITED: BALANCING PROFESSIONALISM WITH GRASSROOTS ACTIVISM

Professionalization. As has been noted, in Latin America the transnationalization of feminism has been accompanied by a process deemed the NGO-ization or professionalization of women's organizations. In Brazil institutional openings in the state that emerged after a political transition to democracy facilitated this process. Working for change within institutional structures became a more viable political strategy after the end of the dictatorship, and women's organizations pushed for legal reforms and used lobbying in order to improve women's gender positions. Such strategies require professional skills and knowledge of the law. We can see a similar trend in the explosion of autonomous women's groups after the political transition in Nicaragua (Lebon 1996; Alvarez 1990, 1994). Autonomy from "mixed" sectoral organizations of the left and the dismantling of the welfare state have meant an increasing dependence of women's groups on international NGO donors for funding. The search for independent funding sources has translated into the need for a "professional," more bureaucratized structure to divide labor tasks such as writing project proposals and reports. Organizational efficiency and accountability increase the attractiveness of the organization to NGO funders (Keck and Sikkink 1998a). This process of professionalization has greatly affected the way that MEC is organized and operates.

The work of many women's organizations has come to revolve around externally imposed deadlines. Preparing for events such as UN meetings and international conferences necessitates a more rigorous work pace and time schedule, which in turn presupposes professional skills. "New" strategies of "information politics" (Keck and Sikkink 1998a; I discuss this in greater detail in chapter 5) also require a certain level of professional skills and formal education. The resulting emergence of more professionalized NGOs can inhibit the entrance of newcomers to women's movements.

Increased NGO-ization has marked new boundaries and tensions within the transnational feminist movement. Some argue that NGOs are becoming "the preserve of middle-class intellectuals," as professionalization accentuates class differences (Lebon 1996: 602). Others have noted that feminist NGOs have access to more international development funding and that these professional, policy-oriented groups have become "privileged interlocutors with public officials, the media, and bilateral and multilateral aid and development agencies," as opposed to the more informally organized, activist-oriented groups (Alvarez 1998: 313).

Despite the populist-feminist collective identity of the women of MEC, the Managua collective has undergone substantial professionalization. As MEC became more institutionalized, the Managua collective became less "activist-oriented," relying on a core of trained organizers and even paid staff to run specific programs for women at the grassroots. A clear division of labor emerged in the Managua office.

For example, Evelyn administered what became the Documentation and Research Center, which was housed in the Managua office and financed by such groups as the Global Fund for Women. Organizers' salaries were paid by the international NGO funds that financed the programs. Petrolina joined the Managua team in 1995 and put her training as an accountant to work administering the revolving credit program and completing bookkeeping for the entire MEC organization. Sara focused on writing project proposals and networking with Northern-based NGOs. In 1996 the Managua collective employed a graduate from the job-training program to work as the office's receptionist.

That year the organization was finally able to obtain a phone line, which contributed greatly to its professionalization and gave organizers access to tools that were critical to implementing the transnational political strategies on issues related to the FTZ. Fax and e-mail became crucial to organizing the meetings of the Central American Network of Women in Solidarity with Maquila Workers and launching public opinion campaigns to raise awareness about conditions in the factories. E-mail helped MEC stay in touch with NGOs, the organizations that made up the transnational anti-sweatshop movement, and other international contacts.

In the daily life of the Managua office the collective increasingly emphasized "professional work" and "rules of the game." At one meeting in which members of the collective evaluated their past performance, participants listed "activism" as a weakness of their organization. Experts at crisis resolution and handling emergencies, the women of the Managua team expressed a need to develop time management skills and learn to plan and work toward future collective goals—skills often associated with (Western) professionalism.

A shift to embracing professionalism was evident in other aspects of the collective's practices. A clear example was a report that Sara presented at a meeting of a group of organizations belonging to the transnational anti-sweatshop movement, on the progress and activities of the program for maquila workers. The entire team worked on preparing this report, but one task—the creation of a visual image that showed the kinds of brands that were produced in the FTZ—was the responsibility of Rosalba, a former maquiladora worker who had lost her job and whom MEC had contracted to help with some office duties. Rosalba glued garment tags on white paper and drew a chart by hand, decorated with hand-done drawings. When Sara saw the visual aid, she indicated that it would have to be redone. Josefina disagreed, "Look at this. This is beautiful, *la compañera* did it with her own hands." But Sara insisted on sending the job to be typed, using graphics from a computer program. "Now this is a *professional* job!" she said approvingly, as she looked over the computer-generated diagrams.

MEC's shift away from activism and toward professionalism, however, is not just the result of dependence on international NGO funding sources. It can be argued that a more professional and bureaucratized organizational structure is better suited to implement the organization's "alternative" political strategies such as media campaigns, lobbying, and negotiation with state agents and transnational capitalists (see chapter 5). In order to become effective negotiators the women of the MEC team have had to adopt professional norms, once considered "bourgeois" and "counterrevolutionary" in the sectoral organizations of the FSLN. In order to help each other convey a more "professional image," members of the collective exchanged used clothes and shoes that they had acquired as gifts from family members in the United States. Sara reminded Josefina to come to the office dressed professionally, in case they were called to meetings with state agents or factory owners without notice.

Many of the tensions manifested in the wider Latin American feminist movement were also reflected within MEC, as its members struggled with issues of accountability, representation, and tensions stemming from institutionalization. Caught in a system in which more professional, NGO-like structures are in a better position to access international funds, MEC organizers struggled to balance their populist and feminist principles with the very real issue of the need for material resources.

The Network as an Alternative Organizational Structure. MEC's organizational structure—bureaucratically organized (in the sense of clearly divided labor tasks) collectives horizontally linked to one another—fits well with MEC organizers' collective identities and with collectively held notions of autonomy. This network structure is common among organizations in Nicaraguan's autonomous women's movement and the stream of groups ("new social movements") that have emerged throughout the South. As an organizational structure, the network fits well with notions of participative democracy, collective decision-making, and respect for diversity.

Although every network is different, the general idea is to allow diverse groups to organize around certain shared basic principles and interests. As feminists in the United States and elsewhere have recognized, loosely coordinated organizational structures, like coalitions, make "the ideal format for uniting . . . various movement actors in collective efforts to achieve concrete goals," since "as a supra-organizational form, a coalition enables distinct parties to mobilize around common concerns while preserving separate political and organizational identities" (Arnold 1995: 276–77). A network does not require ideological agreement or political unity, but instead relies on an overlap of commitments or concerns (Arnold 1995; Red de Mujeres Contra la Violencia 1995).

This organizational structure is compatible with a broadly defined collective identity, while allowing member groups considerable leeway. MEC participants emphasize that they are *not* a union, but an organizational alternative to the traditional labor movement. This collective identification stems from MEC participants' experiences in the CST and their vehement critique of the FSLN's continued use of the "same old" revolutionary slogans and tactics. "So many marches, so many demonstrations, and for what? These things are getting boring [*aburren*]," women in the Managua office would comment.

Despite the fact that the majority of the women of the Managua collective continue to see themselves as Sandinistas—"I'm Sandinista, not 'Danielista,'" Laura would remark (referring to Daniel Ortega)—they would often express deep cynicism regarding the politics of the FSLN. During the electoral campaign of 1996, MEC leaders joked about the Sandinista presidential candidate Daniel Ortega's efforts to rework his public image. The women of MEC were skeptical, interpreting it as another sign that Ortega was willing to say anything to be reelected, that he sold out the revolution for personal and political interests. In a play on a populist, nationalist slogan from the revolution, "Patria libre o morir! (A free country or death!), Laura quipped, "His new slogan should be, 'Patria libre . . . y vivir!'" (A free country . . . and life!). Sara joined the conversation: "Well, I won't die for anyone now—not for any party. . . . Not like when I was a kid. I would say, [bares part of her chest] 'Here, kill me. I want to be a hero of the revolution! Put my name on a plaque!' . . . Not anymore. Now *my* slogan is 'patria libre y vivir!'"

MEC organizers' views regarding the contradictions in Sandinista oppositional politics had deep roots in their experiences within the labor movement, but their comments that those remaining in the party use "un vocabulario que ya aburre" (a vocabulary that has become boring) reflect the desire for alternatives, the need to *romper esquemas* (break patterns). After MEC's formation, founding participants were concerned that they would "repeat the same errors as the men" by creating similar organizational structures. Their network-like organization seemed an innovative alternative.

However, there are drawbacks to networks. The lack of a more strongly defined ideology can be a disadvantage in certain situations. Ironically, it is in negotiations and political lobbying, MEC's primary political strategy, that a strong ideological consensus may be most necessary. Negotiations between groups with highly unequal power relations require "the establishment of consensus and a permanently maintained coherence of negotiated interests" (CEI 1997: 5).

An example of a network within the autonomous women's movement to which MEC belongs demonstrates this point. Shortly before the 1996 elections the Network of Women Against Violence entered negotiations with the Nicaraguan state (in the form of the Nicaraguan Women's Institute [INIM]) regarding the policies of the Comiserias de la Mujer [women's commissaries or police stations]). The representatives of this network who came to the table found it nearly impossible to put forth a clear position, because of the lack of a political ideology and a strong consensus within the network of organizations. The representatives did not feel that they could either reject or accept INIM's proposals. What the negotiators *represented* was not a clear uniform political ideology, but an abstract commitment to broadly stated ideals. INIM played the different individual political interests of organizational members of this network against one another. By promising power over the commissaries in their particular town or city, representatives of INIM began negotiations with individual group members of the network who were willing to compromise in some instances when others were not, causing confusion amongst the women's groups and putting the state agents at a decided advantage. Eventually, negotiations broke down. Later the new president, Arnoldo Alemán, dissolved INIM, making it part of the new Ministry of the Family. Although it is unclear if in this case network consensus would have made a difference, given Alemán's actions, the example illustrates the difficulties facing coalitions that attempt to engage in negotiations with the state.

MEC's changing relations with international and Northern-based NGOs show how transnational relations of power have shaped MEC's internal organizational processes. NGOs have formed complex and wide-ranging linkages with one another as well as with state agencies, social movements, and international development organizations. Such linkages often span multiple international borders in transnational networks and frequently involve the transfer of material resources from NGOs in the North to either social movements or other NGOs in the South. Along with material resources, these networks facilitate the transnational circulation of ideas, knowledge, and discourses, which in turn has provided new possibilities for collective practices.

The case of MEC shows how this has occurred and illustrates some of the power dynamics between progressive NGOs in the North and social justice groups in the South. Like all the mass-based organizations of the FSLN, the Women's Secretariat of the CST relied heavily on international funding from solidarity groups in Canada and Europe for many of its projects and programs. When MEC formed as an autonomous organization in post-Sandinista Nicaragua, however, it was even more dependent upon funding sources from the North. Indeed, the organization could not exist without this support.

External dependency has had important effects. Although Sara and the other organizers are adamant that MEC should administer the services and programs that it offers, it is clear that dependency on external funds affects the kinds of programs that they implement. MEC organizers are very conscious of what kinds of programs are "fundable" and what is "in style" for international donors. They formulate goals and programs after conducting needs assessment in their social base, but they are equally aware that certain kinds of services are more attractive to funders. Thus, in seeking funds from a German church group in which many members are active in unions, Laura and Sara were careful not to include any language that would sound anti-union in the proposal. They astutely sprinkle their proposals with fashionable "sound bytes," like "sustainable development," "participative, democratic organization," and "local autonomy."

In addition, the members of the Managua collective spend a great deal of energy and effort in maintaining "public relations" with international visitors and funders, often holding receptions for them or calling together program participants to *intercambiar experiencias* (exchange experiences) with them. In addition, many funders require MEC to provide spaces for NGO representatives to hold private evaluation sessions with participants to assess the effectiveness of the programs.

The women of the Managua collective often expressed resentment at having to spend so much time on impression management for *las chelas* (white women).[6] MEC organizers have had to negotiate how much autonomy they are willing to sacrifice in exchange for funding. In the programs for maquila workers, for example, Canadian and European funders were often organizations affiliated with labor groups and tended to support union activity. On a number of occasions Sara and Laura had to defend their reasons for not cooperating with the Nicaraguan trade union movement and for not implementing unionist strategies like forming trade unions within the FTZ. Sometimes this led to conflicts with some members of international NGOs, and the women of the Managua collective felt they had to remain firm and not accept working with the labor movement as a condition for funding, maintaining their desire to organize autonomously around the needs and realities of women in the maquila factories. A continual tension resulted from MEC's "can't live with 'em, can't live without 'em" relationship with international NGOs. Within MEC the women's use of *chele/a* as synonymous with "international funder" reflected their recognition of the neocolonial and racial aspects of this dependent relationship and of international power relations.

Requirements of external funders raise problems of accountability for feminist organizations (Acker 1995; Mansbridge 1995), which become even more complicated when North/South dynamics are added to the equation (Mendez and Wolf 2001; Lebon 1996; Safa 1996). As Ann Ferguson observes, problems and contradictions emerge from development projects that are "designed almost exclusively by women in the North as paternalistic gestures meant to benefit women seen as Other, as objects of relief rather than as subjects" (1996: 575). Such problems are salient in Women in Development (WID) models that uncritically incorporate elements of the modernization paradigm in their approach to incorporating women and their needs into development projects (Mohanty 1991).

Despite the best intentions of funders from the North, the dependency of groups in the South on external funding limits the range of activities that they can engage in and strongly shapes their internal practices (Chigudu 1997; Stewart and Taylor 1997). Programs must be designed to fit funding agency requirements and be compatible with the principles and goals of international donors (Sethi 1993: 234).

Although MEC operates in an extremely specific local setting, its search for an appropriate organizational structure is shaped by processes occurring at a transnational level. Reliance on international NGO funding has influenced MEC's shift to a "network-like" structure. As a Uruguayan feminist observed at the 1995 Beijing conference, this trend reflects changes in "cycles of fashion of the agencies of international cooperation . . . which went from [support for] research centers, to grassroots organizations, to NGOs, to local networks, to regional networks, and now global networks" (quoted in Alvarez 1998: 308–9).

As women from poor backgrounds of the developing world, MEC organizers' engagement with feminism and feminist ideas challenges the myth that feminism is a Western or upper-class phenomenon. MEC's struggle to define itself as an autonomous organization and construct an organizational structure fluid enough to reflect its shifting collective identity is directly linked to the group's formulation of gender interests (Molyneux 1998: 76). MEC's experiences support arguments against the practical/ strategic interest distinction as a rigid binary. As Cecelia Blondet (1995) has also demonstrated, women can engage in struggles that simultaneously involve practical and strategic interests. As MEC developed as an autonomous organization, it struggled to address issues that affect women's abilities to feed and clothe their families, such as shrinking public services and women's unemployment, while at the same incorporating notions of gender as a system of power into their programs.

Further, as MEC came into its own as an autonomous organization, internal tensions emerged, stemming from extremely local issues, such as different individual experiences as political actors and varied concepts of the meaning of local autonomy. At the same time transnational processes, such as reliance on international external funding and the influence of discourses from the wider national and global women's movement(s), have affected the way that MEC leaders think about their issues.

Many analysts tend to categorize NGOs as being more bureaucratized and "professional," whereas social movements are seen as more activist-oriented and loosely structured. Like many Latin American women's organizations, MEC has indeed undergone NGO-ization, becoming more professional and providing services rather than solely engaging in political activism. At the same time MEC organizers in Managua and the regions continue to identify with and as "women of the base" and derive their identities from connections in grassroots communities, in this regard remaining closer to a social movement.

Although some scholars view NGOs as potentially able to create alternative development discourses and practices (see W. Fisher 1997; J. Fisher 1993; Wignaraja 1993), others note that the proliferation of NGOs has coincided with the increasing dominance of neoliberalism and shrinking state responsibilities (Petras 1997). Feminists have viewed the NGO-ization of the Latin American women's movement with differing degrees of concern (Alvarez 1994: 49). Some worry that the reliance on external funding of increasing numbers of more professionalized women's organizations stimulates clientelism and requires shifting energy to accountability to international donors and away from grassroots constituencies at the cost of abandoning feminist principles (Lebon 1996; Safa 1996). MEC's experiences show the complexities of these issues for women's groups. Issues of co-optation, representation, democratic participation, and loss of momentum come to the fore as organizers walk a tightrope between accountability to their constituents and their political principles, and accountability to international donors.

The NGO has been seen as supplanting the more "radical" social movement to the detriment of social justice projects. As MEC became more like an NGO and less like an "activist" organization, its shift could be viewed as a reorientation away from *real* issues of social justice. But this view may be too simplistic.

MEC has strong ties in local communities in the regions where it has offices as well as in barrios in and around Managua. The lower-class origins of MEC leaders and the recruitment of new organizers from MEC programs and local communities suggest a different picture, defying a simplistic contrast between an NGO and a social movement. As MEC leaders commit to "rompiendo esquemas," the breaking of patterns, they are attempting to create an organization that merges the commitment to populism practiced within the mass organizations of the Sandinistas with the bureaucratization and professionalism that are increasingly necessary for social justice organizations, and perhaps democratic politics, in a context of the developing world under conditions of globalization.

Of course, this amalgam is not without its problems, imperfections, and internal contradictions. Nonetheless, the oppositional binary of NGO versus social movement can become the basis for a "grassroots enough" yardstick used by international organizations to determine which organizations are "worthy" of funding or solidarity (Mindry 2001). Thus, it can be used to reproduce a neocolonial pattern of "the West knows best" within transnational organizational relations and so deserves critical scrutiny.

FIGURE 1. The Managua office of The Working and Unemployed Women's Movement, "María Elena Cuadra" (MEC), 1995. (Photo by author)

Unidas y fuertes
contra la
discriminación de
las mujeres

MOVIMIENTO DE MUJERES TRABAJADORAS Y DESEMPLEADAS
"MARIA ELENA CUADRA"

FIGURE 2. MEC's logo, which was selected from drawings submitted by MEC participants from local communities. The slogan states, "United and strong against discrimination against women." (Used by permission)

FIGURE 3. The national headquarters of the Sandinista Workers' Central (CST) in Managua, where the founders of MEC had been the leaders of the National Women's Secretariat. (Photo by author)

FIGURE 4. Maquila workers give testimonies about working conditions in the free trade zone after an evaluation session with the MEC team. (Photo by author)

FIGURE 5. Maquila Workers register for a MEC workshop. (Photo by author)

FIGURE 6. The programs at MEC's regional offices often emphasize training in more traditionally gendered skills, such as this workshop in Chichigalpa, which taught young women to cut and style hair. (Photo by author)

FIGURE 7. This woman used an initial loan from MEC's microcredit program to establish a tiny outdoor eatery. After repaying her first loan, she received more credit and expanded to sell cold drinks and grocery items. (Photo by author)

FIGURE 8. Sewing machine operators like this one in Nicaragua's nationally owned free trade zone must work fast to keep up with production quotas. (Photo by author)

FIGURE 9. Except for a noontime break, many workers like this one who adds rivets to jeans stand at their work stations during their entire shift. (Photo by author)

FIGURE 10. A gendered division of labor exists in the garment assembly factories in Nicaragu's free trade zones. Men often work ironing or cutting fabric, while women are usually sewing machine operators and fabric markers. (Photo by author)

FIGURE 11. Scene of a 1997 press conference held in Managua and organized by the Central American Network of Women in Solidarity with Maquila Workers to announce the launch of the campaign: "Jobs, Yes . . . But with Dignity!" (Photo by author)

FIGURE 12. This game of musical chairs symbolizes "win-win" postrevolutionary oppositional strategies in a context of globalization. The participants in this game (author appears) were attending a 1997 meeting of the Central American Women's Network in Solidarity with Maquila Workers. (Photo by author)

FIGURE 13. Images like this one taken from "Gender and Discrimination in the Free Trade Zone" (MEC 1997c) appear in MEC's publications used in workshops for maquila workers and other participants. In the first frame the words "Free Trade Zone" appear on the woman's bound mouth. In the background voices call out "Silence!"; "No talking!"; "More production!" "Work!"; and "Don't lose time!" The same woman later labors in the home, completing housework and child care, while behind her a man idly reads a newspaper. (Used by permission)

FIGURE 14. This illustration appears in the MEC publication "Gender, Discrimina-tion, and Human Rights" (1997b). The man at the podium declares: "Those who have signed have committed to respect ALL . . . Hear me well! ALL rights of ALL." He uses *todos*, the masculine plural form of the word in "rights of all." The balloon indicating a voice coming from outside the cartoon frame corrects the man: "y todas," the feminine form to include women. (Used by permission)

5 "Rompiendo Esquemas": MEC's Political
Strategies and the Free Trade Zone

The merengüe music blasted as the six of us danced around the line of five chairs in a Central American–style game of musical chairs. When the music stopped, each of us scrambled to find her own seat, so as not to be the one left standing. In the free-for-all that ensued, players' high heels went flying into the larger group of workshop participants who were cheering us on. By the time the majority of us had been eliminated and the two remaining finalists competed for the last chair, the room was in an uproar. But the game did not end when Andrea, a cooperante from Canada, used her hips to bump the very petite Rosa María from Guatemala from the last chair.

"Now we're going to change the rules and play again," the workshop leader explained. The new object of the game would be for everyone to find a place to sit as fast as possible, regardless of whether or not she had a whole chair to herself. Though after each round one chair would be removed, no one would be eliminated. The rest of the workshop participants howled with laughter as the first few rounds ended with larger women sprawled on top of one another in disarray. By the last round, however, we had organized, and when the music stopped Marta from Nicaragua stepped forward to quickly direct us so that the six of us fit on the last chair. The observing women jumped to their feet in an emotional standing ovation, as Andrea balanced the whole stack of us on her lap, and we swung Rosa María to the top of the pile.

This was the scene at a two-day workshop organized by the Central American Women's Network in Solidarity with Maquila Workers. Organizers from MEC were among the participants in this workshop, which was designed to teach practical negotiation and lobbying skills. This exercise was more than an ice-breaker. In the context of the workshop it became a particularly apt metaphor for the ways in which globalization has brought a change in the "rules of the game" for oppositional groups.

The first game represented the way oppositional groups, particularly labor organizations, did things "before"—that is, in the war-torn 1970s and 1980s. The subsequent version symbolized the "new" rules of the game. The goals of the first game were competitive, but the second game involved cooperation and compromise. Tactics for winning the first game included confrontational actions like strikes, marches, and demonstrations. Negotiation and mediation tactics were the winning instruments of the second game. We could interpret each player of the first game as representing an oppositional group, struggling more or less individually to claim its own space in the national political sphere. Transnational organizing strategies within the newly configured political and economic landscape in Central America were represented in the second game, as women from different nations of origin cooperated to carve out a collective oppositional space.

As MEC underwent internal struggles to establish an organizational structure, organizers began the process of developing plans for outreach programs and political work. The priorities of MEC's regional offices varied and focused on income-generating possibilities, such as job training and credit. The Managua collective's efforts focused largely on programs for workers in the maquila factories, most of which were located in the state-owned free trade zone. This national program for women maquila workers involves all the components of the organization's work: education, income generation, credit, and job-training in traditional and nontraditional areas. The heightened politicization of the issues surrounding the free trade zone required the organization to continually engage with political forces emerging at the national, regional, and transnational levels and forced the organizers to reformulate and adapt their political strategies accordingly. Repeatedly they found themselves, as they like to say, "rompiendo esquemas," breaking patterns and finding new ways to pursue their goals.

In this chapter I examine strategies and practices that MEC has implemented in its efforts to improve the situation of female maquila workers. As I will argue, MEC follows a larger trend. As grassroots politics have become globalized (Smith 1994), social movement actors increasingly engage in what Margaret Keck and Kathryn Sikkink (1998a) call "information politics." Information becomes an instrument of power, as social movement organizations struggle to gain access to different national and transnational public spheres, using communication technology and transnational linkages with other, often more powerful and influential organizations. Their object is often to pressure state or global institutions (as we have seen in the recent mobilizations around the issue of global justice in Seattle and around the world) or even specific corporations to bring about change (Brysk 1993: 261). The practices involved in such politics include negotiation, lobbying, media campaigns, and electronically disseminated action alerts. Social movements and other groups in civil society depend on information to challenge institutions; they achieve impact through persuasion and the changing of perceptions and values.

These strategies have a reformist flavor because they involve working within existing political and economic structures. MEC's strategies with regard to the problems in maquila factories demonstrate some of the challenges and opportunities that globalization has brought to social movements. The case of MEC shows the importance of historical and national context, even when combating "new" issues facing workers in the global assembly line.

MEC'S PROGRAM FOR MAQUILA WORKERS

When I returned to Nicaragua in 1995, movement organizers were in the process of interpreting the results of the anniversary congress and commemoration that had occurred a few months earlier, in which several hundred women had taken part. To meet the demands that the women from the discussion groups had expressed, the Managua collective was hard at work defining projects and programs and seeking international funding in order to implement them. At a meeting between the Movement's regional leaders and Managua's core group, MEC organizers developed plans for educational programs, such as a job-training program, training of community-based legal and health promotoras, and a leadership formation program; income-generating programs, such as revolving credit funds for the establishment of microenterprises and housing improvements; and special programs for domestic workers and workers in the free trade zone. The broad goal of these programs was to "improve the condition and position of women within civil society" (MEC 1995).

In addition to the congress of 1994, the 1993 strike in the FORTEX factory had been a major turning point for the leaders of the National

Women's Secretariat who would later form MEC. The incident, which is described in chapter 2, was pivotal for MEC leaders because it showed them that the CST was willing to completely turn its back on the Women's Secretariat and on unionization efforts among maquila workers, and it had dramatic strategic implications for MEC's political strategy. Although the strike did result in some changes in the more heinous working conditions in the state-owned FTZ, especially in shop-floor violence, the gains were minimal given the high costs of the action (workers losing their jobs, some being severely injured). Many of the core group of workers who sought to represent the union lost their jobs, and the union itself never achieved official recognition. The continued threat by factory owners to relocate production seemed to be a major factor in the Ministry of Labor's refusal to legalize the union and in state agents' reluctance to hold managers accountable for their violent acts.

The police did little to investigate the charges against the Taiwanese factory owners and supervisors who injured Sara and a group of workers. Indeed, they appeared at the scene in order to protect the armed managers, rather than the unarmed workers and union organizers. Subsequently, they "lost" crucial forensic evidence pertaining to the case. The leadership of the CST did not stand behind the strikers, because they did not want to endanger their negotiations with the Chamorro administration over the social contract (the concertación), which were taking place at the time.

For MEC leaders the failure of this large and widely publicized strike was an epiphany. First, it marked a profound betrayal for these women organizers in confirming for them that the CST leadership was willing to sell out workers in order to protect their own interests. Second, it demonstrated what MEC leaders came to see as the inadequacy of "traditional" tools of the labor movement in a system of global production, which caused them to conclude: "Our people are tired of these confrontational methods. We need to propose alternatives."

MEC organizers' commitment to improving women's daily lives and their work with communities in which large numbers of maquila workers reside made them extremely sensitive to the fear of female workers (many of whom are the sole providers for their large extended families) that they would lose their jobs. In the words of one female worker: "We may have dignity, but we also have need. If we have four children to support and even though what we are doing hurts, it also hurts when we don't have anything to feed our children. So we put our dignity aside and look for a way to feed our children" (quoted in MEC 1996: 16). Over and over again, women workers expressed sentiments like these to MEC organizers, who could not justify implementing strategies that risked leaving women workers with no way to provide for their families. "*We* cannot offer these women employment," Sara and her compañeras would often remark.

MEC organizers used their years of experience in the popular organizations of the FSLN as a springboard for formulating "a new type of organizing strategy that would permit the claiming of women free trade workers' strategic gender, labor, and social interests" (MEC 1996: 59). Thus, this new political vision incorporated feminist ideals by acknowledging and drawing connections between women's reproductive and productive roles and recognizing the gendered power structures in various spheres of women's lives. By developing and implementing alternative, nonconfrontational strategies, MEC organizers were attempting to reconfigure class-based revolutionary ways of "doing" politics to address both the expressed needs of their social base (which included a recognition of women workers' gender *and* class experiences) and a transformed political and economic landscape.

These alternative practices involved negotiation and lobbying, rather than using demonstrations and strikes as tools for meeting their objectives. Organizers looked to institutional channels, including pushing for changes in labor legislation, to achieve their demands. A MEC publication describes this strategic re-orientation: "The Working and Unemployed Women's Movement, 'María Elena Cuadra' of Managua is not opposed to the existence of free trade zones, since these generate employment for thousands of women who have no other alternative in our country. This Movement contends that it is necessary to influence with a positive and nonconfrontational attitude of basic respect for the human, constitutional, and labor rights of women workers in the Free Trade Zone" (MEC 1996: 59).

As a MEC organizer and long-time unionist Laura explained to a group of FTZ workers: "[We are adopting] another more proactive [*propositiva*] attitude in order to look for a more efficient way . . . without arriving at the point of holding a strike." Sara, MEC's coordinator, rejected the suggestion of Dora María Téllez, a candidate for deputy to the National

MEC's Political Strategies **137**

Assembly from the Sandinista Reform Party (MRS), that the workers of the FTZ demonstrate in the streets for their rights. Sara's comment was: "We already know that doesn't work. So many times we have done that, and it serves no purpose [*no sirve*]. We have to use legal mechanisms to make change."

MEC organizers developed a concept of "integral work." They devised programs that would address women workers' needs and interests, not only in the workplace, but at home, and within communities in civil society. The educational component of MEC's program for maquila workers involved not only workshops on the National Labor Code but also training concerning domestic violence, self-esteem, and reproductive health. Within the autonomous space of MEC, these new practices challenge modernist notions of the separation of spheres and make connections between what occurs in the home, in local communities, and on the shop floor and women's position in society in general (Lowe and Lloyd 1997a). Recognizing the interconnections between women's reproductive and productive roles reflects the feminist notion of the personal as political and calls into question narrow conceptualizations of what constitutes "the political."

THE "OLD" IN THE "NEW": MEC'S ORGANIZING
STRATEGIES AND THE FSLN

However, MEC's efforts did not represent a clean break from the oppositional tradition of the FSLN. If MEC was a "new" social movement, then it was also an organization that emerged from the revolutionary tradition of the Sandinista mass organizations. In the years following MEC's formation, the "oppositional networks" that organizers had formed during their participation in the revolution and within the mass organizations of the Sandinista front were crucial to MEC's political work. Indeed, the reactivation of these long-standing latent networks allowed MEC to implement its early programs and mobilize participants. Although the leaders of MEC saw themselves as offering oppositional alternatives, the development of these new strategies and practices relied heavily on a base of networks and organizational resources established within the revolutionary politics of the 1970s and 1980s. Thus, MEC participants constructed their "self-limiting radicalism" upon a basic framework established during the Sandinista years.

In the case of the program for maquila workers, community networks established by MEC organizers and their work in the labor movement were extremely important. In the mid-1990s a large part of the labor force in the FTZ was composed of workers formerly employed in what had been the state-owned textile industry. The great majority of workers resided either in Tipitapa, a small city located approximately forty miles to the northeast of the center of Managua, or in the barrios on the northern side of the city. Because MEC founders previously had worked in the National Women's Secretariat of the CST as well as the regional secretariats of the union federations, they had a large number of contacts among these workers and in their communities.

When Laura, a former member of the CST's textile federation and a leader within the Women's Secretariat, established contact with a German church group that granted funding for an educational program for the women of the FTZ, she and Sara began to plan both the program's implementation and how to organize the workers along "alternative" political lines. MEC sought to organize maquila workers from outside the workplace. The contacts and personal networks of organizers like Laura in the communities surrounding the zone were crucial to this endeavor. Laura and Josefina, another organizer, began meeting with family members and with women they knew who worked in the assembly factories. Sara and the other MEC organizers also contacted women in other communities to spread the word about the organization's programs and mobilizing efforts.

In general, production in FTZs takes place under extremely restrictive conditions. Situated outside the airport on the Northern Highway leading to Managua, the Free Trade Zone "Las Mercedes" offers only limited access to visitors, and armed guards patrol the entrance, requiring identification for those seeking to enter.[1] Though the factories occupy state-owned land, the state-appointed Corporation of the Free Trade Zone administers it as private property. "Our free zone is as private as private can be," boasts the corporation's Web page.[2] In the early and mid-1990s, though the labor code assured FTZ workers the right to free association, in the context of labor's extremely vulnerable position and the anti-labor policies of the Chamorro and Alemán regimes, factory management showed very little tolerance for the threat of worker organization.

Because traditional shop-floor mobilization strategies would prove ineffective, organizers used their "oppositional networks" as a means to gain information about shop-floor conditions and to mobilize workers. For example Josefina, also a former textile worker, had a rich personal history of political activism that included being a union organizer in a paper products factory during the years preceding the revolution, as well as an active member of the textile federation in the state-owned factories during the Sandinista years. A highly respected community leader who also was involved in several initiatives to protest for improved water and sanitation in her barrio, Josefina lived in the same community as many factory workers and had family members who worked in the FTZ. Given her influence and reputation in the community, she was able to mobilize several women to attend the first meetings to launch MEC's program for FTZ workers.

Likewise, Sara and the other members of the Managua collective called upon seasoned activists like Mayra to get the word out about MEC's program and mobilize prospective participants. Mayra was a leader in the Sandinista Defense Committees during the revolution and had years of community organizing and union experience under her belt. In addition, MEC organizers used their contacts developed during their involvement in mass organizations such as AMNLAE and within the literacy and health brigades of the Sandinista years to mobilize women.

Later, Mayra was transferred to work for the job-training program. Participants in this program were recruited from specific poor barrios. Some, like Rosalba, who had been fired for suspected union activity, were former FTZ workers. The program funded the women's technical training with the National Technical Institute (INATEC), a national vocational program, and Mayra accompanied the women as the MEC representative.

One day after Sara observed me conversing with Mayra, she pulled me aside. With a twinkle in her eye she said, "Jennifer, ask la Mayra to show you her little notebook." When she saw my questioning look, Sara described to me with pride an incident that had occurred at INATEC. "Es que la Mayra es bien organizada," she explained—Mayra is very well organized. Apparently, there had been some confusion at INATEC about how many women were registered for the program from each sponsoring organization. One of the technical trainers had argued that there were too many participants from MEC's groups and that there must have been some new women who had not shown up at earlier trainings who were attending class. Mayra quickly produced a small hand-held notebook in which she had documented the names of each woman who had attended the training sessions on each day, effectively showing that everyone present from MEC's group had been attending all along and had the right to keep her spot in the vocational classes. The trainer was so impressed that he contacted Sara. "That woman keeps better records than we do!" he told her. "You see, Jennifer," Sara told me. "She learned that in the unions and the defense committees [CDS]. As a cadre, you are taught to document everything! These are the kinds of women that we need working with us," she said with satisfaction.

These practices counter generalized theoretical conceptualizations of women's movement participants as *new* political actors. Unlike the Madres de la Plaza de Mayo in Argentina, who were new to grassroots politics, the women of MEC have been able to implement alternative strategies precisely because of well-established roots in popular organizations. Here the salience of historical specificity is revealed in the legacy of the revolution and its continued impact on popular organizing in Nicaragua. It shows the importance of locality to social movement strategy— even within a globalized context.

In 1996 MEC gradually began to implement its educational program for maquila workers, revising it according to participants' suggestions and evaluations. Laura's and Josefina's community ties facilitated communication with participants about their needs and evaluations of the program, which consisted of weekly workshops, treating topics such as the National Labor Code and reproductive health. A later addition was a credit program, granting small home-improvement loans. Workers' daughters could apply for a job-training program to develop other skills in fields like auto mechanics and word-processing. Finally, at the suggestion of program participants, MEC contracted with a martial arts expert to teach self-defense skills and tae kwan do.

After participating in an initial series of workshops, workers could opt to become part of the more active component of MEC's program and join the network of human rights promotoras. In order to serve as the bridge between the Movement and the affiliates (workers who participate in

MEC's activities), promotoras completed a series of more advanced training sessions. They were in charge of inviting other workers to the program's weekly activities and workshops, documenting and reporting labor and human rights violations in the factories, alerting MEC to changes and issues from inside the FTZ, and planning and organizing recreational activities for the workers.[3] The role of the promotoras was developed and defined by workers themselves through a series of meetings with Laura, Josefina, and Jill, the Canadian cooperante. Jill confided to me after one of these weekend sessions, "We are inventing as we go along." Workers discussed "morally supporting our compañeras" and "seeking out our compañeras at work and in their homes to talk to them about the Movement." This group met once a month in MEC's Managua office.

In addition, a MEC organizer (first Laura and later Josefina) visited the FTZ twice per week and met promotoras at a spot outside the entrance. Promotoras also spent time visiting maquila workers at their homes, and many had family members who were also employed in the FTZ. In addition, they acted as liaisons between MEC organizers and workers who wished to file complaints at the Ministry of Labor, referring workers with grievances to MEC's office for organizers and later a legal team to assist them with the presentation of their cases.[4]

Though the promotora system was meant to represent an alternative to unions, and the promotoras insisted that they did not represent "una organización sindical," this strategy reflects the Sandinista tradition of forming cadres. The strong parallels between promotoras and *cuadros* (cadres) represents an important instance of "the old in the new," again demonstrating the importance of historical continuity to initiatives like MEC.

MEC organizers' oppositional networks have also created spaces within state institutions. Many of the inspectors and administrators in the Ministry of Labor have histories in labor organizing stemming from the Sandinista years, and MEC has been able to take advantage of sympathetic contacts within the Ministry. Josefina, who in November of 1996 took over the facilitation of the national FTZ program (when Laura moved to support Sara in other regional and international efforts), met with a surprise when she accompanied a fired worker to the Ministry of Labor to seek her severance and vacation pay.

The inspector in charge of the case was a former union organizer with whom Josefina had worked years before when she was a union organizer at a paper products factory. The inspector greeted her affectionately and offered to facilitate the resolution of the aggrieved woman's case. Indeed, in the following week the worker received payment of a large part of her severance pay and eventually was able to receive the rest. In addition, the inspector pledged future support to MEC and even agreed to give a series of workshops regarding the current labor code—which she conducted using an assumed name and reminded workers that if they ever saw her on the grounds of the FTZ, "I won't know you."

INFORMATION POLITICS AT WORK

The efforts of the promotoras in the factories and communities, however, represent more than a mechanism to educate workers and refer them to MEC organizers. These women are a principal source of the information that MEC organizers employ in their information politics. To implement their alternative strategies, MEC organizers had to obtain concrete information about work conditions in the FTZ. As Keck and Sikkink (1998a: 19) point out, through information politics nonstate actors gain influence by serving as alternative sources of information, but to be credible the information produced must be reliable and well documented—and promotoras were the primary source of this information. Carrying notebooks with them to work, they documented changes in working conditions, worker grievances, and management practices as well as in pay scales and production quotas. They also collected pay stubs, garment tags, and social security statements from workers, which they handed over to MEC's Documentation Center to be archived.

These alternative sources are important, because little or no publicly accessible data existed, even on such quantifiable indicators of working conditions as injuries on the job, salary levels, overtime hours, and health insurance benefits. As MEC continued to develop and grow, promotoras also came to be important data collectors. In 1998, 2001, and 2002 the organization conducted a series of diagnostic studies that (along with the media and public awareness campaigns launched as part of the Central American Network of Women in Solidarity with Maquila Workers) served as the basis for proposed legislative reforms, including an initiative to reform the republic's labor code.

The increased importance of the production and control of information has become a defining characteristic of the global system. In the economies of industrialized countries a dramatic shift has occurred from material production to information-processing. Indeed, to a great extent the burgeoning so-called service sector consists of information production activities (Castells 1993; Sassen 1991). Within the world economy, as competition is played out among transnational actors, information technologies make possible the extremely flexible, decentralized, and customized strategies of production coordinated among multiple locations (Bonacich et al. 1994; Castells 1993).

In the garment industry such extreme flexibility is reflected in "just-in-time production" strategies and the increasingly shortened fashion seasons and trends. When a customer buys a clothing item from a large retailer like Wal-Mart, information regarding the purchase is electronically transmitted to the home company. Information about retailers' inventories and production needs is disseminated to contractors in various locations around the world, establishing production allocations that can change from day to day. Wal-Mart's data-storage capacity is rivaled only by the U.S. government, and the company spends half a billion dollars a year on information technology (Palmeri 1997).

Control over information, however, is crucial not only for economic competitiveness. In the reconfigured global political arena, information represents a key resource for the struggles of disenfranchised peoples. Obtaining the necessary reliable information with the goal of improving work conditions in transnationally owned maquila factories is not an easy task. Conditions from one factory to the next within the same FTZ could be very different. It proved very difficult for MEC to have contacts in every factory in the nationally owned zone and the other private zones that began to crop up in the mid-nineties. Even within factories working conditions varied considerably from production line to production line, depending upon the supervisor for that line as well as other factors. Even in Nicaragua, where in 1997 there was only one FTZ with eighteen factories and a handful of separate maquila factories (or *puntos francos*) that were located outside of the zone, keeping abreast of the changing policies, pay scales, and conditions and obtaining verifiable information was an arduous task.[5] Often workers themselves did not know if they had received payment for overtime hours or how such payment was calculated, and pay rates were determined by a complicated system of piece-rate wages sometimes combined with base-pay scales that varied from factory to factory and frequently changed. Thus, simply keeping track of what happened within the walls of the maquila factories represented a crucial project for improving working conditions and a fundamental component of MEC's lobbying and negotiation strategies. Conducting diagnostic studies became an important part of MEC's work as the organization matured and developed.

MEC's documentation center supplemented promotoras' efforts at being "inside informants." One of the first tasks assigned to me when I worked with MEC in 1995 was to help Reyna and Evelyn with organizing the records, documents, and books that MEC organizers had managed to salvage from the office of the National Women's Secretariat at the CST's headquarters in Managua, as well as to plan how to establish and organize their own documentation center. With the help of Evelyn I wrote one of the original proposals for the center, a twelve by twenty-five foot room that was constructed as an addition to MEC's one-room office in early 1996. I continued to work with Evelyn in the Documentation Center in 1996 and 1997.

Evelyn, as director of the center, combed newspapers and government publications daily seeking articles regarding changes in government policy, new legislation, and any other reported happenings in the FTZ. In addition, the center purchased books and articles on free trade, neoliberalism, and the maquila industry and was able to purchase a computer to create a database of information regarding factories' sizes, workforce composition, and wages. This center represented the most complete public collection on the zone's history and composition in the country. In 1998 the Documentation Center conducted MEC's first diagnostic study to generate more complete and concrete data on working conditions, pay scales, and benefits within each factory (MEC 1999).

Sara and the other organizers put this information to use in their principal political work, which consisted of an ongoing national and international lobbying campaign to improve conditions for maquiladora workers. In the first phase of this campaign, from 1996 to 1998, MEC focused on lobbying for factory management's commitment to a code of ethics, guaranteeing compliance with local labor legislation and respect for the human rights of workers. Given the ever-present threat that companies would simply relocate if faced with the possibility of worker mobilization, it became clear to MEC organizers that their work had to extend beyond the country's national borders. Here organizers' regional and international solidarity networks came into play. Sara and Laura used their contacts to expand their networks outside Nicaragua to include other women's organizations that work with maquila factory workers.

THE CENTRAL AMERICAN NETWORK OF WOMEN
IN SOLIDARITY WITH MAQUILA WORKERS

Through her work in the Women's Secretariat of the CST, Sara had cultivated extensive networks with other women unionists in Nicaragua and within the Central American region. In 1986 she co-founded the National Committee of Women Syndicalists of Nicaragua. Outreach through involvement with this group led to her participation in regional meetings of the Women Syndicalists of Central American and the Caribbean. In 1996 she and Laura were invited to attend a meeting in Mexico organized by a group of women's organizations from the Northern border whose work centers on the situation of maquila workers to discuss creating regional networks of women's groups concerned with workers in maquila factories.

Funded by NGOs based in Canada and Europe and organized by Sara and leaders from groups in El Salvador and Guatemala, the first meeting of the Central American Network of Women in Solidarity with Maquila Workers (hereafter, the Network) was held in El Salvador in September 1996 with representation from autonomous women's groups from Nicaragua, El Salvador, and Guatemala. Subsequently, a group from Honduras, two groups from Guatemala, and another group from El Salvador also joined the coalition. The founders outlined the Network's purpose:

> Given the situation of discrimination and superexploitation in which women maquila workers live as a result of the process of globalization of the regional economy and given the lack of proper spaces and conditions that permit them to make demands and proposals and stake claims regarding their rights as women and as workers; we have come together in order to analyze, generate, and contribute by means of this organization a space which could serve this purpose. . . . [T]his space permits us to share and coordi-

nate efforts in the search for alternative proposals in order to confront the problems of the maquilas and improve the conditions of women workers in the Central American region. (Red Centroamericana de Mujeres 1997: 1)

The formation of this regional network was only made possible, however, through the transnational linkages that MEC and the other organizations involved had cultivated with activist NGOs from the North. Their first meeting was funded by the OXFAM family, which had been a faithful supporter of MEC organizers' efforts since long before Sara and her compañeras had left the Women's Secretariat of the CST to form the autonomous organization. In addition, the Network's emergence fits conditions that Keck and Sikkink suggest are the most favorable for triggering the formation of transnational advocacy networks: (1) channels between domestic groups and their governments are blocked or hampered, or such channels are ineffective for resolving conflict; (2) activists believe that networking will further their missions and campaigns; and (3) conferences and other forms of international contact create arenas for forming and strengthening networks (1998a: 12). However, the particularities of labor issues in maquila factories do not entirely coincide with the kinds of political strategies that other transnational networks have found to be effective, as discussed below.

Although they are diverse in history, work focus, and national origin, the autonomous women's organizations that make up the Network share certain commonalities. All worked with and/or in communities in which large groups of women were employed by maquila factories, and the principal organizers of all the groups had substantial experience in popular movements, particularly in trade union federations. In addition, like MEC, the majority of the other groups of the Network formed as the direct result of gender conflicts within organizations of the left. For example, the Association of Women in Solidarity (AMES) split from a trade union federation (Syndical Federation of Food, Agricultural, and Related Workers, or FESTRAS) in Guatemala as the result of male leaders' decisions to change the federation's political orientation and strategy. By cutting off support to the Women's Committees that had formed to organize women in the maquilas, the union abandoned one of the few successful efforts to organize female maquila workers that existed at the time. In addition, union leaders replaced the committees with a women's secretariat to which they appointed leaders, at the same time making all projects of the secretariat subject to approval by the male leadership.

An expressed commitment to "improve the conditions of women (maquila) workers of the Central American region" as a broadly defined principle formed the unifying thread of the Network (Red Centroamericana 1997). Each organization belonging to the Network was autonomous, and, in the words of one participant, "The Network is not above [*encima de*] any one group." The horizontal, umbrella-like organization of this coalition allowed organizations with diverse histories, affiliations, perspectives, and priorities to come together around overlapping commitments and concerns in order to work together toward a broadly defined objective (Red de Mujeres Contra la Violencia 1995).

The Network organizations' views of feminism varied. Some groups embraced typically feminist approaches to issues such as reproductive health, domestic violence, and sexual abuse, and many organizations identified as "feminist," but other group organizers remained suspicious of feminism. These women criticized the liberal orientation and priorities underlying feminist struggles and the privileged class position of many feminists. Many nodded their assent when at the third meeting of the Network an organizer from Guatemala expressed the view that "feminist organizational practice in Central America has never been 'of the masses.'"

Indeed, many Network organizers were more likely to identify with class-based projects than with feminist ones. An organizer from Honduras, who had worked in the maquilas located near Choloma outside of San Pedro Sula, criticized upper-class feminists: "We have lived the experience in the flesh. They do not have any idea what it is to live poverty and work in the maquilas. They are 'of computers.' [*Son de computadoras.*] They do not speak from lived experience. We speak about what we have lived. All we have is our experience. How can they transmit this experience if they themselves do not even know it firsthand? They don't know what it is to have to travel by bus—sometimes without a dime for the ticket. They don't know what it is to carry the big jug of water on their head when there is no water in the neighborhood (*colonia*)."

On the other hand, most of the women expressed extremely ambivalent and complex positions regarding unionism, at once highly critical of the traditional labor movement for its rigidity, corruption, and sexist practices, yet acknowledging that in many cases "the first political organizing experience for [Central American] women was in unions." The diverse positions of the women organizers and their experiences as political actors challenge notions of orthodox Marxism regarding class antagonism as the exclusive site of contradiction (Mouffe 1995).

Rosa María, an organizer from Guatemala, described the culminating meeting that resulted in the formation of AMES. "They told us, look, compañeritas [expressed in the diminutive to indicate condescendence], we're sorry but we are going to restructure in this way, . . . And if you want to ask for authorization for your projects, fine, if not you will have to leave." Many Network members held views similar to those that Rosa María expressed in a conversation with participants at the coalition's fourth meeting: "I'll tell you something, compañeras, I still believe that syndicalism is the only mechanism that truly represents the workers. Now, that unions have not properly involved women is another matter (*otros cinco pesos*). . . . So, perhaps we are not against unions, as such. We are opposed to methods and attitudes, but we are not against the ideology of the unions. We have lived in the flesh the attitudes of the men and have a different approach."

A common experience among Network organizers within the labor movement was their exclusion from decision-making power. Manuela, from El Salvador, contended: "We were always the ones serving the coffee. We lived that. First they [union leaders] would tell us that, yes, they wanted to talk [about women's issues], then they accused us of being *divisionistas*."

But access to decision-making aside, the women of the Network saw the coalition not only as an alternative to traditional labor organizations and labor organizing methods, but also as a means to make visible "the social and labor reality of women." For the organizations that made up the Network, the coalition incorporated a "vision for addressing integral problems associated with the women of the maquilas and of developing processes of collective leadership." Indeed, the women described a main purpose of the Network as being a means to make women visible within popular organizations. In the words of one organizer, "Now we are giving a face to our work. We have always been there, but now we want to receive recognition."

Network members criticized both unions and Central American governments for leaving out women maquila workers from their political agendas. In their view it was only when it was "fashionable" to work with this sector that the unions turned to address their needs. Still, the Network's members criticized the unions for their overly confrontational methods without considering carefully enough the impact on workers' vulnerable positions and for their failure to incorporate a gender perspective into their strategies for organizing this predominantly female sector.

The transnational organizing efforts of the Network represent alternative modes of opposition that recognize a "new" laboring subject, constituted by multiple, intersecting axes of domination. Creating and taking advantage of a globalized political space through localized grassroots initiatives, this transnational coalition is an example of "globalization from below." The Network is only one example of many such transnational initiatives in the struggle to improve the situation of transnational factory workers. As Mary Tong, the director of the Support Committee for Maquiladora Workers of Mexico, argues: "Solidarity among workers should cross the border as easily as companies move production" (quoted in Lowe 1996: 167).

A "network" as an organizational form is characterized by the flow of information and services among members (Keck and Sikkink 1998a; Sikkink 1996). At their semiannual meetings members of the Network share reports on the latest changes and issues regarding the maquila industry in their countries and circulate different materials that they have developed for use in workshops and training sessions with workers. The location of these meetings rotates, and the hosting organization(s) coordinates them by e-mail, fax, and telephone. Indeed, the establishment of communication technology (including telephones) was one of the coalition's first priorities. Members recognized the importance of communication among Network members, but also that the rapid communication of e-mail and fax would match the rapid mobility of capital within the Central American region. Thus, members could warn and inform each other about factory conditions and relocations.

The coalition devoted its first main efforts to an international campaign to raise awareness about the conditions in the maquila industry of the Central American region. The cornerstone of the campaign involved the Network's development and dissemination of its own code of ethics, the endorsement of which it planned to seek through lobbying international organizations like the International Labor Organization and the Central American Parliament.

Although the Network acted as a transnational and regional coalition in launching its international campaigns, each organization decided how best to implement the campaign within its home country. In Guatemala, for example, a large number of minors were employed in maquila factories. Girls sometimes as young as eleven or twelve years of age would forge birth certificates or simply lie about their age in order to work in the factories. Not only were these children superexploited and exposed to extremely harsh working conditions, but they were too young to receive social security benefits in the form of medical coverage. At the time of the formation of the Network the situation of these child workers was a major concern for the Guatemalan groups, while child labor was not considered to be as prevalent in Nicaragua and El Salvador.

Local groups coordinated negotiations with state agents and factory owners to coincide with the regional meetings of the Network. The transnational scope of the Network strengthened and legitimated the position of the individual organization in these national-level negotiations. For example, at the Network's third meeting held in Nicaragua, members formed a negotiation team to meet with the Minister of Labor. As the coordinator of the hosting organization, Sara acted as the head negotiator. The women from Guatemala and Honduras, countries in which the maquila industry had had a much longer presence, testified to some of the exploitative management practices and working conditions in the factories there. For example, they told the minister of forced pregnancy tests required by managers in Guatemalan factories. In order to verify the authenticity of specimens, supervisors would often require workers to urinate in front of them. Sara and Josefina would then chime in, warning that to prevent conditions reaching such a point in Nicaragua measures like the code of ethics must be taken.

As a resistance strategy the organizational form of the Network seems to coincide with the particular conditions that have arisen under global capitalism. The flexible accumulation strategies of contemporary capitalism involve subcontracting practices that place renewed importance on small businesses producing for larger corporations. At the time of this writing even the biggest of the factories in Managua's largest FTZ employs only about a thousand workers (Comisión Nacional de la Zona Franca 2002). Arif Dirlik (1997) and other analysts of Asian production systems have noted the suitability of "network-type"—as opposed to central-ized—organizational structures for subcontracting production. By the same token, we might view the flexibility and horizontal orientation of networks as oppositional organizational structures as being better suited to resist transnational capitalist forces than the highly centralized organi-zations of the traditional labor movement.

In order to implement the campaign at national and international levels, Network members needed training in negotiation and lobbying skills. At each meeting the group took part in in-depth workshops on negotiation, lobbying, and mediation techniques. The host organization was in charge of arranging these workshops, which were conducted by locally based NGO's or local consultants. The skills imparted at these workshops became extremely important, not only for the Network's in-ternational and regional work, but for individual organizations that then incorporated them into their national-level campaigns.

NEGOTIATION TECHNIQUES:
NEW TOOLS FOR SOCIAL JUSTICE?

To learn to become effective negotiators, the women of MEC and the other members of the Network had to learn and adopt a "changed language."[6] This shift in idiom constituted part of an overall ideological strategy to incorporate globalized and nationalist discourses. MEC's change in vocab-ulary, however, also represents an approach to collective resistance that is markedly distinct from revolutionary politics. Through workshop train-ing Josefina, Sara, and the others learned to frame their arguments in the language of negotiation, replacing words from "before" like *cadres* and *bourgeoisie*, to speak instead of "creating a bridge between us," "putting oneself in the shoes of the other," and "paraphrasing."

This change in idiom played a role in an incident that occurred dur-ing the Network's negotiations with the Nicaraguan Minister of Labor. Before the negotiations began, the team had discussed the importance of symbolic demonstrations of respect such as the use of the minister's official title of "Señor Ministro." As the negotiations played themselves out, however, and the women began to put forth their arguments, Sara forgot herself in a moment of excitement, blurting out, "But, compañero . . . !" The other team members kicked her under the table to remind her to revert to "negotiation" language. Later, the other women laughed and chided Sara about the slip, remarking how deeply instilled in them was the "language of before."

Similarly, the mediation skills represent a radical departure from revolutionary orientations. In a mediation workshop Network members learned that the goal of mediation is to "transform conflicts" and that to be effective mediators they had to develop "the skill of emotional self-control" (CEI 1997). As mediators of a conflict the women were not to "tener una opción" (take sides). Some of the women of the Network reacted strongly to this. Given the context of a conflict between groups from such unequal positions of power, as in labor conflicts, how could they remain impartial? A running joke at the activities of one of the Network's meetings masked more serious concerns about "the language of negotiation." The women would say: "We have to learn to put ourselves in the shoes of the other . . . even if those shoes stink!" Some women opined that if justice was their true objective, they could not be objective mediators or maintain the impartial attitude of negotiators. They expressed a belief that it was their duty to intercede in workers' favor. Still, Sara and Laura remained convinced that it was possible to construct relations with employers without necessarily taking their side.

In a discussion with members of the Managua team after a workshop on negotiating techniques, Jill and I expressed surprise that these techniques were so new to the women of MEC. "In all your years in the CST, you never received training on this topic?" Jill asked. The women shook their heads. "Even in the university, I never studied these themes," said Petrolina, MEC's accountant and the coordinator of the credit program. The women explained that though collective bargaining had always been the linchpin of trade unionist strategy, given the gender hierarchy and centralization of power within the Sandinista labor movement, only the upper level of union leadership was groomed for participation at the negotiation table. Women, even those who were leaders, were excluded from this process.

Despite essentialist notions of women, who are thought to be more embedded in social relations, as being more empathetic listeners and so better suited to be negotiators, the women of MEC perceived the language and techniques of negotiation as being "masculine" (Hardy-Fanta 1993; Hamilton 1989). In Sara's words: "In this country everything that moves around negotiation is really 'masculinized' [*masculinizado*]." Josefina exclaimed: "The men know how to call you a 'son of bitch' without saying it."

MEC organizers found learning about negotiation techniques profoundly enlightening. They expressed amazement when they reflected back on negotiation sessions that they had observed between male union representatives and government officials or employers. After learning about the theories behind negotiation, the women came to see these interactions in a different light. Before, they had seen male union representatives as "selling out" their unionist principles, but they now recognized in the men's words and actions some of the techniques that they were learning. For negotiation always involves compromise, and the women learned that in prior meetings the negotiation team had probably established a list of priorities and points about which they were willing to compromise. Nonetheless, even given this insight, the MEC women remained critical of the men's priorities, in their eyes based on self-interest, not on the needs or interests of women workers. MEC organizers thought that negotiation techniques were potentially an extremely useful tool for women's grassroots organizing, and Sara later began conducting negotiation workshops with the promotoras to "take this theme to the base" and provide women organizers the tools that male leaders had always had at their disposal.

But by adopting negotiation techniques, MEC did more than just appropriate "male" tools and put them to use to achieve gender- as well as class-based objectives. MEC and the other Network participants were replacing the revolutionary and/or class-based discourses and confrontational tactics of the 1980s with the active listening skills and smooth talking of a "politics of persuasion." The use of such strategies occurred in a transformed political arena, markedly distinct from that of the 1970s and 1980s. Negotiation techniques are oriented to "winning the game," that is, making the fewest compromises in working toward a "mutually beneficial" agreement. By contrast in revolutionary contestations "the goal of the challenging team is not only to win the game (seize power, smash the state, and so forth) but also to alter the structure of the game" (Kearney 1995).

This shift in political strategies marks changes in the political landscape of Central America as a region. Negotiation and lobbying as political tactics require certain conditions—spaces in which to dialogue and a political structure which allows for the active participation of civil society. The context in which these groups now negotiate is different from union negotiations that took place in earlier periods. In the latter, although negotiators from oppositional groups did not come to the table holding equal levels of power as their adversaries, they did hold an important trump card—the threat of a strike or walkout. In the new transnational context oppositional negotiators no longer hold this card. In a context of strong unionization, like the Sandinista years and even the earliest years of the Chamorro regime, force in numbers was the key to power at the negotiation table. In the new context of labor weakened by the heightened mobility of capital, information used to support lobbying and to change public opinion becomes the key commodity, and the dissemination of this information represents an all-important endeavor.

THE CAMPAIGN "JOBS, YES . . .
BUT WITH DIGNITY!"

Operating simultaneously at various levels of the global system, the Network's campaigns highlight the challenge that their political practices pose to neatly bounded conceptualizations of "local," "national," and "global." In conjunction with the plans established in the meetings of the Network, Sara and the Managua team developed a strategy for implementing a national campaign in Nicaragua.

MEC's strategic orientation regarding the maquilas is encapsulated in the campaign slogan "Jobs, Yes . . . But with Dignity!" Thus, MEC does not call for the removal of the assembly plants, as this would leave women workers with no means of generating income. Instead, MEC organizers publicly denounce the maquila factories and their owners, pointing out the violence and the unfair and extremely harsh working conditions within them and calling for factory owners to respect national labor legislation through support of a code of ethics.

At its second meeting in Guatemala, the Network established four basic points to include in its code of ethics, which were adopted by MEC for its own national code of ethics:

1. The assurance of pregnant women's right to employment and to maintaining their job positions without suffering harassment or restrictions of their labor rights.

2. The assurance that women maquila workers receive legal wages and payment for overtime hours worked.

3. A guarantee that women maquila workers not suffer from any type of physical, psychological, sexual, or work-related violence.

4. The assurance that workers be registered for social security and that they have access to the services offered by social security. For those too young to receive benefits, the employer will provide services free of charge.

In addition, endorsement of the code was to serve as recognition of the Network and its members as independent monitors to ensure compliance with the agreement.

Compliance with national labor legislation was also part of the code of ethics, since all these points were in fact reflected in the Central American countries' labor codes. On April 14, 1997, just before the Network's third meeting, in an event which would have significant impact on the strategy of the coalition and its members, U.S. President Bill Clinton endorsed the Apparel Industry Partnership Agreement (AIP). Participants from fashion companies, labor organizations, consumer groups, and human rights organizations drew up this agreement, which included a workplace code of conduct as well as the establishment of independent and internal monitors for garment assembly factories.

The organizations of the Network then added two points from this agreement: language regarding safe working conditions and freedom from discrimination based on pregnancy, race, religion, age, disability, and sexual and political orientation. Although the AIP included recognition of workers' rights of freedom of association and collective bargaining, a cap on mandatory overtime, and prohibitions against child labor, the Network decided not to incorporate these points into its code. Each national group member of the Network agreed to include the now six basic points in their national codes of ethics, but was free to add other points such as child labor.

Back in Nicaragua I participated with the Managua team of MEC as they developed a national campaign strategy. Using techniques that they had learned in the Network's last meeting, Sara and Laura led the group in constructing a "map of power" to determine who MEC's allies and adversaries might be and how to deal with them effectively in meeting the goals of the campaign. The national campaign was designed to sensitize national and international public opinion regarding work conditions in the maquilas in order to achieve two main objectives: to effect changes in these conditions and to bring about factory owners' signing the code of ethics

Despite MEC's local focus, this initiative clearly reflected transnational dimensions. The very language of the demands of the code of ethics came from UN and other international ordinances. The introduction to MEC's Nicaraguan code of ethics cites the Convention on the Elimination of all Forms of Discrimination Against Women and the Universal Declaration on Human Rights, calling on the Nicaraguan government as a "state participant in international human rights agreements . . . to guarantee that men and women exercise equal economic, social, cultural, civil, and political rights" (MEC 1997a: 1). This tactic demonstrates what Keck and Sikkink term "accountability politics" (1998a: 24), whereby networks use a government's public commitments to expose the discrepancy between discourse and practice.

In order to exert an impact on national public opinion, the team turned its attention to a media strategy. Once again, MEC organizers' personal oppositional networks came into play. MEC organizers reactivated old ties with members of the press from their years of involvement in the labor movement. Certain Sandinista journalists and radio announcers had been sympathetic to Sara and her supporters during conflicts with the male CST leadership. One writer for the opposition newspaper *La Barricada* pledged continued coverage of the campaign in her weekly column. In addition, MEC solicited space in the feminist magazine *La Boletina* (1997a), which ran an article about the situation of maquila workers and the campaign. In addition, after 1990 there was a virtual explosion of independent media in Nicaragua, including the birth of several unaffiliated television stations and newspapers and a plethora of tiny radio stations. To kick off the Network's international campaign, MEC organizers called together their journalist contacts as well as other members of the media for a press conference.

MEC's strategy regarding the media built on a base established by the revolutionary politics of the last decade. The revolution left in its wake an extremely politicized and participative public sphere. Media reform initiated during the Sandinista period and the proliferation of new independent radio and television stations after 1990 enhanced and contributed to this locally oriented public sphere. There is great deal of public accessibility to the many tiny radio stations in the country, and it is common for individuals to use the airways to *hacer denuncias* (make public denunciations). Individuals do not even have to have money for a phone call or access to a telephone, as most radio stations allow written notes to be passed to announcers and read over the air.

As others (Urla 1995; Guattari 1984) have demonstrated in the case of the free radio movement of Europe, radio can be instrumental in constituting alternative oppositional public spheres. Countless tiny radio stations exist in Nicaragua. Indeed, one need barely nudge the dial to tune in to one station after another. These stations have extremely limited range, and owners often operate them from their homes.

Other oppositional groups in civil society, including women's groups, have taken advantage of this politicized public sphere, primarily relying on the myriad of small radio stations to reach "the public." For example, in its yearly campaigns against domestic violence, the Nicaraguan Network of Women Against Violence flooded the airways with campaign slogans like "My body is mine" and paid radio spots depicting domestic violence situations and calling for an end to violence within families.

Locally oriented small stations, and even larger stations, frequently broadcast calls to political action. For example, during the general strike of April 1997, demonstrators coordinated efforts at various barricades and kept supporters informed through radio broadcasts—particularly through the Sandinista stations like Radio Ya, located across the street from the University of Central America in Managua, a hotbed for political organizing. In this way, oppositional groups from civil society use the newly expanded national media to address "the distinctive . . . interests of local and regional communities" (Morley and Robins 1995).

Using their personal networks, Sara and Evelyn, the director of the Documentation Center, contacted journalists from various media to invite them to a press conference and luncheon. The invitation was to cover the third meeting of the Network and the national and international campaign. In addition, Sara and Evelyn promised journalists the opportunity to interview a group of maquila workers, some of whom chose to wear masks to disguise their identities. Sara was also able to call upon some other contacts to arrange an appearance for a group from the Network on the Sandinista television station's morning program.

At the press conference, held the day before International Labor Day (May 1), journalists were able to ask questions of the various representatives of the Network. Referring first to Clinton's endorsement of the AIP, the women of the Network read aloud the code of ethics and made a call to the government and administrators of the zone to support its signature. Before the conference the women of the Network met with the Minister of Labor to present him with the code of ethics and ask him for his support. The press conference was also timed to coincide with an upcoming summit of Central American government representatives. On the agenda for this summit were early talks about the initiation of what would later be dubbed the Central American Free Trade Agreement (CAFTA). The issue of free trade, then, and the maquila factories in particular, were in the forefront of the state officials' political agenda.

At the press conference Sara called attention to the minister's expressed support of the Network's efforts and his commitment to publicize it at the upcoming meeting of Central American labor ministers. "We have opened a bridge of communication with the Ministry," Sara announced. The minister had in fact instructed his staff to be sure to receive anyone coming from MEC and assist them in any way possible. "We went in there and no one knew us, and we came out recognized," said Josefina. "Now they know who we are."

After asking other questions about work conditions and goals of the Network, the press was able to enter a room where the group of maquila workers had assembled. The promotoras had agreed to be interviewed, though Sara announced to the journalists that cameras would not be permitted. Some workers who had been unfairly fired were willing to give their names, and one appeared on television. One worker had brought with her a memo from factory management requiring workers to make up time lost due to a power outage. In violation of national labor laws, the obligatory overtime was to take place on a Sunday with no overtime compensation.

The media gave wide coverage to the activities of the Network. Members of the press expressed how impressed they were with the bravery of the promotoras and the organization of the Network. They had been disappointed with what they deemed a pathetic show on the part of the Sandinista unions who had called for press coverage of their march on International Labor Day. According to the reporters, few people showed up, and the march was extremely disorganized.

Sara and the others also scheduled this media event to publicize the Network's meeting with the vice president of the Free Trade Zone Corporation. In the first days of the Network's meeting, the negotiation team had spent hours preparing for this meeting. The two-day workshop practicum on negotiation skills gave them the opportunity to engage in role-playing and other exercises to practice for this encounter. Although the administrator would not commit to supporting the code of ethics, he did indicate that he would send a copy of the document to the association of factory owners who were meeting in order to draft their own workplace code of conduct in anticipation of the aftermath of Clinton's endorsement of the AIP and resulting creation of the Fair Labor Association (FLA).

MEC followed up this free publicity from the media with paid newspaper ads featuring the code of ethics and a call for its endorsement by state officials and factory owners. In addition, MEC implemented a petition drive. Promotoras, organizers, and program participants collected thirty thousand signatures, which they presented to the Minister of Labor. The petition further circulated information about the work of the Network within grassroots communities and other organizations in the autonomous women's movement.

In addition to placing issues facing female maquila workers on the public agenda, the campaign had other concrete results and was recognized internationally as a success story. (Indeed, in 1998 MEC was given the Human Rights Award of the Canadian Council for International Cooperation [CCIC] for its work on this campaign.) The media campaign raised public awareness about the working conditions of female maquila workers, and MEC affiliates and organizers attributed a drop in shop-floor violence to this increase in awareness. The Ministry of Labor opened its doors to MEC, allowing organizers privileged access to inspectors. Organizers were also allowed access to the free trade zone and could pass through the front gate unquestioned. In a landmark victory Nicaragua's Minister of Labor Wilfredo Navarro was the first state agent to endorse the coalition's code of ethics, which he signed on February 1, 1998. Later the ministry adopted the code as a ministerial resolution, which all factory owners within the free trade zone eventually signed. It also paved the road for the drafting of a bill to reform the laws that govern the FTZ that was eventually passed (Anteproyecto de Ley 1999).

Despite these successes, the political tools that MEC has chosen pose certain difficulties. For instance, the negotiation techniques that the women are learning to employ are borrowed from the business world and are designed to reach an agreement between relatively equal adversaries. It is unclear that negotiation in and of itself can be an effective instrument for bringing about changes in social structures. The danger is that those in positions of power have much more about which they can compromise. The oppositional groups have less to begin with and have few options for "cutting a deal."

COMPETITION AND CONFLICT
IN TRANSNATIONAL POLITICS:
MEC AND THE LABOR MOVEMENT

MEC experienced other obstacles in the implementation of its strategies. In its work within the free trade zone, as well as with the national and international campaign, it had repeated encounters with the traditional labor movement. If the women of MEC had long-standing networks within the popular movements of the FSLN, they also had many adversaries. Movement organizers were vocal in their positioning of MEC as an alternative to trade unions, typically presenting the organization in such terms as: "We are not a unionist movement, nor do we have anything to do with unionism. They have their organizations and we have ours. We are offering an alternative by and for women." The fact that MEC had emerged from conflicts in the labor movement meant continued tense relations with traditional labor organizations. These tensions came to a head as the CST-affiliated Textile and Apparel Workers' Federation, led by Pablo Alvarez, began to try to form unions within the FORTEX factory, the site of the nationally publicized strike of 1993, which at that time the CST had refused to support.

MEC's organizational identity and alternative work strategies transcend the territorial boundaries characteristic of groups that have their roots in the mass organizations that formed after the 1979 revolution. These popular organizations had divided society into sectors: industrial workers (CST), agricultural workers (ATC), youth (JS-19), women (AMNLAE), and barrio dwellers (CDS) among others (Saakes 1991: 175). The structural origins of the mass organizations corresponded with one aspect of an individual's lived experience or identity—that is, with his or her membership in one particular, relatively homogeneous sector.

MEC's democratic struggle addresses inequalities in both class and gender relations, and, thus, does not fit into the "separation of spheres" approach of the popular organizations. The CST and the other labor organizations continued to see factories and other workplaces as their organizational domain, separate from that of women's organizations. A leader of CAUS, a union with a history of communist affiliation, expressed a typical attitude of union organizers. In a conversation with Sara about union organizing in the FTZ he commented: "You *do* know that the maximum organizational expression for workers, be they women or men, is through syndicalism?! Is this or is this not the case?!" Representing a "bigger package," MEC's integral approach to improving maquila workers' lives challenged traditional Marxist notions of a privileged revolutionary subject as constituted solely by economic relations and the division of society into spheres of the Sandinista mass organizations.

In the 1980s there was competition among some mass organizations to recruit affiliates and extend their social base. The CST was no exception, and, indeed, the history of trade unionism in the Sandinista era is one of intense competition for worker affiliation. As the official labor organizations of the FSLN during the 1980s, the federations of the CST usurped what had been the domain of the communist unions like CAUS. In 1996 when the textile federation of the CST began organizing efforts in the FTZ, union leaders applied the same competitive methods to deal with MEC, which by that point had an established presence in approximately half of the factories of the FTZ.

Even before confrontations with Pablo Alvarez and the Textile and Apparel Workers' Federation, MEC organizers had anticipated opposition from the traditional labor movement. In the campaign planning meeting the women of the Managua collective had listed the unions under "potential adversaries." By the late 1990s, as Pablo and his supporters were able to form unions in three factories in the zone, the traditional labor movement came to present one of the greatest threats to MEC's work.

Turf wars have been prevalent within the Nicaraguan labor movement since even before the revolution. Such conflicts were frequent even between Sandinista organizations. For example, in the early 1980's the ATC and the CST battled over who would organize sugarcane workers, with the CST eventually winning recruiting rights within the sugarcane processing plants (Luciak 1995: 65). As noted earlier, the CST's presence within these plants would become the basis for a major scandal during the concertación talks of the 1990s when tripartite negotiations took place regarding the privatization of state-owned plants. Workers were left with no shares in them, and CST leaders were able to privately obtain a major portion of shares in several of these plants. The workers, left jobless, responded in protest, constructing and living in a tent city on the South Highway into the city where they remained for over a year.

By February 1997 rumors flew that Pablo would send spies to infiltrate MEC's activities in an effort to destroy it and "take over" the factories. The atmosphere at the Managua office was tense, and the Managua team met alone and later with the promotoras to discuss the organization's plan of action should it be faced with an onslaught by Pablo and his supporters. Some members were even in favor of screening new participants in the maquila worker program. Eventually, the other members of the collective convinced them that no such drastic measures were necessary. Jill opined: "They are playing the same old dirty game as always. . . . We should ignore them. . . . We have nothing to hide."

In one case a MEC promoter, Rosalba, was fired after talking to a solidarity delegation from Canada in a conversation arranged by a group of workers who were in touch with the Textile and Apparel Workers' Federation. Rosalba's general manager called her to his office and informed her that she was being fired for being a unionist. Later, she learned that her name had appeared on a list of potential union activists, which was being circulated among the managers of the zone's factories. Rosalba was convinced that textile federation supporters had handed her name over to management. Whether or not this was the case, the incident caused great concern and anxiety in the MEC office in Managua. "If they are going to sink, they want to bring us down with them," mused Sara, who worried that such incidents would drive away MEC's constituency of maquila workers.

Other incidents occurred in which supporters of the CST textile federation confronted MEC organizers. At a meeting before a special commission of the National Assembly, Pablo and his supporters blasted MEC's use of the code of ethics, declaring that "the only document that needs to be respected is this country's labor code!" In a culminating encounter Pablo and a group of his supporters clashed with Josefina and a group of promotoras at the entrance to the free trade zone. Pablo told Josefina: "Whether or not Sara Rodríguez likes it, we are entering the zone!" He then pointed to Josefina and the promotoras calling out, "These women are trying to destroy syndicalism!" As Pablo and the other unionists hurled taunts at Josefina and the promotoras, the encounter nearly became a physical confrontation between the two groups.

Meanwhile, the Textile and Apparel Workers' Federation began to mount its union-organizing campaign in a number of FTZ factories. In 1997, to support their efforts, Pablo and other federation members used the Sandinista media to publicize management's anti-union tactics, as targeted factories repeatedly fired all workers who led the union drives. Pablo appeared repeatedly in the media, threatening to shut down factories in which unionizing efforts were being mounted. In addition, the textile federation tapped into long-standing transnational solidarity networks in the United States and Canada, to exert international pressure to support unionizing in the zone. Later, in 1999 and 2000 groups like the Campaign for Labor Rights (CLR) and the National Labor Committee (NLC) waged fax and e-mail campaigns, targeting the Corporation of the Free Trade Zone and the Ministry of Labor as well as the home companies that produced in the zone.

By March of 1997 three legally recognized unions had formed in the zone. Despite the media and internet hype, MEC promotoras and orga-nizers felt that the unionizing efforts were reaching a minuscule social base. Most promotoras from factories with supposed union representa-tion had never heard of the union drive until they were told by MEC organizers. The union that formed in the FORTEX factory was initially established with signatures of only thirty-five members, though more workers eventually joined. (Nicaraguan law allows for the creation of unions with as few as twenty worker signatures; Bellman 2003). Although women were well represented among the rank and file of this union as well as the other unions that subsequently formed in the FTZ (see Bellman 2003), the leadership of the federations to which these unions belonged continued to be men—whose past histories, attitudes towards women, and leadership styles were quite familiar to the women of MEC. There was little or no evidence that gender issues were taken into consideration in the unions' practices or strategies. Given their years of experience in the CST and their familiarity with leaders of the federations that sponsored unionization drives in the FTZ, the women of MEC, though voicing re-spect for women workers' choice regarding which organizations to join, remained extremely skeptical about the degree to which unions would take gender issues into account or represent the kinds of needs and prior-ities that women workers had repeatedly expressed in MEC's workshops, consultations, and forums with them—issues like not being docked for time spent at home caring for sick children or for visits to the clinic and keeping her job when a woman becomes pregnant.[7]

For example, one of the first unions to gain legal recognition in the FTZ, the Union August 16, was successful in negotiating a collective bar-gaining agreement. Josefina was able to obtain a copy of the agreement, which promotoras and MEC organizers found severely lacking. For the most part, the contract was taken word for word from the national labor code. The only specific language that it contained regarding working conditions concerned the provision of masks and special shirts for iron-ers. The promotoras scoffed, since in the segregated division of labor of the factory, the vast majority of ironers are men (who incidentally were known to make more than seamstresses, the majority of whom were mostly women). And even though most of the agreement's language was taken directly from the state's labor code, the provisions that specifically address women workers were absent from the contract. The promotoras were indignant. "¡Que chanchado, ese sindicato!"—That union is such a pigsty!—a worker from FORTEX exclaimed.

Still, despite the extremely limited gains of the agreement, one aspect of it was especially worrisome to MEC organizers: it established the union as "the only representative of the workers of FORTEX." MEC organizers feared that this staking out of organizational territory could have a possible negative impact on their negotiations with factory owners and state agents. The question of who were the "true" representatives of maquila workers was clearly what was at stake during this conflictive period of relations between MEC and the unions. What concerned Sara, Laura, and Josefina was that the confrontational methods of the labor federations and what they saw as their extremist positions would threaten MEC's delicate negotiations with factory owners and state officials.

After the April 1997 meeting of the Network and the recognition that MEC received through negotiations with state officials and FTZ administrators Josefina and Sara had better access to the FTZ, obtaining appointments with human resources administrators and even some upper-level managers and factory owners. Taking advantage of Pablo's and other federation leaders' militant appearances in the media, the women presented the code of ethics as a "proposal," and suggested MEC as an alternative to the confrontational tactics of the unions. Sara and Josefina's use of the language of negotiation and expressed desire to establish a bridge of communication with managers and their positioning of MEC as an alternative by and for the women, made these managers and owners more willing to hear their arguments. "The unionists don't work with proposals, but with shouts," commented the factory owner who accepted Sara's copy of the code of ethics and promised to present it as a proposal for the workplace code of conduct at the next association meeting. Another upper-level manager of ECCO, the only shoe-producing factory in the FTZ, agreed to meet with Sara, offering MEC organizers access to the shop floor with the understanding that they would publicly proclaim "the truth" about work conditions there. National managers were concerned that their factories were acquiring the same poor image as the Taiwanese and Korean factories, in which they believed the work conditions were far worse. By differentiating their movement from traditional labor unions, MEC opened some negotiating space with FTZ administrators and some managers. As we shall see, however, this differential positioning was not always advantageous.

"SELF-LIMITING RADICALISM" AND TRANSNATIONAL POLITICS

Competing national and transnational interests have prompted diverse and shifting alliances among the various actors involved in the struggle over working conditions in the maquila factories. The principal actors have included state elites, traditional local trade union organizations, autonomous women's organizations, Northern-based labor organizations, and international solidarity organizations—often Northern-based NGOs. MEC and the other members of the Network had to position themselves within this national and international political field of allies and adversaries.

The "radical reformism" of MEC and the Network affected their ability to implement strategies at the transnational level. MEC's stance regarding the maquilas—that they remain in the country but respect local labor laws and improve work conditions—meant that organizers had to be extremely careful in their lobbying efforts not to pressure the factories to the point where they would relocate production. This limited the ability of MEC and the Network to engage certain political strategies that have been successful for some campaigns, such as international boycotts in the case of the Nestle corporation (Keck and Sikkink 1998a). MEC organizers and other members of the Central American Network were very aware of this. As one participant put it, "We are asking for the minimum. We aren't even questioning the exploitation of workers." Another leader chimed in: "We accept that the transnational corporations superexploit us, but we have no choice [*no hay de otra*]."

Other transnational campaigns, like the ones launched by coalitions of human rights organizations or of students groups, labor organizations, and other NGOs within the anti-sweatshop movement, have used "leverage politics" in order to change the behavior of target actors (Keck and Sikkink 1998a). However, given MEC's "self-limiting radicalism," transnational leverage was harder to elicit. To date neither MEC nor the Network has ever issued a clear public message regarding how international individuals and groups can support their campaigns. The Network's campaigns have gone beyond the regional level only insofar as they have disseminated information about work conditions and the code of ethics through linkages with groups and individuals in the North. In keeping with their position of "jobs but with dignity," the only thing that MEC and the organizations of the Network have clearly articulated is that they do not support consumer boycotts or direct action such as leafleting retailers as a way to exert pressure on factories. Coalition organizers acknowledged that the real power did not reside with the factory subcontractors, but in the so-called mother (*matriz*) companies, the transnational corporations like GAP and J. C. Penney. The fear here, however, was that under boycott pressure, these companies would simply turn to other factories for their production needs—once again leaving Nicaraguan workers jobless. This fear was not unfounded, as there had been several cases in Central America in which boycotted companies had withdrawn contracts from subcontractors, eventually shutting them down (Köpke 2000; Molina and Quinteros 2000).[8]

There have been other obstacles. In 1997 Network members decided to enter negotiations with international organizations and to present their code of ethics to the Central American Parliament and the ILO, asking for political support from these institutions of "global governance" (Drainville 1998). But they found it difficult to gain access to these institutions or to other transnational political spaces such as summit meetings of Central American ministers of labor or presidents.

The ILO, for example, continues to adhere to the model of tripartite negotiations—in which the participants are representatives of the state, business, and unions—as the proper method for achieving changes in workers' situations. This formula excludes autonomous women's organizations. For example, when the ILO held a conference in Nicaragua, only representatives from the labor movement and the media received official invitations. Evelyn was able to attend after pursuing contacts through friends in the labor movement, who were able to secure an extra invitation for her.

In the late 1990s the Network sought to establish alliances with other regional and transnational networks, but was not successful. For example, ICIC (Iniciativa Civil para la Integración Centroamericana, or the Civil Initiative for Central American Integration), a coalition of twelve Central American NGOs, was eager to meet with representatives from the

Network. Members were disappointed, however, when ICIC's invitation was not to join the initiative as an autonomous organization, but to become part of a "women's branch" of ICIC, along with the women's wings of the other organizations. They were not invited to join ICIC at the 1997 summit of Central American presidents held in Costa Rica, but instead were asked to participate in a women's forum to be held in Guatemala. ICIC's call for a unified political agenda for Central American civil society sounded all too familiar to the women of the Network. "We haven't forgotten about the important role of women in civil society," commented the ICIC representative at the meeting with Network representatives. It seemed clear that this "we" did not include women.

Nor did it seem that MEC was fully welcome within the transnational anti-sweatshop movement. In the late 1990s the NLC and other labor organizations involved in formulating the AIP began focusing on establishing independent monitoring teams within the maquila factories in order to ensure compliance with the AIP's code of conduct. Overwhelmingly, these groups turned to the traditional labor movement and human rights organizations to form independent monitoring teams. In the majority of cases autonomous women's organizations were excluded from this transnational political initiative.[9] (The exception was Honduras in which the women's collective CODEMUH, a member of the Network, was included in the independent monitoring team; Köpke 2000.)

In 1998 the NLC initiated efforts to establish independent monitoring teams in Nicaragua's maquila factories. They turned to the Sandinista unions, which had been the traditional counterparts of the Central American solidarity movement in the North and set up meetings with CST organizers. The NLC also approached the human rights organization CENIDH (Nicaraguan Center of Human Rights) to play a major role. Because of the deep divisions between the CST and MEC, and CENIDH's strong ties to the FSLN, the NLC did not invite the women of MEC to participate.

Some women's groups have been included in some independent monitoring teams (most notably in Honduras), but a gender perspective has largely been absent from these efforts. The "gender blindness" of transnational organizing efforts at monitoring conditions within maquila factories and the continued adherence to the traditional organizational structures and political orientations of the labor movement have prompted the Network to keep promoting its independent efforts at negotiating its own code of ethics and to search for other mechanisms for monitoring factory conditions (Mendez and Köpke 1998).

An event in November 1997 crystallized how sharply the independent monitoring initiatives differed from MEC and the other members of the Network. The NLC, working with Witness for Peace, a U.S.-based social justice organization with a long history of solidarity work with the Sandinistas labor movement, facilitated a visit to the FTZ for a team of reporters from the U.S. television program *Hard Copy*. In a three-part series reporters used hidden cameras to expose the working and living conditions of employees. To add more shock value to the series, reporters exaggerated some of its claims, reporting that minors as young as thirteen were employed there and taking workers' comments out of context. Because it mixed inaccuracies with reports of real labor and human rights violations, the program lost a great deal of credibility, especially when it later aired in Nicaragua.

A national uproar ensued when a local television affiliate picked up the segment and broadcast it in Nicaragua. Public opinion was split, and the issue polarized people into pro–or anti–Free Trade Zone. Supporters of the maquilas, including representatives of the government, pointed to *Hard Copy*'s relations with the NLC and described the report as a plot by U.S. unions, whose workers are threatened by off-shore production. Meanwhile, the Sandinista labor movement, spearheaded by Pablo Alvarez, called for the ouster of the foreign-owned factories. The headline for an editorial in the opposition newspaper *La Barricada* by the former Minister of the Interior Tomás Borge read "¡Que se vayan!" (Get out!) Borge's editorial took a hard line: "The benefit received by the country is insignificant. Our national dignity is of greater value" (1997). Sandinista union and party leaders exchanged accusations of national betrayal with state representatives, and each camp struggled to use the maquila issue to demonstrate their representation of true national interest.

In response over 350 male and female workers marched in front of the Ministry of Labor calling for the factories to remain in the country (Barreto 1997). The Sandinista media portrayed them as manipulated by the Free Trade Zone Corporation in order to protect their jobs, while supporters cited the march as evidence that Nicaraguans supported maquilas (Meza 1997). The national media sought out the women of MEC for their view. "We felt like a sandwich," said one MEC leader, and the group remained silent rather than have their views distorted in order to fit within the binary frame of the public debate. Thus, the more middle-of-the-road position of MEC—that the factories remain in operation but improve conditions—was effectively excluded from public discourse. Several workers who appeared in the broadcast segment were fired from their factory jobs after the report aired in Nicaragua (*La Barricada* 1997b). "Are *they* going to give these people work?" MEC organizers wondered of the CST and the Sandinista leadership. In addition, the scandal caused MEC organizers to fear greatly that the publicity and confrontational methods of the textile union would jeopardize their delicate negotiations with factory administrators and representatives of the state.

The tense relations between local and international labor organizations and autonomous women's groups and the exclusion of women's organizations from the independent monitoring groups prompted MEC and the other members of the Network to consider briefly an affiliation with the Council on Economic Priorities Accreditation Agency (CEPAA). CEPAA had drafted a system defining a universal set of auditable standards and an independent auditing process to protect workers' rights, known as the SA 8000. The agency accredits qualified commercial auditing firms to conduct SA 8000 audits and certifies companies and contractors who successfully pass the independent inspections.

Like other corporation codes of conduct, CEPAA's efforts have been vehemently criticized by the international trade union movement and solidarity NGOs. Its advisory board includes representatives from human rights organizations and NGOs, but also from various corporations. It is accused of excluding unions and other labor organizations, of vertical decision-making based in the North (Labor Rights in China 2000), and of failure to consult with groups from the South in drafting the SA 8000 guidelines. Critics further claim that the SA 8000 does not provide a means to obligate companies to disclose the full number of their suppliers and subcontractors, so a company could be SA 8000 certified while still subcontracting with uncertified suppliers (Clean Clothes Campaign 1998).

In the end, the Network decided against pursuing SA 8000 accreditation. Instead, MEC and other Network members sought to work with other organizations throughout the region to create a new network of independent local monitors (Köpke 2000) and insist that monitoring standards must include a gender perspective.

Northern-based solidarity organizations are the source of MEC's funding, and many within such groups continue to take the narrow view that unions are the only truly appropriate organizational model for protecting workers' rights. Due to their greater access to material resources, these "global agents" have considerable influence over the form, content, and personnel of transnational initiatives (Nelson 1997). The incident of the *Hard Copy* report is an example of the continued narrow unionist orientation present within some Northern NGOS.

International funders have exerted indirect and direct pressure on MEC and other members of the Network to change their strategies. After returning from a trip to Europe to meet with solidarity groups and funders, MEC leaders talked about their frustrating and sometimes humiliating experiences with these groups. Some individuals within them repeatedly sought explanations for why MEC and the Network did not coordinate their efforts more closely with the labor movement. In fact, one group that had funded the initial phases of the campaign "Jobs, Yes . . . But with Dignity!" informed Sara that the code of ethics, which had been carefully and laboriously constructed within the Network and within each member organization, should be changed to include the freedom to organize unions. Sara and the others held firm, explaining that the points included had been decided upon in collective meetings and could not be revised.

Laura and Sara were discouraged that individual members of organizations that were among their closest allies were so invested in the outdated ways of "before": "They have all these theories about the transformation of society, but . . . This is a process. It is step by step. It's not true that we are going to change the whole world—the whole economic system—from one day to the next." Sara scoffed at the use of the "language of before" by some Europeans: "This language from before . . . 'Patria libre o morir,' me choca a mi (really rubs me the wrong way). Let *them* die. *We* want to keep living!"

In MEC organizers' view, international supporters spent more time talking than taking action and yet wanted to control MEC and the Network's plans. This was partially responsible for MEC's decision not to employ international pressure on factory owners and the state, a technique that would be consistent with strategies employed by transnational advocacy networks in which leverage is sought against targeted institutions through the application of pressure from other more powerful governments (the boomerang effect; see Keck and Sikkink 1998a). Instead, MEC focused on the Network-based national and regional campaign, which enjoyed international support, but did not involve directing pressure from outside the country at the Nicaraguan state or FTZ factory owners. At one point MEC had hoped to launch international fax campaigns, a technique that would be taken up later in 1999 by groups like the CLR and the NLC in conjunction with the Textile and Apparel Workers' Federation. However, in 1997 MEC's Managua team decided against fax campaigns, turning their energy instead to negotiations at the national level with factory workers and state representatives like the Minister of Labor.

These examples show the complexities involved in "globalization from below." Other scholars (e.g., Nelson 1997) have noted these types of tensions within transnational networks, pointing to the conflict as well as the cooperation that occur within transnational partnerships. Despite the conflict, linkages among local groups across national borders continue to be a highly significant and powerful form of oppositional organization. Thus it is important to find ways to confront and deal with these tensions.

WHAT DO MEC'S political strategies tell us about how power and resistance operate under globalization? At this point MEC's alternative practices have been effective in calling state and local public attention to the situation of women maquila workers and to gaining space within state institutions, most notably the Ministry of Labor. On the other hand, because of its autonomy and reformist orientations, MEC has had difficulty fully entering the transnational political arena. Unlike human rights networks and other oppositional groups such as the Zapatistas of Mexico, they have been unable and, at times, unwilling to employ transnational strategies for fear that they would compromise their approach, opting instead for local negotiations and media coverage. MEC and the Network have experienced difficulties in engaging international supporters and NGOs within the campaign for "Jobs, Yes . . . But with Dignity!"

As has been noted the problem that MEC faces is how to effectively implement accountability politics around women workers' issues in the maquilas (Keck and Sikkink 1998a). In the current context of global capitalism, is the most effective lobbying strategy to focus on state institutions or global institutions? On national or global civil societies? MEC's self-limiting radicalism, although it has at least opened spaces at the national level—both in the state and with private factory owners—limits their ability to gain material leverage either nationally or transnationally.

MEC's immediate goal to improve women's daily lives, their approach to gender and class interests, and the conditions in the global economy do not lend themselves well to the types of strategies that other transnational networks have found to be effective. For example, human rights networks used information politics to target specific states which then exerted pressure on the Argentine state to end the torture and disappearances of citizens. Boycott strategies have also been effective for other networks (see Keck and Sikkink 1998a). But given the objectives of MEC and the issues of women maquila workers, these strategies may lose their material punch because of the mobility of factories and the ever-present threat that they will relocate. Thus, MEC constantly struggles to find strategies that pressure factories sufficiently to implement changes but not so much that plants will close or leave the country.

If Keck and Sikkink's (1998a) assessment of transnational politics is correct, the problem becomes formulating a "causal story" regarding who is responsible for remedying the situation. Large companies like J. C. Penney can easily point to subcontractors, who can in turn just as easily blame individual supervisors for rights violations. Likewise, assigning blame to the state can be difficult, especially when protesters call for factories to remain in operation.

Other actors have stepped forward to fill the void left by noninterventionist neoliberal state regimes, including NGOs and labor organizations. However, their strategies for holding corporations accountable for labor and human rights violations exhibit contradictions. Gender blindness continues to be a problem within the international trade union movement. The SA 8000 and other voluntary corporate codes of conduct also pose serious dilemmas and have been accused by some labor organizations as being simply a case of "the fox guarding the hen house." Tensions between North and South cross-cut both of these transnational initiatives.

The tensions experienced by MEC and the Network call for an analysis of the power relations that occur within transnational organizing initiatives. A gender-blind analysis of the initiatives making up "globalization from below" is inadequate for understanding power and resistance in the global system. The transnational political terrain is a highly gendered terrain. Structures of power and hegemonic definitions of the split between public and private construct certain political spaces as "male domains." We see this in the exclusion of autonomous women's groups from various political spaces, such as ICIC, most independent monitoring teams, institutions of global governance like the ILO, and transnational or regional forums like summits of Central American presidents.

The *Hard Copy* example illustrates the internal power dynamics of transnational political organizing, serving as a reminder that public spheres—local, national, or transnational—are based on systemic exclusions (Guidry et al. 2000a: 10). Gaining access to a transnational public sphere can also have unforeseen and sometimes adverse consequences for local actors.

Domestically, unions were willing to devote considerable energy to undermining MEC's work. By contrast, government representatives actually showed support (although the women are ever suspicious), which further shows that "globalization from below" can be a complex, multilayered process.

Tensions between the autonomous women workers' organization MEC and labor federations with continuing ties to the CST reflect contestations over how workers, and women workers in particular, should be represented. What is partially at stake is the definition of a "true" worker's organization.[10] Labor federation leaders, MEC organizers, international funders, and U.S.-based independent labor organizations have different views and differing stakes in the debate. And they bring different kinds and amounts of power to bear in influencing it.

Assessing transnational political organizing efforts, what works and why, depends on the character of the issues themselves, but also upon timing and on the interarticulations among the political conditions at the national, transnational, and local levels. Local political history remains extremely significant in gauging the impact that a given strategy will have. The framing of issues is an important aspect of such political strategies. The following chapter continues the examination of MEC's "self-limiting radicalism" through an analysis of the discursive framing strategies that the organization has employed.

6   MEC and the Postsocialist State: Democracy, Rights, and Citizenship under Globalization

"¡Voto por la democracia en el país, en la casa, y en la cama!" (I vote for democracy in the country, in the home, and in the bedroom.)—Slogan for 1996 campaign of the Network of Women Against Violence

My very first encounter with a MEC organizer was especially memorable because it introduced me to the ways in which local public spheres operate in Nicaragua. Newly arrived in the country and seeking to establish the groundwork for a research project, I was struggling to locate organizers of the domestic workers' union that had formed in the early 1990s. At that time few people in Nicaragua had phones, and cell phones were not widely owned. My very *gringa* strategy for obtaining meetings or interviews was that I needed to call people first in case they were busy. For that reason, during my first trip to Nicaragua I stayed with Myrna, my husband's aunt, who had a telephone in her house, where she also operated a small beauty parlor. I quickly came to realize, however, that face-to-face visits were going to be the best way to reach potential interviewees.

After one particularly trying day in which I had made little progress finding contacts, I flopped into one of the makeshift salon chairs in frustration to recount the difficulties I was having to Myrna and her assistant, who were busy cleaning hairbrushes and sweeping hair from the entrance way that served as the tiny beauty parlor. I knew the name of the leader of the union (Reyna, a founding member of MEC), but I did not have the slightest idea how to find her. Myrna and her assistant both suggested that I visit Radio Ya, the Sandinista radio station across the street from the University of Central America. I was reluctant, but the women assured me, "If you are looking for someone in Managua, this is the best way." Coming as I did from a context of corporate-owned-and-controlled media and used to access to communication technologies like e-mail that even by the mid-1990s had made letter writing and even most phone calls obsolete, it would have never occurred to me to use the radio as a way of contacting people.

After a short ride in Myrna's husband's red Volkswagen bug, I found myself sitting in the waiting room of the radio station. Three or four other women were also waiting. I learned later that they were probably domestic workers who used the radio as a way to look for work or to denounce employers who had not paid them their earnings. Because they had no way to be contacted by phone, after their ads were read on the air, they waited at the station to see if any prospective employers would respond, or they hoped that the public embarrassment would cause employers to pay their missing wages.

I wrote my message to Reyna along with Myrna's phone number on a piece of paper and was told that it would be read on the air free of charge later that afternoon. Skeptical that this trip would yield any results, I left. The very next morning I received a call from Reyna. "I heard that you were looking for me," she said. "My neighbor heard your message on the radio."

Globalization is replete with contradictions. The spread of communication technologies has caused the world to become smaller for those with access to them, but the digital divide and growing disparities between rich and poor seem to be pulling the world's people apart as much as cultural, economic, and political integration are supposed to be bringing them together (Barber 2001). Communication technologies have transformed the ways in which people can interact in real time, but, especially in the North, the growing corporate control of the global media has meant that these media seem less and less a "public" sphere to ordinary people. Yet, as the example of the Radio Ya illustrates, global corporate control is far from absolute.

Paradoxically, increased corporate ownership of the global media has occurred alongside the spread of democratization to many parts of the world. According to the United Nations Development Programme (2002: 15), between the years of 1980 and 2000 the number of democratic regimes doubled (from forty-one to eighty-two), while the number of authoritarian regimes fell from almost seventy to fewer than thirty. In Nicaragua "democratization" has meant a transition from an authoritarian to a revolutionary regime and then from a revolutionary regime to a polyarchic regime—in which a small group actually rules, and participation by the majority is constrained (Robinson 2003: 53, 71). Nicaragua's postsocialist governments have promoted neoliberalism, as an emergent global capitalist order has supplanted both dictatorial and revolutionary regimes.

The discourse of rights has taken on new prominence in this context. The emergence of a universalized set of international norms and rules, based on a notion of individual bearers of unalienable rights, has transformed national and international spheres of political activity (Lipschutz 1992). The discourse of human rights has become a crucial idiom for disenfranchised people to frame their claims and demands in both national and transnational political arenas (Keck and Sikkink 1998a).

Nicaragua's transition to "democracy" (read, polyarchy) allows for a space for marginalized groups to make claims on the state based on their equal rights as citizens. In Nicaragua, as in other newly democratized countries, state actors and social justice groups use a common language of rights and citizenship but for radically different purposes, imbuing the terms with distinct meanings (Schild 1997: 606; and see Dagnino 1998). Groups like MEC posit alternative conceptions of citizenship (Schild 1998), calling for the extension of rights to excluded groups—in this case poor women and women workers—and emphasizing social and economic rights (Jelin and Hershberg 1996). Articulating demands in this way feels new on the tongues of marginalized people. The language may be new, but, in the postrevolutionary context of Nicaragua, what is not new is the politicization of such groups for whom participation in certain public spheres is not foreign and who are familiar with the use of the media as a tool for political mobilization, an important legacy of the revolution.

States in Latin America have also used a vocabulary of rights in their dealings with civil society, but as part of an overall neoliberal agenda and a new "politics of exclusion," which has generated and maintained social polarization (Robinson 2003: 314). For example, neoliberal governments often emphasize the right to private property, a major issue for the Alemán administration, which proposed legislation that would give land that had been redistributed by the Sandinistas back to its prerevolutionary owners. They often celebrate the political right to participation in highly controlled elections between competing elites. Or they place weight on a notion of "active citizens" who have the responsibility to position themselves entrepreneurially in the economy, a process said to be facilitated by free trade and comparative advantage and which shifts responsibility for social reproduction from the state to marginalized communities themselves (Schild 1998; Robinson 2003: 314).

This chapter uses the case of MEC to examine more closely the implications of democratic transition and struggles over citizenship for social movements under globalization. I analyze MEC's deployment of rights and citizenship discourses as it makes demands of a neoliberal state regime and discuss the conundrums that MEC has faced in reconciling the use of these discourses with the organization's aims to create a more just and democratic society, particularly for women workers in the FTZ. MEC's framing strategies raise questions about the limitations and strengths of the discursive tools of citizenship and rights (including human rights) for social justice projects in a context of globalization. And MEC's successes and failures reveal how state power has been reconfigured in a postsocialist context as well as the changing relationship between the state and civil society in a country that has made the transition to a neoliberal democracy.

MEC AND THE LANGUAGE OF RIGHTS

When I returned to Nicaragua in 1996, I strolled into MEC's newly renovated office where Evelyn, Sara, and Jill greeted me warmly. The changes since I last had worked in the office were striking. The Documentation Center that Evelyn and Reyna had dreamed about in 1995 had been constructed as an extension of the small building that had hosted all of MEC's Managua-based programs. The office itself had also been significantly enlarged, with a new lobby-like room that was separated from the rest of the space. In this more public area Magdalena, a graduate of MEC's job-training program, attended to visitors who came to MEC to seek services, meet with MEC organizers, or visit the Documentation Center. Though MEC still did not have telephone service (they obtained a phone line later that year), now there were three new computers.

I arrived just after the Managua team had hosted a Canadian delegation of visitors. Soon, Jill and Sara took me to the back. In what in 1995 had been a backyard of weeds there now stood a tiled outdoor patio area, a small garden, and a new conference room used to hold workshops and other activities. In 1997, yet another conference room would be constructed, and MEC would build another small office next door to the main office in order to house its microcredit program.

The patio and conference rooms displayed small plaques on the walls recognizing individual friends and supporters of MEC. Most of these individuals were major players in the NGOs or foundations that had financed MEC's projects. MEC organizers explained to visiting groups that "before" they followed the Sandinista tradition of naming organizations and buildings after those who had died, the heroes and martyrs of the revolution. MEC itself, as we have seen, was named for an organizer who had been killed. "But she was not a hero or a martyr," said Sara. "She was a great fighter for women's rights and a leader in the struggle of domestic workers. . . . But that is the last time that we name anything after someone who has died." "We shouldn't have to wait until someone dies to recognize their accomplishments," agreed Evelyn. Thus, as part of MEC's growth as an autonomous organization, the newly constructed facilities were dedicated to the living.

I eagerly entered the tiny space for the renamed Center of Documentation and Research, and Evelyn showed me examples of the different publications that MEC had produced in the last year, including a draft of one of the very first studies completed on women workers in maquila factories. Later that afternoon Sara updated me about the programs that the organization had launched and described the new workshops that were offered as part of MEC's job-training, leadership, and microcredit programs. She and the other members of the Managua team were leading educational workshops on the Nicaraguan Constitution, human rights, and the National Labor Code.

A quick glance through MEC's educational materials showed the importance of a concept of rights—civil, human, political, and economic—in the organization's work with women from local communities. The educational programs were designed to introduce women to their rights and to use this knowledge for empowerment in their daily lives. The preface to one MEC publication, entitled "Gender, Discrimination, and Human Rights" (1997b) reflects the organization's strategy with regard to rights, education, and democracy: "May this educational booklet serve as a working tool and promote knowledge of our rights with the goal of producing changes in the conceptions and practices that foment discrimination, subordination, prejudice, and inequalities in our society. Our Movement takes up this effort to strengthen our Network of Promoters in Human Rights in the Free Trade Zone so that through study and discussion we can contribute to the knowledge and defense of our rights to be able to advance *together* toward the construction of a free, just, and humane society" (emphasis in original).

As mentioned above, in Nicaragua, as in other recently democratized countries, state actors and groups seeking social justice use a common language of rights and citizenship but for radically different purposes. Social movements often use the language of citizenship and rights to seek to "define new political identities and thus to expand citizenship," while states use these discourses to support the neoliberal goals of privatization, public sector downsizing, and foreign investment (Schild 1997: 606).

Nicaragua's political history imparts a particular character to contested meanings of citizenship. In the 1990s neoliberal state actors framed projects and ideologies in opposition to a particular construction of *sandinismo*, the political and economic ideology of the Sandinista regime. Negative images of *la Piñata*, that is, the private appropriation of state-owned property,[1] and the scarcity experienced by the general population during the trade embargo of the 1980's were the background to neoliberal definitions of democracy and calls for policies to encourage foreign investment, dismantle the cooperative system, and drastically reduce the public sector. In short, in Nicaragua in the 1990s neoliberalism had to be understood in its oppositional relation to sandinismo. Autonomous women's organizations like MEC were caught in the middle, for they were critical of the methods and ideologies of "before" (i.e., the Sandinista period) but also recognized the dire consequences of neoliberal projects for women, especially poor women with children.

The use of the citizenship and rights frames is, of course, not particular to MEC. Indeed, discrimination and equality have long been the master frames of women's movements in the United States and Europe. The transnational movement to oppose violence against women has appropriated human rights discourse as a means to put women's rights on national and international political agendas (Keck and Sikkink 1998a: esp. 168). Like many other organizations within the transnational women's movement, then, MEC's vision involves the transformation of society through the empowerment of citizens by learning their rights. A pocket manual developed by MEC leaders explains: "We are conscious that Nicaraguan women and men workers do not have power in this country, nor in any country in the world. However, it is necessary for us to gradually construct this power, learning and getting to know our rights so that *together* we can construct a new labor society [*sociedad laboral*]" (MEC 1998b: 1–2; italics in original).

The emphasis on civic education, however, at times struck participants as both confusing and ironic. At a workshop on the National Labor Code that I attended, Lola, Claudia, and María Luisa, MEC organizers from Granada, could hardly keep still in their chairs and whispered back and forth to each other during the presentation by the workshop leader, an inspector with the Ministry of Labor. As former FSLN cadres, these women had worked within the state-owned textile factories in Granada, where they had held leadership positions in the trade union federation. As the workshop leader outlined the many rights "guaranteed" by the National Labor Code, the women smiled to themselves and exchanged incredulous glances. At the break, as we sipped sodas and ate packets of cookies, we huddled in a corner to discuss the session. "In what way do these 'rights' serve us?" exclaimed Lola. "Especially in the free trade zone where workers' rights are never respected." Claudia scoffed at what seemed like the speaker's naïveté: "Es como si no fuera Nicaragüense," she said—it's as if she weren't Nicaraguan.

The Granada organizers' comments point directly to the contradictions faced by social justice initiatives within neoliberal democracies. These women questioned the workshop organizer's knowledge of the lived realities of poor Nicaraguans. They knew firsthand that all the supposed rights held by citizens under Nicaraguan democracy meant little in women's daily struggles for survival on the shop floor, in their communities, and in their homes. In their minds it is these struggles that constitute what it is to be Nicaraguan, not some abstract claim to rights based on citizenship and encoded in distant laws.

It is, however, precisely this contradiction between state discourse and laws and the actual enforcement of those laws that MEC has capitalized on in its use of the language of rights. MEC organizers, then, have taken advantage of the language of civil society and citizenship that both social movements and the neoliberal civilian governments of Latin America use, one struggling to achieve social change, the other to keep democratic demands in check (Schild 1998). MEC's use of rights discourse has been effective at gaining the attention of particular targeted state actors and in opening negotiations between MEC participants and certain state agents (witness the alliance between MEC and the Ministry of Labor). For example, the media attention surrounding the international campaign for the code of ethics yielded an invitation to members of the Central American Women's Network in Solidarity with Maquila Workers to meet with members of a commission of the National Assembly and later an invitation to appear in front of the assembly to present their demands. In addition, the National Assembly's Commission on Peace and Human Rights agreed to visit MEC's headquarters and hear the testimonies of women workers.

The commission's president, Carlos Guerra of the Liberal Alliance party, addressed the two hundred women who gathered to give testimony about working conditions and human and labor rights' violations in the zone. Guerra's opening remarks use notions of citizenship that both converge with and diverge from the language used by MEC and the Central American Network:

> It is very important that this free trade zone where you currently work complies with the requirements of our prevailing laws in the country. That is, it is not that the free trade zones are independent states. Rather, these are concessions that are given to certain businessmen for the creation of jobs. . . . We believe that the solution is neither completely capitalist, nor is it to go to a state-run economy. We consider the state to be a bad boss, a poor administrator. But we also think that "savage capitalism" is not the solution. . . . We do not intend for the Asian managers to leave the country. What we intend is for them to comply with all labor regulations. Nor do we believe it to be good for our country that they are taking advantage of the nonenforcement and nonobservation of the labor norms as established in our labor code. . . . We cannot permit that. Our sovereignty begins with the defense of the rights of our citizens! And if we, the deputies, cannot do anything on this front, we will be failing in our obligation as representatives before the National Assembly. . . . We are Nicaraguans, and we should protect ourselves, the Nicaraguans, first and foremost!

Let us look more closely at how neoliberal state agents like Guerra and social movements such as MEC deploy notions of rights and citizenship for radically different ends. As scholars like Verónica Schild and Evelina Dagnino have pointed out, a redefinition of citizenship as an active exercise of responsibilities is central to neoliberal projects. Neoliberal state actors actively foster this concept of what Brian Turner (1990) has labeled "active citizenship," in which citizens are held to be autonomous individuals and bearers of rights who must entrepreneurially position themselves within the economy and "fashion their overall personal development through wider relations to the marketplace" (Schild 1998: 96). At the same time, neoliberal projects entail an assault on institutions and practices of the so-called statist period, systematically eliminating consolidated rights and "transforming their bearers/citizens into the new villains of the nation, privileged enemies of the political reforms intended to shrink state responsibilities" (Dagnino 1998: 49). In Nicaragua, of course, there is a direct reference to the Sandinista era.

Contestations about the meaning of citizenship shape the ways in which marginalized groups frame their demands and struggles. MEC organizers promote a notion of citizenship based on a right to dignity and respect as well as economic and social rights. A brochure articulating the position of the Network and its members (including MEC) puts forth specific demands made to the governments of Central America based on human rights: "It is important to remember that the governments of Central America have participated in the ratification of [international] conventions . . . , and therefore, they are obligated to guarantee for men as well as women *equality in the enjoyment of all rights*, whether they be economic, social, civil, or political" (Colectiva de Mujeres Hondureñas 1998; emphasis in original).

This emphasis on social and economic rights challenges the neoliberal definition of citizenship as based solely on civil and political rights. Furthermore, MEC's use of rights discourse and the concept of citizenship represents part of a larger vision of social change and radical democratization of all sectors of society in which "all of us would be seen as subjects of rights, not just the one who has money, nor only the one who holds a public office, but all women and men citizens can make use of our rights as is established in the laws of our beloved Nicaragua" (MEC 1998b: 2).

The different projects behind the way neoliberal state actors and MEC use the concepts of citizenship (the former to maintain competitiveness in the global market and the latter to promote radical democracy) are in conflict. For example, at the end of the session held by the Commission on Peace and Human Rights, Sara stood up and asked the women in attendance to raise their hands if they had ever held a copy of the Constitution of the country. No one raised her hand. Sara then turned to Carlos Guerra and told him that she, as the coordinator of MEC, was making a formal petition to the commission to "place the Constitution in the hands of the people" and donate copies of the document.

Without hesitating an instant, Guerra flatly turned down her request. His reply was: "All of us have an obligation to learn the law." He also suggested that MEC solicit funds from international NGOs, as the government lacked the finances necessary to make such a donation. The not so subtle implication was that it is the responsibility of civil society, not the state, to find the means to educate citizens regarding their rights. Thus, neoliberal "active citizenship" fits nicely with privatization projects and global competitiveness. Responsibility for the "public welfare" shifts from the state and becomes the responsibility of "active citizens," legitimizing the downsizing of the public sector.

Furthermore, Guerra's suggestion regarding international NGOs shows how the creation of a "global civil society" can work to the advantage of neoliberal projects of privatization. A national civil society may not have the resources to provide for the needs of its citizens, but the existence of an international NGO community allows neoliberal states a convenient justification for eschewing their public service functions.

What is being contested here is not just the meaning of rights and citizenship but how certain rights can realistically be granted in an era of dramatic global and national inequalities of wealth and resources. In a context of global capitalism, poor, indebted states like Nicaragua simply cannot feasibly meet the social needs associated with the rights to jobs and healthcare.

In other cases, the common language of rights has been effective in countering some negative effects of neoliberal reforms, highlighting contradictions in neoliberal discourse. For example, human rights discourse shifts the focus away from economics and challenges neoliberal conceptualizations of a naturalized and benign global market. Rather than making demands for higher wages, MEC leaders and other Network members argue for guaranteeing the universal human rights of workers.[2]

One of my jobs as a cooperante was to act as an interpreter for MEC organizers when they received international brigades of visitors. These often consisted of student and religious groups interested in international development and social justice who were participating in programs and tours that allowed them to meet and talk with local organizations about the political, economic, and social conditions in Nicaragua. As an educator in the United States, I was not surprised when nearly every student group asked questions like: "Isn't a job in the free trade zone better than no job at all?" or "Isn't it the Nicaraguan government's responsibility to enforce labor laws?" These comments reflect classical economic and liberal assumptions about employment and the role of the state characteristic of mainstream, middle-class views of the last twenty years in the United States.

Sara's passionate responses to these questions changed the frame of the debate. A charismatic speaker even in translation, Sara spoke in ways that created a charge in the air: "Even if the Nicaraguan state shares some responsibility, the great transnational companies are taking advantage of our poverty in order to use up our labor force and send the product elsewhere. These companies make a huge profit, and don't leave behind anything except the bill that Nicaraguans must pay with their taxes because the corporations are exonerated from all custom taxes. So, I ask you, jobs at what cost? At the cost of our women's lives and health? At the cost of the human rights and dignity of the women workers?" Sara's use of human rights discourse breaks out of the framework of the posed questions, shifting the focus from the market to a common human experience based on liberal concepts of equality. Thus, using human rights discourse to frame arguments about working conditions in the maquila factories uses liberal notions of equality and justice to confront neoliberal discourses about the benefits of unfettered markets, an example of the oppositional potential of human rights.

Invoking the language of rights also highlights contradictions in neoliberal state ideologies and practices, which is an important strategy for holding states accountable for human rights abuses. For example, deputies from the national assembly as well as inspectors and agents from the

Ministry of Labor criticized the campaign for a code of ethics. They argued that, since the requirements of the code of ethics were already contained in the Constitution and the labor code, the code of ethics was unnecessary. MEC organizers, however, quickly pointed out that since the state has been unable or unwilling to enforce the laws, civil society has had to look for alternative mechanisms for ensuring the respect for workers' rights. Such a claim directly challenges the state's claims to sovereignty; it addresses the state in its own terms and invokes a discourse of civil responsibility. MEC's widespread *sensibilización* (raising public awareness) regarding this contradiction has largely been responsible for drawing state agents, such as the Minister of Labor and different deputies in the National Assembly, into a dialogue.

A major challenge that MEC and the other members of the Central American Network have faced is to find appropriate mechanisms for enforcing national and international laws and ordinances within maquila factories. In Keck and Sikkink's terms (1998a), they have sought to implement effective "leverage" and "accountability" politics. Who will hold the transnational corporations accountable for the violation of workers' rights? MEC focuses on the role of state institutions. Although the state is not directly *responsible* for the violations that occur in the factories, organizers argue that the state is *accountable* for violations that occur within its territory. (See Jelin 1996a: 112 for a brief discussion of the difference between responsibility and accountability.) The difficulty here is that the strategic deployment of civil and political rights discourse in much of the developing world has historically entailed a preoccupation with constraints on the power of the state such as in cases of state-sponsored torture and other human rights violations rather than an emphasis on its affirmative duties to ensure rights (Sullivan 1995: 127). MEC organizers try to goad state actors into intervening in the sphere of the maquila workplace to protect the rights of workers. At media events and public presentations MEC organizers often introduce the problem of human rights violations in maquila factories as an issue of sovereignty and adopt a nationalist discourse to shame state institutional actors into enforcing labor legislation. The universal and globalized language of human rights then becomes nationalized in its political implementation.

The code of ethics that MEC and the Network developed is also firmly based on rights discourse; as noted in chapter 5, the preamble cites international ordinances such as CEDAW and the Universal Declaration of Human Rights. But the document goes on to address the state's obligations. For example, it calls for equal protection under the law for men and women: "the government of Nicaragua, as a state party in international human rights agreements has the obligation to guarantee the equal enjoyment of men and women's economic, social, cultural, civil, and political rights."

The six demands of the code of ethics (see chapter 5) all address the enforcement of current national laws from the Constitution of Nicaragua as well as the National Labor Code.[3] In January of 1998 the Ministry of Labor, in partnership with MEC, presented a ministerial resolution to the employers of the factories of the FTZ. The ten articles of the resolution are based on MEC's code of ethics, which the Labor Minister himself had endorsed a few months earlier. Like MEC's code of ethics, the language of the resolution—the result of a state-civil society partnership—frames demands in terms of rights and discrimination under the law.

The articles include the following conditions:

1. Employers must ensure identical work conditions for all workers without discrimination for reasons of pregnancy, race, religion, ages, disability, or political orientation;

2. Employers must guarantee that pregnant workers maintain their jobs without suffering violations of their rights and that they not be fired during their pregnancy or during their postnatal maternity leave, as stipulated by law;

3. Employers are responsible for maintaining a respectful work environment free of physical and psychological abuse, verbal abuse, and any other acts or lack thereof that might affect the dignity and rights of workers;

4. Employers must create a safe work environment that guarantees the physical integrity, health, and hygiene of workers and reduces the risk of accidents on the job; further, to maintain the health of workers, employers must provide medical checkups that consist of routine exams as well as any that may be prescribed, and continuing education and in-servicing of employees in the area of health, directed at preventing occupational risks in each factory and common illnesses that affect production;

5. Employers must guarantee workers' right to social security benefits and services and register workers with social security;

6. Employers must comply with laws regarding the payment of overtime hours. (Ministerio de Trabajo 1998)

All employers in the state-owned FTZ subsequently signed the resolution.

Thus, the ministerial resolution reflects MEC's conception of rights in general and the organization's emphasis on social and economic rights. These concepts represent a key element of MEC's view of democracy and social change. For example, MEC's publication "A Pocket Manual of Labor Rights" articulates the organization's democratizing vision: "We Nicaraguan women . . . maintain that it is vital for us to support our children and our families. We need to eat, to clothe ourselves, to buy medicine, to have a dignified dwelling, to send our children to school in order to live a better life. The women of Nicaragua demand *dignity* in our workplaces; we demand dignified treatment within our homes. . . . We want liberty and solidarity in order to transform our world and finally achieve social justice" (1998b; emphasis in original).

MEC uses the language of citizenship and rights as part of a larger vision of social transformation—one which would involve extending rights to the domestic sphere and empowering women through civic and human rights education. This same vision was encapsulated in the 1996 campaign of the Network of Women Against Violence, of which MEC is a participating member. The campaign, which was held in commemoration of the International Day Against Violence Against Women and Children (and beginning before the elections of October) had the slogan: "I vote for democracy in our country, at/in the home and in the bedroom," clearly articulating a political agenda that bridges public and private life.

WOMEN'S RIGHTS . . . HUMAN RIGHTS?

In workshop materials on international ordinances and women's rights published by MEC appears a cartoon showing an elderly, bearded man clad in formal robes like a judge or professor, standing at a podium that supports a huge book, presumably an international convention. The man proclaims: "Los que firmaron se comprometieron a respetar a TODOS . . . ¡Oigase bien! *Todos* los derechos de TODOS." (Those who have signed have committed to respect ALL . . . Hear me well! *All* rights of ALL.) *Todos*, however, is the masculine plural form of this word. A balloon indicating a voice coming from outside the cartoon frame corrects the man: "y TODAS," or *all* in the feminine form, to include women (see figure 14).

The cartoon can be read in multiple ways. If we view the bearded (white) man as symbolizing state (read also: male) power, then the faceless voice coming from outside the (master['s]) frame could symbolize that of marginalized female "others" clamoring for inclusion. But also captured in this image are dilemmas stemming from notions of sameness, difference, and equality as they relate to democracy and rights. For the cartoon highlights the implicit assumption within human rights discourse that equality is analogous to sameness.

The equation of sameness and equality is problematic for MEC, as many of the organization's demands are based on a conceptualization of gender difference. For example, the campaign for the code of ethics calls for pregnant women to retain their positions of employment and be granted maternity leave without dismissal—different, not equal, treatment. Women who are primary caregivers are not "equal" as workers. Maquila workers in MEC's programs complain of losing pay, or even their jobs, when they become pregnant or must miss work to care for children who are ill.

Organizers, then, face the challenge of using *human* rights discourse to argue for *women's* rights and for collective as well as individualist notions of rights. In classical liberal discourse, inequalities derived from gender, race, or class are ignored and are viewed as irrelevant in determining an individual's equality as a citizen. Citizens are assumed to be the same—based on a white male individual (Yuval-Davis 1997b: 6). Since they require states to ensure and respect rights but also to take differences, such as those based on gender, into account in ensuring rights, CEDAW and other international conventions such as the International Convention on the Rights of the Child and the International Convention on the Elimination of All Forms of Racial Discrimination are powerful tools for social movements who make rights claims of neoliberal states. For example, in order to ensure women's effective right to work, CEDAW requires that states take measures to "encourage the provision of the necessary supporting social services to enable parents to combine family obligations with work responsibilities and participation in public life, in particular through promoting the establishment and development of a network of child-care facilities" (CEDAW Article 11.2c). Such a provision recognizes women's socially assigned gender role as caretaker of the family, reconceptualizing rights so as to include women's gender experiences.

The introduction to MEC's code of ethics draws from CEDAW to define discrimination against women as "any distinction, exclusion, or restriction made on the basis of sex which has the effect or purpose of impairing or nullifying the recognition, enjoyment, or exercise by women, irrespective of marital status, on a basis of equality of men and women, of human rights and fundamental freedoms in the political, economic, social, cultural, civil or any other field" (Women's Convention, Article 1). The MEC publication "Gender, Discrimination, and Human Rights" explains how gender differences become the basis for discrimination:

> We women have rights because we are people!! Since we are people, we are equal to men in intelligence, capacity, and dignity. But why do men seem to have more rights than obligations, while we women have more responsibilities than rights? There exist certain physical differences between us and them, like sexual organs and the capacity for reproduction. . . . Unfortunately, these physical differences between men and women have been used to treat some differently from others. . . . But these differences do not make us any less nor do they give other people the right to mistreat us, to impede our educating ourselves and working, to sexually abuse us, or to obligate us to have sex when we do not want to. In other words, these differences do not justify discrimination. (1997b: 11–12)

The idea of discrimination encoded in the Women's Convention exposes "the myth of rights" and equality contained in bourgeois liberal notions of citizenship that assume equality rather than creating the conditions to ensure it. That is, by highlighting the presence of patriarchal structures, the women of MEC "expose the gap between liberal concepts and their actual realization" (Romany 1994: 87). MEC's publications use the terms *ciudadanas y ciudadanos* (male and female citizens), rather than just the male form of the noun (*ciudadano*) to refer to citizens. This challenges the assumption of a universal male norm that underlies Western definitions of citizenship (Pateman 1988).

Although in some situations MEC's use of rights discourse involves references to international ordinances and the use of globalized discourses like human rights, in other contexts participants use images of gender difference that draw on gendered understandings of nationalism. The creation and use of gender ideologies are a crucial part of the state-building enterprise of the modern nation-state. Nationalism and the sovereignty of the nation-state accord responsibility for protection of the family and private sphere to the state (Pateman 1988: 11), allowing women to make claims on the "male" state. At particular moments MEC organizers have tapped into these responsibilities by positioning the young single mothers who work in the factories and who lack male breadwinners as in need of patriarchal protection from the state.

In a session before the National Assembly, representatives invited MEC organizers and affiliated workers, as well as unionists from the newly formed Sandinista textile union and a group of male workers who had been fired, to testify about the social and working conditions in the FTZ. Deputies of the Nicaraguan National Assembly were much more sympathetic to the testimonies of the young single mother workers than they were to those of recently laid-off male workers. "If they want us to play the part of the poor little orphans, that's who we'll be," remarked a MEC leader after appearing at the Assembly hearing.

Because of nationalist ideologies surrounding women, as well as cultural constructions regarding the sanctity of motherhood, the women workers, who addressed the state as patriarch, were effective in gaining the deputies' sympathy. After the hearing the members of the human rights commission of the National Assembly requested a meeting with MEC, but not with the male workers who were also present. As Sallie Westwood and Sarah Radcliffe point out, "in Latin American history, men and masculinity are tied to the defense of the nation and the protection of family, home and the people, while women are cast not as defenders, but as reproducers of the nation as wives and mothers" (1993: 12). Thus, images of the family represent an important contested ideological terrain in Latin America and can be appropriated for a variety of political ends (Radcliffe 1993; Schirmer 1993). Here the neoliberal state's alliance with transnational capitalist interests was challenged by the state's own rhetoric regarding gender roles and its responsibility to protect women as "reproducers of the nation."

The deployment of gendered nationalist images to frame class interests has been effective in gaining access not only to state institutions but also to FTZ administrators. For example, in the campaign promoting the code of ethics MEC organizers approached national administrators and owners of maquila factories to negotiate their support. Sara and Josefina set up a meeting with a co-owner of one of the factories of the state-owned FTZ (a Nicaraguan national and a woman). After the meeting Josefina and Sara returned to MEC's headquarters flushed with excitement, and the rest of the team gathered around them to hear how the encounter went.

Sara described meeting the well-dressed, fully made-up business-woman, decked out in elegant gold jewelry. We all giggled as she imitated this upper-class woman—*una burguesa prepotente* (an arrogant bourgeois woman) and her high-society mannerisms. At the beginning of the meeting, the administrator was quite cold and unreceptive. Indeed, at first she did not seem to understand why a "woman's organization" like MEC would be interested in maquila workers. Sara told us, "She said: 'I recommend that you work with other women. Here in the Free Trade Zone there are lots of eyes on us [a reference to recent media attention around working conditions in the zone]. Why don't you work in the communities?' " The tone of the meeting changed dramatically, however, when Sara explained that, *as* a women's organization, MEC had specifically sought a meeting with *her*, a Nicaraguan woman, to seek her help in negotiating with the *other* (foreign) factory owners to support the code of ethics.

The administrator brightened and changed her attitude completely once they called attention to their shared identity as Nicaraguan women. The factory owner said that she was proud to be a Nicaraguan woman and that, perhaps by being MEC's voice to the other factory owners in meetings of their association, she could "do something positive for other Nicaraguan women." As Sara reported, "She said that she wants to become our *sucursal* [subsidiary or branch office] and support the women in the meetings with the other administrators. 'Those *chinos* [referring to the Taiwanese and Korean factory owners and administrators] need to be controlled,' she said. 'In our association meetings I'll tell them, No, no *chinito* [little Chinese man], not like that, that isn't possible and remind them of labor laws and women's human rights.' "

Thus, a gendered (and racist) nationalist discourse resonated with this member of the Nicaraguan elite, who took the code of ethics from Sara and promised to support it. As Sara and Josefina left the meeting, the factory administrator urged them to teach women to work hard "and be responsible so that Nicaragua will advance in economic development," further illustrating the convergences and contradictions between nationalist ideologies and transnational capitalist interests. Such contradictions can represent sites for oppositional intervention, providing opportunities for challenging the exploitation of FTZ workers (Lowe and Lloyd 1997a).

MEC has also strategically presented its struggle as that of *women*, not of workers, in negotiations with managers within the free trade zone. Mobilizing and drawing from their personal networks and after careful negotiations and hard work, Josefina, Sara, and Laura were able to obtain permission for MEC organizers to have regular access to the state-owned FTZ. Sara and Josefina successfully negotiated with administrators in the human resources departments and with individual factory owners in order to schedule lunch hour meetings with groups of women workers.

But organizers also met with obstacles in their negotiations with managers and administrators, as they were often forced to draw on gender ideologies that regard women's issues as inherently apolitical. Josefina had a meeting with the general manager of FORTEX, the Taiwanese factory that was the site of the 1993 strike in which several MEC organizers were involved and injured in the violence that broke out. At first, Stephen Chang, the general manager, was very receptive to Josefina's presentation and was particularly interested in MEC's efforts to help women find access to gynecological checkups as well as its workshops on reproductive health. The reason, Josefina presumed, was that pregnant workers represent a liability to profit margins. Josefina enthusiastically handed over samples of MEC's workshop materials, thinking that she could perhaps gain permission to meet with women workers. Her mistake, she told us later, was enclosing materials about the Nicaraguan Constitution. Chang's attitude and manner changed abruptly when he saw the materials. He told Josefina, "I thought that you said that your women's center wasn't political!" Although Josefina tried to smooth things over by saying that the Constitution was something that everyone had a right to learn about, the damage was already done. Chang cut the meeting short and made a quick exit. Later, a friend and promotora from another factory chastised Josefina: "*Caballa* [loosely translated: you're as stupid as a horse], no one likes to be called exploiter to his face!"

MEC's demands, framed simultaneously in terms of "difference" and "equality," suggest an apparent contradiction. On one hand, MEC employs a concept of discrimination to call for gender equality based on citizenship and human rights. On the other hand, MEC calls for state protection of young single mothers, and its negotiations with FTZ administrators highlight gender differences, calling for rights to be enforced, not so much as citizens and workers, but as women and mothers.

Perhaps more significant than the tension between equality and difference is the contradiction between the strategic use of nationalist narratives, which runs the risk of reinforcing gender inequities, and MEC's feminist vision for the reconstruction of society. MEC organizers exploit the conventional public/private dichotomy, which is reinforced by the state. Their vision for social change, however, is directed toward challenging the separation of spheres in the call for democracy in the home, the workplace, and other areas of public life. The fact that MEC organizers have had to position themselves as struggling women, and downplay maquila workers' status as workers, seems to go against the very raison d'être of MEC.

Ironically, MEC founders and supporters broke with the traditional labor movement because it left gender off the political agenda. Now as an autonomous women's organization, MEC participants sometimes find it difficult to articulate demands based on their class experience. Although the work, mission, and objectives of MEC transcend notions of class and gender as distinct categories of experience, hegemonic ideologies about the separation of spheres shape the ways in which MEC positions itself, often requiring participants to frame their demands in ways that rely on the dichotomized parameters of public/private, class/gender or worker/woman.

NEOLIBERAL STATE PROJECTS

Although some state officials have responded to nationalist and gendered images of women workers that portray them in need of paternal protection and have opened a dialogue with MEC leaders, the neoliberal agenda of Nicaragua's postsocialist regimes has prompted them overwhelmingly to favor foreign investors. In accordance with structural adjustment policies, both the Chamorro government and the subsequent Alemán regime crafted laws to attract foreign investment and to implement the privatization of the country's formerly extensive cooperative agricultural system and worker- and state-owned enterprises. The general strike of 1997, which paralyzed transportation of goods and services between Managua and the rest of the country, was in response to Alemán's proposed laws to further displace peasants from cooperatively held land and return property to the "original" prerevolutionary owners. Another proposed law would have ended many state-provided benefits and subsidies for worker collectives, while tax breaks would have been granted to the private sector in order to stimulate economic growth. Policies such as these reflect the state's response to transnational capitalist interests.

In the late 1990s the Liberal Alliance, the majority political party, clearly demonstrated its support of foreign investors. In 1997 President Arnoldo Alemán traveled to Taiwan to negotiate incentives for more investment in the Nicaraguan economy. Shortly before Mother's Day in 1997 Alemán paid a visit to the Free Trade Zone. Women workers were indignant when Alemán headed straight for the upstairs administrative offices, without even making an appearance on the shop floor or addressing the workers. When administrators made the announcement over the intercom system that the president was in one of the factories, workers simply kept their heads down and continued working. Apparently, the president and the managers were angered when the workers did not applaud the president. After Alemán departed, (never having addressed the workers), managers informed the employees that they would be required to work until 3:00 P.M. on Mother's Day, instead of being allowed to leave at noon as had been scheduled. Women workers saw this as a clear punishment for their less than enthusiastic reception of the president and also as a reflection of the state's close alliance with maquila factory management.

In Nicaragua, and in many places in the world, the political and economic neoliberal agenda (i.e., export orientation, privatization, and the reduction of the role of the state) have gone hand-in-hand with extremely conservative social policies to regulate the private sphere and control women's lives and bodies (Marchand and Runyan 2000a: 18). In Nicaragua and elsewhere religious fundamentalism and ethnic-nationalism represent the political counterpart of global economic restructuring (see Barber 2001). These forces blame "both the welfare state and feminism for the breakdown in the social and moral fabric" (Brodie 1994: 57).

After taking power in 1997, Alemán proposed extremely conservative legislation based on ideologies of "family values" and control of women's sexuality. Closely allying itself with the conservative Catholic hierarchy, Alemán's party promoted and implemented a blatantly antifeminist agenda (Kampwirth 2003). The administration promoted an image of the nuclear family composed of a male breadwinner and a wife-and-mother who is relegated to the private sphere of the home. Together, Church and party propagated an antifeminist platform that was "pro-family" (i.e., nuclear family), anti-abortion, and heterocentric.

In 1997 Alemán sent a bill to the National Assembly to restructure the Nicaraguan Fund for Children and the Family (FONIF) and the Nicaraguan Women's Institute (INIM), making them subunits of a new Ministry of the Family. The introduction to the law explained that the "state recognizes that the mission of the couple . . . is the formation of a community of love and procreation" and that the "state has the obligation of protecting and defending the family against any form of aggression that seeks to manipulate or deviate it from its mission." One of the expressed objectives of the Ministry was to be "to promote in couples who live together in stable unity the formalization of their relationship through matrimony, in order to strengthen the legality of their bond." In addition, the objectives of the Ministry would include protecting "dispossessed sectors, especially single and abandoned mothers" (quoted in *Boletina* 1997b: 14, 13, 16, 17).

Although women's groups, particularly feminist collectives and NGOs rallied against the creation of this ministry, declaring it inconsistent with international norms, some of the objectives of the ministry resonated with some poor single mothers. At the time, women headed approximately one third of Nicaraguan households, and were among the poorest of the poor.[4] In Nicaragua informal unions of poor people are more common than formal arrangements, and many couples with six or more children have never established a binding civil or religious agreement. In a context of a system of machismo, informal unions coincide with irresponsible sexual behavior on the part of men, who may have several children by different women and may barely contribute to any of their upbringing (Lancaster 1992: 92). For single mothers who are in situations of extreme poverty, the idea of enforcing paternal responsibility is greatly appealing. So, while feminists from organizations like the feminist collective las Malinches denounced the proposed law, stating that "the idea of a traditional nuclear family as the only model . . . is a proposal that is foreign to Nicaraguan reality" (quoted in *Boletina* 1997b: 13), poor women like the ones who took part in MEC's programs did not widely support this position or resist the idea of associating women with family.

The proposed Ministry of the Family, which eventually was formed in 1998 and is known as MIFAMILIA, though explicitly antifeminist in its equation of women's interests with the family, resonated with the articulated needs of poor women.[5] And although the traditional nuclear family with a male breadwinner is far from the norm in Nicaragua, for poor women the *idea* of a breadwinning husband is attractive. Indeed, an extremely popular workshop organized by MEC involved a visit from a lawyer who worked with INIM. The lawyer presented information on women and the law to a group of MEC program participants. The room became most animated when the lawyer opened up the floor for questions, and the topic that sparked the most interest was how to go about getting married and how much it cost. The lawyer's offer to marry a group of women and their partners the next day free of charge in MEC's office elicited a round of cheers from the entire group of women. Thus, these women were very interested in forming nuclear families and formalizing their unions and had only failed to do so because of the prohibitive cost of the civil ceremony and marriage license.

The state's fixation on male responsibility might seem to contradict its strong support of foreign investment in maquila factories, which target a mainly female workforce and leave males largely shut out of the economy. On the other hand, the Liberal Alliance's pro–nuclear family construct jibes with neoliberal notions of "active citizenship" and is indicative of the degree to which the identities and conduct of individuals matter to the state in Nicaragua. Making men responsible for assuming the social reproduction costs of raising and caring for children supports neoliberal projects and a reduced role for the state. Rather than developing public programs or providing employment in a public sector, the state assigns the responsibility to men as supposed breadwinners and heads of households.

But given cultural, nationalist, and religious notions of the sanctity of motherhood and the need for protection of women as the "mothers of the nation," single mothers' demands on the state for assistance in meeting the costs of (re)producing the labor force / nation / culture are culturally legitimate. Through the rhetoric of the Ministry of the Family, Nicaraguan state agents, then, appeared to champion women in the search for "subsidization" of (re)production costs, shifting blame from the state as failing to provide social investment to "dead-beat dads" who fail to meet their paternal responsibilities.[6]

The focus on individual fathers counters state-centric models of the Sandinista era, in which the state provided health insurance, child care, and even basic foodstuffs. Thus, as Elizabeth Jelin points out, "While neoliberalism implies a reinforcement of duties and responsibilities on the part of the family, it also erodes the capacity of households to command the resources necessary to meet domestic needs" (1997: 75). Not surprisingly, the Liberal Alliance's support of responsible fathers did not include any means for these so-called breadwinners to engage in formal employment. This example demonstrates that under the "new world order" states are not weakening but merely reconfiguring their role. Neoliberal conceptualizations of "active citizenship" are consistent with this overall project, as the focus becomes "family responsibilities" rather than social and economic rights of individuals.

Although liberal ideology formally discourages state intervention in the realm of the private sphere, as is evident in the case of the Ministry of the Family, the state regulates and intrudes on family life when such interventions serve larger political, social, and economic goals (Mertus 1995: 135). And Nicaragua's neoliberal, socially conservative state with its discursive emphasis on family values heightens the state's interest in protecting and defining the private sphere. Thus, both the economic and social orientations of Nicaragua's neoliberal regimes have provided MEC organizers with some room to maneuver, as they call on the state to intervene in "private" transnational corporations in order to protect single mothers.

The image of the family codified in the laws that created the Ministry of the Family conveys state elites' imagining of the domestic sphere as well as the gender-specific aspects of citizenship (Joseph 1997), allowing MEC organizers to make claims on the state according to these gendered citizenship roles. Organizers were conscious of this when writing the code of ethics. With demands that reflect the "natural" association of women with the domestic sphere and as reproducers of the nation, the code of ethics has a "moral economy flavor." For example, the demands that women workers be protected from all forms of violence on the shop floor, that pregnant women maintain their job positions, and that women be free from harassment invoke the state's duty to protect mothers and the private sphere with which they are associated. Although the women of MEC are contesting traditional notions of citizenship, they base some of their claims on the state's definition of a gendered domestic sphere.

RIGHTS DISCOURSE: MASTER'S TOOLS OR TOOLS OF LIBERATION?

What, then, can we make of MEC's use of liberal strategies and discursive tools borrowed from classical liberal discourse? Are these simply the "Master's tools" that will never bring down the "Master's house" (Lorde 1984)? Does the liberal "baggage" that comes along with these discourses deprive them of all transformative potential, making them dangerous to feminist social justice projects?

Despite what might appear to be accommodation to dominant discourses, like other organizations that form the larger Latin American women's movement, MEC has promoted new forms of citizenship by "empowering" women as political actors (Schild 1997: 614). MEC's educational programs, offered to all the organization's participants, focus on issues such as domestic violence, gender roles, feminism, and reproductive health and use rights as a tool for bringing about a vision of social justice. This feminist curriculum, which also includes *capacitación* (educational training) regarding women's human rights as well as their rights under the Constitution of the Republic and the National Labor Code, is subversive in promoting the redefinition of citizenship and challenging dominant gender ideologies through consciousness-raising.

A case can be made that MEC is challenging the dichotomy between "reformist" and "transformative." MEC organizers do not see themselves as changing social structures "de un día pa' otro" (from one day to the next), but it would be a mistake to dismiss their actions as devoid of transformative potential. If we view rights and citizenship as the result of concrete struggles, then the on-the-ground practices of MEC are significantly expanding the meaning of citizenship.

On the other hand, the conservative language often used to define rights and citizenship in Nicaragua suggests the strength of antifeminism and the continued hegemonic power of the state, framing the very demands that social movement actors are able to articulate. Despite the threat that economic globalization poses to some aspects of state sovereignty, the hegemonic power of the state continues to shape the terms under which resistance occurs. Some aspects of globalized discourses such as the liberal tenets of human rights fit nicely within neoliberal states' economic and political projects—such as privatization and cutting back the public sector as a strategy to address the country's economic crisis.

The case of MEC's negotiations with state agents also reveals important aspects of the relationship between global, national, and local discourses. The ways in which rights are constructed and in which actors make demands depend upon the specific local (or national) context. The Liberal Alliance's use of a concept of citizenship based on the responsibilities of "active citizens" can be juxtaposed with ideologies and policies of the Sandinista period. Notions of personal responsibility and "active citizenship" resonate in a particular way among the Nicaraguan public and converge in some ways with the claims-making language of groups that oppose the policies of the regime. The Liberal Alliance has capitalized on dissatisfactions under the Sandinista regime and bases its view of citizenship and the proper role of the state on an ideological alternative to a "litany of horrors" under the Sandinistas—"la Piñata," forced military service, corruption, and problems associated with state-provided land, housing, benefits, and goods.

One example is the national scandal revolving around the Sandinista party's executive director, Daniel Ortega, and his stepdaughter, Zoilamerica Narváez Murillo. In 1998 she publicly accused Ortega of having sexually molested her since she was eleven years old. In the national uproar that ensued, the Liberal Alliance could articulate a moralist position of "family values" and portray Ortega as corrupt and immoral. For example, in the days following the outbreak of the scandal, President Alemán issued this statement to *La Prensa*: "We must meditate deeply upon the rescue of moral and ethical values. . . . As Nicaragua's president, I make a call to the whole nation to consolidate familial unity and return to the ethical and moral values which have characterized the Nicaraguan people and which his Eminence Cardinal Miguel Obando [y Bravo] has so strongly urged us to restore" (Canales 1998a: 1A). Vice President Enrique Bolaños attacked the Sandinistas more directly, commenting that Narváez's accusations did not surprise him since "The Sandinista Front . . . is a movement with immoral foundations" (Montoya 1998: 4A).

Once again women's organizations were caught in the middle, as they supported Narváez's breaking the silence regarding sexual abuse but rejected calls by the Liberal Alliance and Catholic Church to return to "family-oriented" morals, which include a view of the man as the head of the household and translate into male control of women's bodies and sexuality, curtailing their reproductive rights (Canales 1998b). Thus, the ways in which rights and notions of citizenship are framed, interpreted, and contested develop within a specific historical, national, and local conjuncture. Despite globalization, a diversity of normative orders prevails (Wilson 1997; Hannerz 1996).

MEC's complex discursive strategies reflect the ways in which articulations between the national and transnational present marginalized groups with strategic spaces for presenting demands and making claims. MEC actors easily switch between globalized discourses of human rights and nationalist discourses of women as the reproducers of the nation. Though hegemonic power may shape what kinds of demands these actors make, MEC organizers have been able to exploit contradictions between state discourses about women and the family and transnational capitalist interests.

A grounded, situational analysis of rights and citizenship discourses reveals important implications for the deployment of these discourses as part of specific oppositional projects. When compared to other struggles, such as the Madres de la Plaza de Mayo and transnational organizing efforts surrounding violence against women, the use of rights discourse to make claims for female maquila workers carries with it specific advantages and limitations.

The human rights frame has been effective in countering the state's inclination toward ensuring global competition in a free market rather than protecting its citizens from abuses in Nicaragua's current neoliberal democracy. Nicaragua's ratification of international conventions has provided MEC the opportunity to engage in "accountability politics," calling on the state to adhere to international law. Finally, MEC's use of a gendered, nationalist discourse to call for state intervention to protect maquila workers has garnered the attention of government officials.

Yet, the interarticulations of national and transnational discourses have confronted MEC with obstacles. MEC has appropriated strategic tools that contradict its own radical democratic vision for social change (including transcending the public/private split as defined by bourgeois liberal ideology). In its negotiations with state agents, MEC has had to operate within the parameters established by the neoliberal state. Although MEC's vision for change involves extending democracy beyond the "public" realm, which contradicts the "family values" ideology of the state, at times their demands involve recognizing and even incorporating the very dichotomy that they seek to transcend.

Human rights as a "master frame" does not consistently support struggles for women workers' rights. MEC organizers have used an approach that not only reifies a state-regulated "private" sphere, but accepts a kind of "strategic essentialism" (McRobbie 1985), in which actors base claims on both equality and gender differences but downplay class-based aspects of their experiences. Gendered citizenship and human rights are not necessarily effective frameworks for some demands that the organization also has an interest in making. For example, "living wage" demands come head-to-head with neoliberal conceptualizations of an unfettered global market, and it would seem unlikely that these frameworks could trump neoliberal states' agenda of attracting foreign investment to create jobs.[7] Thus, the political openings that rights discourse offers to marginalized groups come at a price, and groups like MEC face the challenge of balancing their long-range goals and principles with the necessities of each strategic moment. Exigencies arising from the national political sphere may cause them to use a global or nationalist discourse that resonates in that particular context with state decision-makers or factory management, but can compromise the organization's vision of social change and gender equality.

7 Resistance Goes Global: Power and Opposition in an Age of Globalization

When I left Central America in 1997 I wondered what the future would hold for the group of dedicated MEC activists. The organization's unique approach to the situation of women workers in Nicaragua was playing an important role in civil society, filling what seemed to be a gap between the labor movement and the autonomous women's movement. But in the late 1990s, though MEC in many ways had come into its own as an autonomous organization, it was still questionable how sustainable its efforts would be. Would relations with the unions continue to be so tense? Would the organization be able to sustain its activities in the face of funding pressures? Would MEC be able to continue to exist as a network of regional offices? What would be the fate of the Central American Network of Women in Solidarity with Maquila Workers? Would it continue its activities?

Despite the many obstacles that the organization has faced, in the early 2000s MEC has flourished. It is impossible to recount every event and activity in which MEC has been engaged, but here I present a few highlights of the organization's work and struggle since the conclusion of my fieldwork. This account will also serve to illustrate further the theoretical implications of this case for understanding political engagement with globalization.

MEC has faced challenges and opportunities that have not merely originated from "above"—that is, from the state, global institutions, and transnational corporations. Instead, MEC's activities illustrate the many levels and complexities of "globalization from below." Whether or not opportunities for action present themselves within the transnational political landscape depends on constructed categories such as "women's" versus "labor" organizations, or "community" and "grassroots" organizations. These distinctions are constructed and maintained locally (as we saw in chapter 4 with the case of the autonomous women's movement in Nicaragua) as well as transnationally (as in the case of NGO funders in the North) and even globally (through global institutions like the ILO and the UN).

An episode that occurred shortly after I returned from Central America illustrates the pressures that have continued to confront MEC as a result of the way organizations and their activities are categorized by national and transnational actors. In 1998 a small NGO from San Francisco that works in partnership with local organizations to support community development contacted me for help in locating women's organizations in Nicaragua that would make good potential partners. After I suggested the NGO contact MEC, some members of the board expressed reluctance. The board questioned whether MEC's work with maquiladora workers and unemployed women—job training in nontraditional skills; education about labor, reproductive, and civil rights; legal services for support in filing complaints with labor courts; and gender awareness training—could be considered "urban community development." Board members were skeptical about the fact that most MEC organizers were not maquila workers themselves and noted that MEC's office was not located in the main communities where workers reside. Was MEC an "authentic" actor for grassroots development?

The partnership was eventually established, and MEC was funded by the NGO. However, it took a concerted effort on the part of a committed director of the NGO to educate the board and challenge members to think critically about their definitions of "community development." The NGO had to interrogate its assumptions about the relationship between locality and community. It also became apparent that, if the NGO's goal was to form partnerships with a women's organization, they had to move beyond traditional models of urban community development projects that often privilege male voices (Staudt et al. 2001).

In this case, considerable work needed to be done to convince transnational agents to accommodate a local organization—MEC was not "grassroots enough." Yet, as scholars have also noted (and the case of MEC supports this contention), international organizations and donors have also been influential in pushing organizations toward previously unexamined issues, such as those related to gender (see Seidman 1999). Both points indicate the importance of dialogue and exchange between Northern donors and organizations in the South about funding priorities and the implementation of projects. A careful balance must be struck between the Northern organization's principles and the realities that groups in the developing world face that may be specific to their social position as women or ethnic or racial minorities.

Despite the many challenges in securing financial support from transnational donors, by as early as 1998 every regional office of MEC had obtained some kind of funding for projects through long-time supporters, including the OXFAM family, a private U.S. donor, CoDevelopment Canada, and the Canadian International Development Agency. Regional projects continued to be based on credit for microenterprises, job training in traditional as well as nontraditional skills, and home improvement loans (MEC 1998a).

By 1998 the regional offices were all implementing projects, but some regions were more active than others. While Juigalpa, Estelí, and El Viejo seemed to be barely surviving, Granada and León were implementing more large-scale projects. In 1998 MEC reported that ninety-three women in Managua, Juigalpa, and Estelí had received microcredit to fund small enterprises. Loans were for a minimum of US$300 and a maximum of $500 and had to be repaid in six months before new credit could be solicited. The fund's recuperation rate of 83 percent was considered very successful. In the extremely impoverished northern city of Estelí these credits were used to support more traditional microenterprises, like street vending and small grocery stands. In addition a Catholic organization from the United Kingdom had funded the purchase of a small house, which enabled regional organizers to establish a permanent office there. In Juigalpa the credit was used to fund a literacy program, and in Chichigalpa MEC organizers continued to implement training of seventy women in traditional fields like hair styling and sewing.

By the late 1990s the Granada office was involved in the implementation of two projects. In 1998 one hundred and seventy-two women received microcredit loans to finance small businesses, such as those selling traditional "Granadino" handicrafts like embroidery and furniture. In Granada and Managua one hundred and ninety-nine women received home improvement loans, and by 1998 several had repaid the first installation of credit and were about to receive the next disbursement.

The more recent microcredit project that provided funded loans in Juigalpa, Estelí, and Managua followed on the heels of an earlier (1996–97) revolving credit program in which eighty-eight women in Managua had benefited from three installations of credit to fund small businesses like market vending of groceries.

In Managua from 1997 to 1998 seventy-eight women received job training in nontraditional fields like welding, auto mechanics, refrigeration, and electrical installation. After completing training they were given the highest priority to receive microcredit, in order to put their new skills to work in their own small businesses (MEC 1998a: 2, 4–10, 14–26).

In 1998 Hurricane Mitch brought new suffering to Central American populations already accustomed to natural disaster, war, and dire economic hardship. Eleven thousand people died, mostly in Honduras and the northern region of Nicaragua (*New York Times* 1998a, 1998b). Although Managua was not affected as severely as regions like Matagalpa and Estelí, where mudslides wiped out entire villages, the northern barrios and nearby towns (including Tipitapa, where many maquila workers reside) suffered a great deal of damage. As part of the wave of civil society organizations that surged in response to this natural disaster, MEC shifted its efforts to assist women in reconstructing their lives and their homes by concentrating their focus on microcredit and home improvement for those most affected by the hurricane (see Babb 2001: 248). After the hurricane the regional office of León shifted its focus from the environmental effects of the nearby gold mines, supported by CoDevelopment Canada, to diagnostic studies of the emotional and psychological effects of victims of the hurricane (International Development Research Center's Web site, accessed February 1999; *La Prensa* 2003).

Despite this adjustment in focus, MEC's most visible work continued to be its organizing efforts in support of maquila workers. It was in 1998 that MEC received a Human Rights Award by the Canadian Council for International Cooperation for its work on the campaign "Jobs Yes . . . But with Dignity!" By then it had implemented the second phase of the campaign, which focused on lobbying for changes to the laws that regulated the FTZ.

Soon thereafter, following several union-busting activities at the Chentex and Mil Colores factories in the FTZ, the transnational anti-sweatshop movement, led by the National Labor Committee (NLC) and the Campaign for Labor Rights (CLR), both independent North American labor organizations, in conjunction with the CST-affiliated Textile and Apparel Workers' Federation, launched a high-profile campaign, propelling the issue of sweatshops in Nicaragua into the U.S. media. The conditions in the maquila factories in Nicaragua received coverage from a variety of media: from National Public Radio (2000) and the *New York Times* (Gonzalez 2000) to *The National Catholic Reporter* (MacEoin 1999) and the *Nation* (Ross and Kernaghan 2000), and even *Rolling Stone* (Marsh 2000).

U.S.-based activists like Charles Kernaghan spoke out in the media against Target and Kohl's for contracting with the Chentex and Mil Colores factories, and a coalition of organizations—including the Nicaragua Network (a solidarity organization based in Washington, D.C.), Witness for Peace, CLR, United Students Against Sweatshops (USAS), and the AFL-CIO's solidarity branch—launched a massive leafleting campaign at Kohl's and Target stores.

Meanwhile, MEC continued to cultivate networks of supporters and allies who were less visibly pursuing strategies related to independent monitoring and codes of conduct (Nicaragua Network 2000). MEC leaders were highly critical of the more high profile tactics of U.S. activists like Kernaghan. One of the MEC leaders from the Managua team sent me a rather snide e-mail: " 'El Señor Charles' was here again in Nicaragua, and, as usual, he came, said his piece and left . . . while those of us who are always here continued the day-to-day struggle" (personal communication, June 5, 2000).

Because of the NLC's connections with the Sandinista CST, MEC was not included in the dialogues that took place as part of this transnational coalition's efforts to initiate a formal system of independent monitoring within the Nicaraguan free trade zone.[1] In contrast to Honduras and El Salvador, where independent monitoring groups made up of members of civil society organizations were formed, efforts to create a formal system of external monitoring in Nicaragua stalled in the late 1990s. However, MEC continued its separate work of lobbying state institutions for legislative reforms, while still engaging in transnational dialogues and debates about the maquila issues in Central America and globally. One of MEC's current projects involves picking up where the other coalition left off and trying once again to create a network of external monitors in the FTZs (Köpke 2002).

In addition to nationally oriented actions, MEC leaders like Sara, Josefina, and Evelyn, and even a number of promotoras from the FTZ have continued to forge and maintain transnational connections by traveling internationally to attend events, conferences, and speaking tours organized by groups like the Clean Clothes Campaign, Global Exchange, and OXFAM. In 1999 two British organizations, the Central American Women's Network (CAWN) and Women Working Worldwide, organized a conference on codes of conduct, which was held in Managua. In attendance were representatives from the Network as well as long-time supporters like the Canadian Maquila Solidarity Network.

MEC's networks have also extended to organizations in Asia. In 2001 MEC, along with the Asia Monitor Resource Center of Hong Kong, Grupo Factor X/Casa de la Mujer of Tijuana, Mexico, and the Canadian Maquila Solidarity Network coordinated a conference entitled "Breaking Boundaries/Constructing Alliances." Eight women leaders from Asian labor rights and women's organizations and two organizers from Sri Lanka traveled to Nicaragua for a program that included three days of visits to different sites in Managua, including the FTZ, where they met with company representatives, as well as two and a half days of exchanging information and testimony about working conditions, subcontracting patterns, and organizing strategies (Breaking Boundaries/Constructing Alliances 2001).

MEC organizers do not engage in these activities for their own sake or merely to obtain funding. As was the case in the campaign "Jobs, Yes . . . But with Dignity!" international connections and the publicity that they bring have bolstered MEC's national projects. As noted earlier, the Ministry of Labor adopted MEC's code of ethics as a ministerial resolution, which all factory owners within the state-owned free trade zone signed. The campaign also paved the road for legal reforms related to the FTZ (Anteproyecto de Ley 1999). In 1999 MEC's research team conducted a diagnostic study of the social and labor conditions within the factories of the FTZ (MEC 1999; see also Mendez and Köpke 2001) that became the basis for a bill to be sent to the National Assembly. The bill, which proposed reforms to the law that regulates the FTZ by adding further protection for women workers and specifically addressing the issue of gender discrimination in the zone, was signed into law in 2000. MEC also used the results of this study to lobby for an increase in the minimum wage laws, to raise the minimum to C$1,000.00 (approximately $118) per month and to develop a proposal that would reform the country's labor code. This last initiative (which as of the time of this writing has not yet been passed) involved a nationwide campaign in which MEC consulted with three thousand women from all over the country and collected the signatures of five thousand women in support of the proposed reforms (*La Prensa* 2001; Köpke 2002).

The transnational campaigns launched by the anti-sweatshop movement in coordination with the textile and apparel workers' federation and CENIDH have been highly visible in Nicaragua and even in the United States. However, MEC continued to focus its main efforts on the less flashy task of improving the day-to-day realities of workers in the FTZ, such as providing legal support to maquila workers through its legal *bufete* (a legal aid office). The legal desk had been an important element of the CST's Women's Secretariat, and MEC had briefly reestablished it during my fieldwork in 1995. A small team of lawyers reopened the office in 1999, offering consultations to maquila workers (for both labor-related and civil cases), helping them file formal grievances at the Ministry of Labor or advising them how to file civil complaints. MEC organizers have noted that such legal support has meant that workers are better equipped to settle their cases through direct negotiation with their employers or with Ministry of Labor inspectors, avoiding the time-consuming and expensive proceedings in the court system. MEC's gendered approach to women's labor issues is also reflected in its legal support program. In 2001 the legal office began offering consultation in cases of domestic violence, in keeping with MEC's focus on the interconnections between work and the private sphere (Köpke 2002).

After a period of continuing tension, MEC's relations with the labor movement has improved. In 1998 the organization even granted office space to some union organizers and used its Web site to document unionization activities in the FTZ (MEC 1998c). This level of cooperation was short-lived, but as MEC has continued to receive growing national and international recognition, the labor movement seems to have accepted coexistence with MEC, at least to some degree, indicating that MEC has successfully carved out its own space within Nicaraguan civil society.

By 2002 MEC's teams estimated that their number of trained promotoras had grown to around five hundred and that over seven thousand workers had participated in one or more of MEC's programs (Köpke 2002: 10). MEC organizers continue to have access to the FTZ, though not to every factory, and one of its legal consultants created a makeshift office (a desk) to consult with workers on site at the FTZ. MEC continues to be part of the Network, which meets once a year to exchange information and work on campaigns. In an external evaluation in which members of the government, press, and civil society organizations were interviewed about MEC's activities, there was considerable agreement that the FTZ has become more accessible and open to public scrutiny as a result of MEC's campaigns (Kopke 2002). As a sign that MEC has achieved public acceptance as an authority on issues related to women maquila workers, it was able to join government commissions, including the Nicaraguan Commission for Economic and Social Planning (CONPES) and the Minimum Wage Commission. The latter represents an important victory for the organization, as MEC is an addition to the traditional tripartite pattern of representation of labor unions, the private sector, and the government.

POWER AND TRANSNATIONAL POLITICS

To return to the question posed by this study, what does MEC's case tell us about the possibilities and difficulties of organized resistance under globalization? MEC's political strategies and practices illustrate the complex relations between the local, transnational, and state arenas, which are not distinct or exclusive, but overlapping, fluid, and contingent upon one another. This case shows that power differentials—including material and ideological power represented by "globalization from above," but also the power among groups and individuals "from below"—must be taken into account (Smith and Guarnizo 1998). Inequalities of power are dispersed, take many forms, and can stem from race, class, nationality, and gender, among other factors, affecting access to the media, state, and international institutions. Shifting, often overlapping "matrices of domination," to use Patricia Hill Collins's (1990) illuminating concept, operate in complex and surprising ways within transnational politics, as locally formed identities, strategies, and orientations confront each other, but also come into contact with transnationally circulating ideas and discourses about social and economic justice, organizational and strategic priorities, and targets of action.

At any given historical conjuncture these forces may line up or contradict each other in different ways, and collective actors engage in practices based on their interpretations of the conditions at hand, taking advantage of the spaces for action that emerge. These situational practices never represent either "pure" resistance or complete accommodation, but suggest varied meanings at particular conjunctures (Kondo 1990).

We can see an example of a contradiction between different power structures in MEC's use of gendered nationalism to improve work conditions for women in the FTZ. The nation-state's role as patriarchal regulator that constructs women as the repositories of culture and reproducers of the nation conflicts with transnational capitalist interests in reducing production costs, resulting in an opportunity for MEC organizers.

Actors situated in the local can gain access to state and global arenas of contestation by engaging in transnational practices, forming linkages across national boundaries. The transnational linkages formed among the organizations that make up the Central American Network of Women in Solidarity with Maquila Workers facilitated gaining access to state officials and broadened the national political arena for its participants in several Central American states. The transnational linkages between the Sandinista Textile and Apparel Workers' Federation, Witness for Peace, and the NLC are another example. These groups were able to access a more global arena of contestation through the *Hard Copy* report on the conditions within the Nicaraguan FTZ, although their message was different from that of MEC and the Network.

The case of MEC shows that power levels are not equal within transnational political initiatives. NGOs and solidarity organizations from the North have greater access to important resources, including money and the media. Power also influences who can engage in transnational political networks. A particular construction of gender limited MEC's access to a regional arena of contestation when ICIC, a transnational network of

NGOs, invited MEC and the other members of the Network to participate as a women's branch rather than attend the regional summit of Central American presidents, for example.

Our study clearly shows that the global arena is a highly gendered terrain in which the dichotomy of public and private spheres shapes the content and inner workings of transnational politics. Although UN women's conferences have become important global venues, a gender-informed political agenda is largely absent from many globalized political spaces. As in national political arenas, certain political spaces are constructed as male domains, and autonomous women's groups like MEC are excluded from them—for example, ICIC, most independent monitoring teams within maquila factories, and forums and conferences organized by the ILO.

On the other hand, autonomy has opened other important spaces and connections. Because MEC was a "women's organization," it received recognition and support from women's organizations in the United States and Europe. Its local efforts, including revolving credit funds for unemployed women and maquila workers, are made possible by such transnational connections. As Gay Seidman (1999) has argued in the case of South Africa, international attention to women and gender has created "transnational political opportunity structures" for women's groups.

POWER AND FRAMING CATEGORIES IN
TRANSNATIONAL AND NATIONAL POLITICS

The obstacles and constraints that MEC has encountered also illustrate other important elements of power in a context of globalization. MEC seeks to address both class and gender inequalities, making claims and demands about the experience of women *as* women, but also as workers. However, organizers are constantly faced with situations in which they must choose to represent themselves as one or the other—as women *or* as workers. Examples have occurred not only in MEC's dealings with state institutions but even in interactions with feminist organizations.

Connections can be drawn between MEC's struggle and that of women in other geographical contexts. Women of color in the United States, for example, have also confronted "multiple jeopardy" in liberation struggles, finding themselves marginalized in class-based, racial, and feminist movements due to their multiple social positions (King 1988). Feminists of color have demonstrated the problems with additive models of oppression and movements organized around essentialized identities. Instead, they emphasize the complex intersections of multiple forms of power and seek to construct a political practice that provides a basis for solidarity and coalition-building, but does not essentialize identities, gloss over difference, or privilege any one position or standpoint (Sandoval 1995).

The experience of MEC sheds light on the relation between local practices and larger cross-national processes (Alexander and Mohanty 1997: xix). Like women of color in the United States, MEC organizers have created and reconfigured political practices informed by the grounded experience of poor working women. The women of MEC draw from a rich, cumulative oppositional history as political actors in order to negotiate the constantly fluctuating political landscapes under globalization.

NGOS AND PROFESSIONALIZATION

The dramatic increase in number and influence of NGOs represents one of the most prominent social, political, and economic developments of the late twentieth and early twenty-first centuries. The professionalization, or "NGO-ization," of social movement organizations has corresponded well with the kind of "information politics" that has formed the basis of many social movements' transnational political strategies, and both have occurred alongside the global spread of neoliberal policies and reductions in the public sector. Does the organizational rigidity and the exclusion of grassroots actors that professionalization often implies limit the kind of creative and extremely flexible political practices that have characterized social movement organizing in the last quarter of the twentieth century and the beginning of the twenty-first?

NGOs are seen by many as embodying participatory democracy and presenting a solution to the top-down development strategies of previous decades. Yet NGOs do not escape the power dynamics of North-South relations in the postcolonial context. Despite the flow of ideas and resources across national borders, a great deal of power remains in the hands of both state and nonstate political actors in the North. "Global" NGOs based in the North are able to shape both the methods and projects undertaken by groups in the South, who are dependent upon them for resources (Jelin 1998). This lack of financial autonomy greatly affects social movement organizations like MEC. It is an important vector of inequity within "globalization from below." In a dialogue with her colleagues, Parpart sees global funding agencies as "disciplining" small-scale organizations (Staudt et al. 2001: 1255). Accountability to external funders means systems of evaluation that redirect important time and energy away from social justice pursuits and toward satisfying agencies and donors that local organizations are sufficiently accountable to their social bases (as judged by the donor or Northern counterpart) and a range of other requirements imposed by "global agents" (Mato 1998).

Some have worried whether NGOs are themselves democratic and have questioned their self-appointment as representatives of the poor or vulnerable (MacDonald 1997). And feminists have been concerned with the NGO-ization of Latin American women's movements in which organizations increasingly focus on dispensing services to women and less on developing close ties to a social base. As an organization, MEC has struggled with achieving a balance between doing grassroots work and also being "professional enough" to sustain its efforts through continued financial support from NGO donors. This has not been an easy task. And MEC has had to negotiate a new collective identity for itself, based on varied definitions of feminism and on some elements of professionalism—an identity which some members of the collective rejected and which prompted their departure from the organization.

MEC has sought to maintain its connections to its social base by continuing in the Sandinista tradition of integrating promotoras (much like cadres) into the ranks of its permanent collective. But as an organization, it has continued to professionalize since its inception, which on some level has affected leaders' efforts to stay close to the base. The kind of political and community work that it has engaged in—lobbying and negotiation as well as administering job training and microcredit—requires professional capabilities. MEC's somewhat contradictory and tenuous efforts to professionalize while at the same time maintaining connections to its base are nonetheless made possible by the particular class backgrounds of its core leadership and their political socialization within the FSLN.

MEC's efforts to occupy the contradictory position of a "professional" organization with a strong social base must be seen as contextualized within the broader milieu of postrevolutionary Nicaragua. And MEC's professionalization represents neither simply a "natural gravitation" nor a free choice for these women, but a necessity in the postsocialist context, given the organization's dependency on funding from Northern donor organizations.

One of the great ironies associated with MEC is that its creation was the result of a struggle for women's autonomy, yet, it can only exist as an autonomous organization through its dependency on international organizations for financial resources. This means that MEC must strive to represent itself as a worthy recipient of funding that "authentically" represents grassroots communities. Globalization's disruption of a notion of territorialized, bounded communities casts doubt on whether the word *grassroots* continues to carry relevance. Nonetheless, international funders continue to be motivated by an image of a "grassroots enough" version of the local, which is in turn driven by the accountability of foundations to individual donors or of NGOs to foundations and so on. A transnational chain of accountability, then, links global and local actors, with local organizers' political goals making them accountable downward to their base, but also upward to NGO funders, who may have a very different view of what projects should be prioritized, as in the case of Northern union supporters who pressured MEC organizers to cooperate with local unionizing efforts.

In order for social justice organizations to represent themselves effectively as agents of grassroots transformation, they must have professional skills (such as grant-writing abilities) and a working familiarity with the particular language used to describe successful project proposals. Organizers must appear "local enough," or close to the grassroots, and yet "global enough" to keep up-to-date regarding the latest trends in international funding and to be well connected to a transnational network of donors.

WHAT DOES MEC TEACH US?
LESSONS FOR THE NORTH

What does the case of MEC reveal about how to contribute to the empowerment of social movements that address the negative consequences of globalization? Perhaps the strongest lesson can be found in MEC's attempts to create alternatives that break from conventional binary categories such as community organization (coded as feminine) versus union (coded as masculine), public versus private, worker versus woman. Organizations seeking to support the efforts of groups like MEC must not allow rigid funding priorities to become a straitjacket that prevents those working for social justice within local contexts in the South from developing and implementing alternative organizational forms, strategies, and practices. If organizations from the North are to develop effective partnerships with groups like MEC, then it is important that they engage in practices and develop policies that demonstrate "respect for alternative ways of presenting knowledge that are situated in women's experiences" (Ferguson 1998: 103).

As a co-author and I have argued elsewhere, this is no easy task. Development initiatives seeking to implement alternative, participative, and democratic models face serious institutional and structural constraints (Mendez and Wolf 2001). Systems of accountability must be rethought, so that external accountability to funders does not override internal accountability to local groups' organizational principles and strategic visions (Chigudu 1997; Stewart and Taylor 1997). In other words, deep institutional and structural changes must occur for these power inequalities to be sufficiently addressed.

MEC's involvement in transnational information politics suggests other lessons for organizations and individuals in the North, including the anti-sweatshop movement. Many organizations have tried to address the dangers that organized boycotts can pose for workers, but boycotts continue to be seen as a highly effective strategy. In their important book on the apparel industry in Los Angeles, for example, Edna Bonacich and Richard Appelbaum (2000) single out the organized boycott as an effective (if not *the* most effective) method for gaining leverage with transnational corporations.

MEC's struggle provides an important qualifier to this positive evaluation of the effectiveness of this strategy. As Nalia Kabeer notes, boycotting campaigns are "blunt instruments" that leave little room for "nuanced, balanced and differentiated accounts of ground-level realities in low-income countries" (2004: 179). Even if a boycott causes a transnational corporation to change its behavior, should it be considered a success if this change involves propelling women workers and their dependent families into even more dire poverty?

I would suggest that in devising transnational strategies, groups and individuals in the North should collaborate with those in the South in order to develop approaches to improving work conditions that recognize gender and racial differences. Northern groups need to consider carefully the consequences of strategies and tactics, including their gender implications, not just how much pressure they can exert on target actors.

In the transnational political field information is a kind of capital, and inequalities are reflected in who controls the flow of information and who constructs the meanings of information (Melucci 1996: 182). NGOs and solidarity organizations from the North need to become more sensitive to the political implications of their use of information as well as the impact that the transnational dissemination of information exerts within localities in the South. Developing mechanisms that enable local organizations of the South to have more control over information and how it is used seems an important endeavor. This might include facilitating access of local groups to the global media and to communications technology such as the Internet, or funding the education of groups in the use of such technologies (as well as in written and spoken English), or supporting efforts to improve women's international legal understandings.

Recent events point to other important transnational initiatives. In 1999 and the early 2000's the global justice movement has mobilized students, religious groups, and representatives from social justice organizations from all over the United States and many parts of the world to protest the policies and practices of prominent global institutions—the WTO, the World Bank, and the IMF. At the time of this writing it is difficult to foresee the long-term impact that such mobilizations will exert, but it does seem apparent that the large scale and the high level of organization of these initiatives have drawn international public attention to these issues. The large-scale global justice movement may open political spaces that could present important opportunities for local groups like MEC and smaller scale transnational or regional networks like the Network.

However, to be effective in protesting work conditions in FTZs, any transnational movement must do more than portray maquila factories as "showcases of horrors for the labor abuses sanctioned by the global free trade economy" (Ross 1997: 10). Rather, they should acknowledge that, given other available alternatives, or lack of them, in the labor market, for women workers who are the only breadwinners in their large families the maquila industry often presents them with the best survival strategy (Kabeer 2004: 187). Transnational initiatives aimed at combating sweatshop abuses should not compartmentalize gender issues as "particularistic demands" (Molyneux 1998: 81), but should recognize varied perspectives and interests among workers.

This point is particularly relevant for the transnational anti-sweatshop movement, which often presents "women's issues" and "workers' issues" as mutually exclusive. A continuingly pervasive gendered construct of separate spheres (that codes work and unions as masculine and community organizations and the home as feminine) undergirds the definition espoused by many solidarity organizations in the North and labor organizations in Central America of who and what organizations represent workers' interests. These bounded categories marginalize the voices and gender perspective of autonomous women's organizations.

For example, at a 2000 mobilization of the global justice movement to protest the policies of the IMF and World Bank, organizations from the anti-sweatshop movement held a teach-in in Washington, D.C. The forum, which was organized by Campaign for Labor Rights (CLR), an organization that emerged from the Central American solidarity movement, was entitled "Sweatshops: Globalizing the Resistance." This important event marked one of the first times that various organizational actors within this transnational movement had met to take stock of the newly emerged movement and reflect on its trajectory and future strategies. Panelists included organizers from U.S.-based NGOs, unions, solidarity organizations, independent labor organizations, and student groups, as well as several representatives from unions and organizations from Latin America and Asia. Among the speakers were Mariana Rivera, an organizer from the Women's Movement Mélida Anaya Montes (MAM), a Salvadoran member of the Central American Network, and Betina Lucero of the Authentic Workers' Front (FAT) in Mexico (both names are pseudonyms).

In line with the strategic orientation of the Network, Rivera spoke of individual change, reflection groups, and consciousness-raising as playing significant roles in organizational work within the FTZ's. She noted, "All efforts are valid; . . . it's about changing the conditions with or without unions." Lucero, a union organizer, emphasized similar themes, including the importance of the labor movement's building alliances with different sectors of society. Lucero was the only panelist at the teach-in to mention the fact that female workers have faced oppression at the hands of not only managers and supervisors, but male union organizers.

However, the translator omitted her mention of male union organizers as a source of sexual harassment. Although this omission was almost certainly unintentional, gender was only discussed in passing during the entire day, and the idea that women's movements and human rights organizations have a role in changing the conditions faced by sweatshop workers was only briefly mentioned. Although the panelist speaking about Nicaragua made reference to the work of MEC, the male leader of the Apparel and Textile Workers' Federation (known in this book as Pablo Alvarez) had been extended an invitation to attend the event (though he was not able to obtain a visa) while MEC organizers went uninvited.

Despite these women's presence at the conference, the notion that unions are the only true representatives of workers has persisted within the anti-sweatshop movement—particularly in the case of those organizations emerging from the Central American solidarity movement. For example, in his speech at the teach-in, the late Trim Bissell, the former director of the Campaign for Labor Rights, discussed CLR's strategy of launching e-mail and fax campaigns to pressure companies to ensure that subcontractors adhere to local labor laws. Bissell explained that CLR bases its strategies on a solidarity model that takes it cues from workers in local contexts. Thus, CLR mobilizes its networks to implement boycotts or leafleting campaigns only when "the workers ask." The message to corporations is: "If you want this movement off your backs, then you have to bargain a contract with the unions" (Bissell 2000). Although this strategy involves a close coordination between solidarity organizations in the North and groups in the South, CLR deals almost exclusively with unions to plan and implement direct actions such as leafleting campaigns.

Unionization is viewed as benefiting and representing the interests of all workers, and other perspectives—such as those of women's organizations that have formed independently of unions—are marginalized.

In a 1999–2000 leafleting campaign of Kohl's and Target stores in the United States to protest the firings in the Chentex and Mil Colores factories in Nicaragua, all coordination for these actions was completed with the CST and with the Apparel and Textile Workers' Federation. Asked if MEC endorsed this action, a CLR organizer replied by e-mail: "The Target campaign is endorsed only by the federation because we are not launching the campaign simply because a majority of the workers are women, but because they were fired for their attempts to unionize. We see them as *workers first*" (personal correspondence, May 17, 2000; emphasis added). A well-known activist from the Nicaraguan Network expressed similar sentiments when I asked her if representatives from MEC would be included in a group of speakers for the 2000 mobilization in Washington, DC. "We deal with unions, since they are the only organizations that can legally collectively bargain a contract."

Clearly, solidarity organizations like CLR are working toward goals of structural transformation and the empowerment of oppressed workers. These groups face enormous constraints of limited resources, but their "information politics" have been quite effective in raising awareness among consumers, students, and activists in the United States about abuses that have occurred in FTZs in places like Central America. CLR, for example, sponsors speaking tours for maquila and other sweatshop workers to give testimony before groups of students and community organizations, and, in some cases, stockholders in corporations.[2] These events represent an extremely powerful forum for raising sensitivity and awareness regarding the conditions that workers face and their connection to global capitalism.

I recognize the importance of the actions of groups like CLR, and as a supporter of the goals of the anti-sweatshop movement my criticism is sympathetic to the movement's social justice agenda. Although solidarity organizations should certainly be able to choose with whom they establish relationships, the *Hard Copy* example described earlier illustrates the danger of engaging in information politics without careful consideration of the impact within local contexts. Relying exclusively on unions' interpretation of strategies and their impact means constructing a plan of action based on one perspective among many, particularly given the fact that in many contexts the trade union movement has failed to represent the interests of women workers. Further, as the case of the *Hard Copy* scandal demonstrates, poorly informed transnational strategies can have a negative impact on the long-term efforts of other local organizations working for economic justice goals.

In other words, basing strategies on a narrow definition of workers amounts to gender- and race-blindness. Effective transnational strategies for resistance of global processes emanating from global capitalism must include an understanding of how gender and race operate within the global and national economies. Certainly, gender politics throughout the world has taught us that ending class oppression of workers will not necessarily bring an end to the oppression of women. The anti-sweatshop movement cannot ignore the fact that the majority of workers in FTZs are, in fact, brown women who face the harsh reality of having to choose between improved working conditions and the opportunity to work at all (Kabeer 2004: 187).

Scholars and activists have debated the effectiveness of social clauses or codes of conduct for combating the so-called race to the bottom.[3] But an equally important, if less visible, issue is the decision-making process for determining the content of workers' clauses in trade treaties or factory codes of conduct. Social clauses or codes of conduct based on a gender-neutral (read: male) worker will do little to address the intersection of issues related to both the public and private spheres that impacts women workers' daily lives. And in a global production system that makes use of geopolitical power, as well as race- and gender-based structures of oppression, clauses that do not incorporate the particularities of workers' multiple positions—in the home, community, and workplace—will have a limited impact on the conditions that they face. Only through an inclusive and democratic process in which the varied experiences and vulnerabilities that are glossed by a universalized category of "worker" are debated, weighed, and incorporated can social clauses or any other solution to workers' oppression in the global economy be achieved.

To return to the case of MEC, like many other political initiatives "from below," this organization represents a democratic challenge—to both traditional leftist oppositional strategies and neoliberal conceptualizations—in its demands for the democratization, not just of the traditional political regime, but society as a whole. As we saw in chapter 6, this process is being carried out through a redefinition of citizenship and the reinvention of rights and involves a reconceptualization of politics that "challenge[s] the political arena to enlarge its own boundaries and broaden its agenda" (Dagnino 1998: 57).

Some unionists and anti-sweatshop movement supporters have criticized the efforts of groups like MEC for their reformist orientations and have questioned whether "self-limiting radicalism" can bring about social transformation. The case of MEC demonstrates that to dismiss such efforts as *merely* reformist overlooks important aspects of political practice in a transnational context. An expanded analytical perspective would include not only MEC's strategic orientation but also its larger feminist and democratic vision as reflected in its work at the grassroots level, to appreciate the implications of this group's practices for offering new possibilities for struggle and action in the current age of globalization.

REFORMIST OR REVOLUTIONARY?:
POLITICAL ENGAGEMENT WITH GLOBALIZATION

As we have seen, MEC's integral approach to addressing the situation of poor women bridges both a class/gender dichotomy and the public/private divide and also challenges a simplistic binary of transformative versus reformist. Many of MEC's strategies could be seen as reformist in that they address state institutions and do not seem to challenge the capitalist system. And yet MEC's programs and work with women workers and unemployed women challenges the separation of public and private spheres by connecting what occurs on the shop floor and in the local economy to what occurs in the home and community.

As scholars have noted in the case of other women's movements, underlying MEC's practices is a "new way of relating what is political and what is social, the public world and private life" (Jelin 1994b: 3). MEC's feminist vision for change has the goal of empowering poor women by placing tools for change in their hands. Drawing on feminist perspectives provides a meaningful way to view MEC's strategies and practices in that they conceptualize social transformation not as a one-time event but as a process, and view the means and ends of struggle as inextricably interconnected (Eschle 2001: 96).

MEC's formation as an autonomous women's organization involved women's developing a gender and feminist consciousness that emerged from their engagement in political struggle. Through the creation of the women-only spaces of MEC and the Network, women as political actors and the gender and class claims that they articulate became more visible. Women organizers came into their own through this process, asserting themselves as political agents. And although the processes involved were complicated and did not always involve consensus, women formulated their political strategies by applying a gender perspective, created their own organizational forms and practices, and developed their own discourses for articulating their claims. And they did so independently of the heavily male unionist organizations where they had received their political socialization. In order to develop a more complete picture, evaluations of women's national and transnational politics need to employ a gender analysis that recognizes such micro-level processes and the dispersed ways in which power can work within and through social movements.

Adopting a wider and more complicated view of resistance and social transformation that draws from a feminist perspective calls attention to the broader context and framework of meaning of MEC's political practices. Through education and *capacitación* regarding women's rights and in the tradition of feminist practice and ideology, MEC seeks to bring about the transformation of poor women's consciousness in order for them to experience their lives in a different way. MEC educates women about their political, civil, labor, economic, and social rights while putting forth a vision of democracy in which all people can claim this broad spectrum of rights. In the words of MEC educational materials, this vision entails: "Todos los derechos de todos . . . y todas."

In keeping with a more process-oriented view, it is also important to consider the counter-hegemonic properties of MEC's efforts. According to Gramsci, the construction of hegemony is a process of constitution of subjects, continually "submitted to re-elaboration and renewal, conceived as the basis for collective political action toward social transformation" (Dagnino 1998: 42). In this manner both MEC and the Central American Network that MEC organizers helped form can be viewed as spaces for the cultivation of counter-hegemonies, where alternatives to the dominant neoliberal paradigm (Rosen 2002) are formulated, articulated, and disseminated and where politicized subjectivities are forged.

Reconstituting and broadening definitions of rights and democracy and extending the boundaries of citizenship in order to widen a space for political action are important components of such counter-hegemonies (Jelin 1994b: 5). This vision directly challenges neoliberal regimes' definition of citizenship as "less a collective, political activity than an individual, economic activity—the right to pursue one's interests without hindrance in the marketplace" and of democracy as "tied more to representative government and the right to vote than to the idea of the collective, participatory activity of citizens in the public realm" (Dietz 1998: 382).

This book has been an effort to understand better how marginalized people's engagements with globalization are evolving by taking seriously the perspective of those on the ground and in the struggle. Much work remains to gain a better understanding of the conditions and opportunities that confront groups seeking to combat global injustices. My hope is that the case presented here will serve as a learning tool and inspire others to follow the example of the women of MEC and work for change and social justice in a global here and now.

NOTES

1. "MARÍA ELENA CUADRA"

1   The term *maquiladoras* (colloquially, *maquilas*) refers to export-processing assembly factories. In Nicaragua the majority of these factories manufacture clothing.

2   The International Labor Organization (2004) estimates that of the 2.8 billion people that had work in 2003, 1.2 billion were women.

3   Two studies that do look at women's movements are the anthologies by Naples and Desai (2002) and Teske and Tétrault (2000).

4   In this book names of organizations have been left unchanged while the names given for individuals are pseudonyms, except in the case of those who hold public office or who are well-known public figures. To disguise the identities of individuals I have at times changed some factual information about them. All uncited quotations are from interviews or my field notes documenting my participant observation. Translations from Spanish are my own.

5   Not everyone would agree that MEC organizers represent or are grassroots women. In chapter 4 I discuss the idea of *mujeres de base* as being an important collective identity for different factions of MEC organizers and what this means to them. Mindry 2001 describes how the degree of association with the "grassroots" is used as a yardstick by international donor organizations in determining which local women's organizations are considered worthy of funding.

6   "Compañero/a" literally means companion or partner. It is also used much like our "comrade" when addressing fellow revolutionaries or members of leftist political movements. MEC members referred to each other and to their allies and supporters in this way.

7   *Chele* (or the female *chela*) is a Mayan word that literally means *blue*—referring to the eyes of Europeans (Lancaster 1992: 217). In Nicaragua, and indeed Latin America as a whole, racial categories are constructed in ways that differ dramatically from those in the United States. For example, race is tied closely to class, and individuals can "whiten" by moving up the socioeconomic ladder (Wade 1997). In Nicaragua children from the same nuclear family may be considered to belong to different categories of skin color. Nearly every family has a child affectionately dubbed a *negrito/a* (literally, little black one) and a *chelito/a* (little white one). Lighter skin and straight hair—European phenotypes—are more highly valued

than dark brown eyes and wavy hair, associated with indigenous people or blacks. And though Nicaraguans acknowledge a common indigenous ancestry, "indigenous" characteristics are typically spoken of disparagingly. "Se le salió el indio," (his or her "indianness" came out) means that someone lost his or her temper or was loud or crude. See Lancaster (1992 chap. 17) for a more detailed discussion of the terms *chele* and *negro*.

8 The verb *joder* varies in connotation in different parts of Latin America. Although the word literally means "to fuck," it is often used to mean "to pester" or "to screw around." In Nicaragua the sexual connotation is not as strong as in other parts of the hemisphere, which is why I have chosen to translate it in this way. I should also note that Nicaraguans consider the use of *joder* and this saying in particular to be very *pinolero*—typically *Nica*. It is considered to be a "salt-of-the-earth" popular expression.

9 The concept of social capital is widely used in sociology. The French sociologist Pierre Bourdieu, who coined the term, defines it as "the sum of the resources, actual or virtual, that accrue to an individual or group by virtue of possessing a durable network of more or less institutionalized relationships of mutual acquaintance and recognition" (Bourdieu and Wacquant 1992: 119).

10 See Wolf 1996a for an insightful review of the literature on feminist dilemmas in fieldwork.

2. OPPOSITIONAL POLITICS AND MEC

1 It could easily be argued that there are at least two Nicaraguas—the Atlantic Coast, which is populated by descendants of African slaves who mixed with the indigenous population such as the Miskitus and other Afro-Caribbeans (who speak creole English, Miskitu, and other indigenous languages) and the more heavily populated Pacific Coast, which is Spanish-speaking and largely *mestizo*. The two regions have separate and distinct histories, with the eastern coast having been colonized by Britain and isolated from the distant mestizo Pacific. In 1988 after bitter ethnic conflict between the Sandinistas and the Miskitu, who allied themselves with the Contras, the Autonomous Atlantic Northern Region (RAAN) was formed as a largely autonomous region, politically, economically, and culturally, with its own constitution and separate laws. See Lancaster 1992 (especially chap. 17) and Hale 1994. As in other Latin American contexts the construction of racial categories is tied to a dominant ideology of *mestizaje*, or the new cosmic race resulting from the "natural" miscegenation of European, indigenous, and African races. National elites constructed this ideology at the beginning of the twentieth century as Latin American countries were undergoing

the tumultuous process of nation-state building. The idea of *mestizaje*, or a shared and uniquely Latin American racial identity, made possible the notion of a culturally and racially homogenous nation-state, with the *mestizo* as the national subject. In some nations, including Nicaragua, where the indigenous population was largely enslaved in the more heavily populated Pacific regions, mestizos are in fact the racial majority, but in others, such as Guatemala, the large indigenous populations make up the majority. See Gould 1998 for a historical analysis of the creation and power of the myth of Nicaraguan *mestizaje*.

2   For example, such diverse personae as Salman Rushdie (1987) and Ed Asner have been vocal champions of the Sandinista revolution. Among the scholars, journalists, poets, and other writers who traveled to Nicaragua during the Sandinista period and whose work reflects the profound effect that the experience had on their lives are Susan Meiselas (1981), Maxine Molyneux (1985), Margaret Randall (1981, 1992, 1994), and Adrienne Rich (1986). In addition, Nicaragua has a proud, vibrant, and internationally recognized literary tradition. The verses of the country's national poet, Rubén Darío (1867-1916), have inspired generations of artists, nationalists, and revolutionaries. And the revolution also gave rise to such internationally acclaimed poets as Claribel Alegría, Daisy Zamorra, and Ernesto Cardenal. The work of the Nicaraguan feminist writer Gioconda Belli is also internationally recognized and widely translated.

3   Vanden and Prevost (1993: 55) note an inherent tension between, on the one hand, radical participative democracy involving direct participation of the masses and, on the other, vanguardism and centralized decision-making within the Sandinista party and government. They attribute this tension, which is also reflected within the mass organizations themselves, to the multi-class composition of the coalition that overthrew the Somoza regime as well as the different variants of Marxism (including Leninism but also the Cuban revolution, liberation theology, and the ideas of Che Guevara) that underlay the Sandinistas' political ideology.

4   In 1996 the IMF suspended disbursements to Nicaragua under the ESAF program due to failure to meet the conditions of the SAP (Close 1999: 132).

5   In a 1987 study Pérez Alemán and her co-authors found the textile industry to be extremely segregated, with women concentrated in areas in which the salaries were significantly lower than those of the men. The justifications for women's concentration in these lower-paying areas given by directors of human resources in the state-owned factories are strikingly similar to those other researchers have recorded from managers of transnational assembly factories in a variety of contexts: "The men's tasks require more strength, but the jobs of manual skill are women's"; "The women have more manual dexterity.... Men have more physical resilience" (Pérez Alemán et al. 1987: 7; and see Freeman 2000; Wolf 1992).

6 Although by U.S. standards the provision of any food by management might seem unexpected and generous, Nicaraguan workers' expectations are shaped by experiences during the Sandinista era when payment or bonuses in the form of basic foodstuffs and provisions (often the product made by the company) were common. María Luisa and Lola would often reminisce about CST leaders arriving at worker-owned factories with jugs of oil and bags of rice to be distributed among workers. In the mid-1990s one of the complaints that one often would hear among Nicaraguan maquila workers was about the stinginess of factory managers, who never once "gave us even a scrap of fabric or a pair of scissors."

7 On relative wage levels, during the time of my field research nurses and school-teachers earned approximately C$400, or US$47 per month. There are competing statistics regarding the average wages of Free Trade Zone workers in Nicaragua. FTZ employers calculate wages in a variety of ways, including paying a base or minimal wage to which piecework wages are added or simply paying wages based on piecework (as in Isabel's case). In addition, there are complex systems of bonuses and wage deductions that vary not only from factory to factory but from work area to work area. Witness for Peace (1997) documented the average wage to be US$18 per week. Renzi (1996) found wages to average C$700-800 (US$83-95) per month. Finally, a 1998 ILO study reports that the hourly wage for a seam-stress in the maquila factories of Nicaragua averaged US$1.16 (cited in Baumeister 2002: 5).

8 See ILO 1996 for a detailed description of these laws and decrees.

9 It is interesting to compare this figure with the Nicaragua's national budget for 1997 of $585 million and with sales for Wal-Mart (a major retailer of products from factories in the zone) for that same year at $105 billion (National Labor Committee 1998).

10 Though many autonomous women's organizations and their participants self-identify as feminist, I choose to use the more general label of autonomous *women's* movement, rather than feminist movement and then to refer to specific organizations as feminist. (See note 12, below.) The more inclusive category of autonomous women's movement is more often used in Nicaragua by participants in the movement (see Criquillon 1995) and includes all women's organizations that are not affiliated with a political party, whether or not they identify as feminist. Nonetheless, it is important to note as do Babb (2001, 1997) and Ewig (1999) that there is a strong presence of internationally funded feminist NGOs and service organizations in the Nicaraguan autonomous women's movement.

11 Criquillón points out (1995) that the women's secretariats of the Union of Public Employees (UNE) and the National Confederation of Professionals—Heroes and Martyrs (CONAPRO H-M) did at key points ally with the organizations of the

autonomous women's movement. Indeed, some of the earliest feminists to leave the Sandinista organizations left CONAPRO to form the autonomous organization Colectiva Masaya (Ewig 1999: 84). See Isbester 2001 for a detailed description and analysis of these important "semi-autonomous" women's organizations.

12 González and Kampwirth (2001: 15-17) explain the distinction between "feminist" and "gender" perspectives within women's political organizing in Latin America. At the end of the twentieth century the latter term was favored by leftist working-class women as an alternative to the middle-class connotations that the term *feminist* had taken on during the first wave and early years of the second wave of feminism in Latin America. A "feminist" perspective analyzes gender relations and struggles to overcome inequalities between men and women. Although a "gender" perspective, while less precisely defined in its usage, generally holds the same meaning, use of the term also serves to distinguish oneself from the organized feminist movement.

13 Microcredit and microenterprises are development strategies that have grown in predominance along with the emergence of NGOs since the early 1990s. They have been touted as solutions to poverty facing women by such unlikely bedfellows as the USAID and neoliberal state regimes *and* leftist NGOs seeking alternatives to dominant development strategies. In chapter 4 I discuss NGO funding and micro-enterprises in more detail.

14 The union named itself to honor the indigenous leader after she visited the group and spoke of her experiences as a domestic worker.

15 The domestic workers' union did not survive. After union organizers were physically removed from the offices of the women's secretariats by CST leaders, the union gradually disbanded. Although the law establishing December 10 as a paid holiday for domestic workers has not been repealed, in 1994 when I visited the Ministry of Labor and interviewed staff members there about domestic workers' labor rights, none of the interviewees reported knowing about the existence of this law.

3. GENDERING POWER AND RESISTANCE

1 See also Portes et al. 1999; Smith and Guarnizo 1998; Glick Schiller et al. 1995; Kearney 1995; Guarnizo 1994.

2 See for example Smith and Johnston 2002b; O'Brien et al. 2000; della Porta et al. 1999; Keck and Sikkink 1998a; and Smith et al. 1997.

3 As Tarrow (2001: 15) points out, the political process approach to social movements provides tools for understanding how and when domestic actors can develop transnational ties and forge transnational identities. His institutional

approach to transnational politics lists brokerage, certification, modeling, and institutional appropriation as mechanisms for creating transnational horizontal connections.

4 This scholarship is heavily influenced by the work of Laclau and Mouffe (1985), the European new social movement (NSM) tradition, and cultural studies. See Edelman 2001 for a review of the various disciplinary and conceptual splits within the social movement literature and for an examination of the affinity of Latin Americanist researchers (particularly anthropologists) for the European new social movement paradigm because of its emphasis on cultural practice and civil society.

5 It is worth noting that this group of scholars draws on Gramscian, feminist, and cultural studies and European NSM frameworks.

6 For example, groups like the Zapatistas in Chiapas, Mexico (Yúdice 1998), and the Garifuna of Honduras (England 1999), both of which participate in the pan-indigenous movement, also make demands based on their class positions as workers or campesinos.

7 Recent work within social movement theory has highlighted the interconnected nature of culture and social structure. See for example Mansbridge and Morris 2001; Johnston and Klandermans 1995; and Morris and Mueller 1992.

8 The term *resistance* has different conceptual origins and usages. The anthropologist James Scott first used the concept in his study of "weapons of the weak," individualized acts of contention against local power-holders that he maintained existed outside hegemonic relations (1986: 335-36). His followers expanded the concept in examining cultural oppositional practices in the South. In the study of transnational advocacy networks, social movement scholars in political science and sociology have used the term with little theoretical specification (e.g., Tarrow 2002: 232-33). Post-Marxists and cultural studies theorists, however, have waged Foucaultian critiques against this use of the concept, questioning a theoretical construction of subjects as existing outside of power relations (Abu-Lugod 1990; see Ong 1991) as well as the class-reductionist overtones of the concept (Kondo 1990). Others have worked to reconceptualize the term in the study of what has been termed identity and cultural politics (Gordon 1998; see Hale 1997).

9 Foucault's (1980) work regarding power has been decidedly influential here. For Foucault power is ubiquitous, and it is impossible to exist outside it. His work also stresses the multiplicity of forms of power and their inseparability from one another and from other kinds of social relations (production, kinship, family, and sexuality) and highlights the ways in which power operates through discourse to structure subjectivities.

10 For example, Lowe and Lloyd (1997a) are concerned with reconfigured oppositional narratives under global capitalism. Mansbridge and Morris and contribu-

tors (2001), though not specifically examining transnational social movements, bring culture and power to the study of social movements by theorizing oppositional consciousness. The new social movement tradition conceptualizes social movements in terms of collective identity and the goal of creating cultural change (Cohen 1985; Melucci 1985).

11 See also McAdam et al. 2001 for a discussion of contentious politics under globalization.

12 See also, for example, Collins 2003; Mills 1999; Lee 1998; Bose and Acosta-Belén 1995; Safa 1995, 1990a;, Tiano 1994; Wolf 1992; Ong 1987; Nash 1985; and Fernandez-Kelly 1983.

13 Printed copies of such reports on the Maquila Solidarity Network's Web site are in my files. See also Breaking Boundaries/Forming Alliances 2001.

14 For analyses of Latin American women's participation in political movements of the right and left see González and Kampwirth 2001b. For a review of the sociological literature on Third World women's activism see Ray and Korteweg 1999. The scholarship on Latin American women's movements is extensive. See, for example, Lind 2002, 2000; Schild 1998; Dore 1997; Stephen 1997; Alvarez 1994; Jaquette 1994b); Jelin 1994c; Radcliffe and Westwood 1993.

15 Perhaps no one has illustrated this point more vividly than feminists of color and Third World feminists in the United States, who have systematically explained and demonstrated the problematic aspects of unmediated claims to sisterhood that deny the multiple forms of power in women's lives (Mohanty 1991; Trinh 1990). White middle-class feminists have reproduced racism in the movement, and white feminist theorists have put forth an overdetermined conceptualization of patriarchy that has obscured both the way in which white women benefit from racial structures and the importance of allegiances between men and women of color in antiracist struggles. Feminists of color in the United States have made important inroads in theorizing power as taking multiple forms that intersect in context-specific ways (Yuval-Davis 1997a; hooks 1991; Collins 1990; King 1988). Thus, these theorists reject additive models or a notion of a hierarchy of oppression, but have turned instead to debates about how to construct politics built on intersecting, but not essentialized, identities and across difference (Yuval-Davis 1997a; Sandoval 1991). Such politics would be by necessity coalitional and based on a "new subjectivity," what Sandoval (1995) calls "differential consciousness," acknowledging the multiple, partial standpoints of others without privileging any one position.

16 For more on these conferences, or *encuentros*, see Vargas and Mauleón 1998; Sternbach et al. 1992; and Navarro 1982.

17 Feminist scholars have posed different views with regard to political projects involving citizenship rights and differences. For example, Correa and Petchesky

(1994) hold that we should reconstruct, rather than abandon rights discourse. Such a reconstructed discourse would specify gender, class, cultural, and other differences, while recognizing social needs. Eisenstein (1989) holds a similar view regarding the reformulation of human rights. She maintains that some common notion of human beings is necessary, but that what needs to be rejected is a unitary standard against which they all are judged.

4. MEC'S SEARCH FOR STRUCTURE

1   Some scholars have cautioned against essentializing NGOs and generalizing as to their functions (e.g., sustainable development and social justice), organizational forms (professionalized and more bureaucratic than social movements), and orientations (progressive) (see Fisher 1997). Indeed, there is little consensus regarding what an NGO really is. For the purposes of this analysis, I use the term NGO to indicate organizations from the North or South which do not operate as official parts of state institutions, political parties, or trade unions.

2   In the original structure the national office was also the headquarters for what was to be a regional Managua office. However, the Managua office and national office never developed as separate entities.

3   Las Malinches derives from the name of the Aztec woman Malinzin, also known as La Malinche, who served as Cortes's translator during the conquest and who later bore his children.

4   With these scholarships MEC program participants could receive technical training at various training centers along with other paying students, who often included men.

5   In the early 2000s disagreements among regional leaders and the national confederation leadership caused a split in the CST. A faction, including Ana María, then formed a second confederation, naming it the CST José Benito Escobar.

6   Though certainly, not all NGO funders are white, the vast majority with whom MEC organizers came into contact in Canadian, European, and U.S. organizations were. The general use of this term also reflects a racial understanding of international power relations.

5. MEC'S POLITICAL STRATEGIES

1   Relatively speaking, Nicaragua's FTZs have always been more accessible than in other countries in the Isthmus. I myself entered the zone with MEC organizers a number of times as early as 1995 with only minor difficulty, though at other times (especially in the aftermath of incidents such as accidents that drew media attention), visitors were heavily scrutinized. And by the early 2000s in part due to

public attention generated by MEC and the labor movement, the FTZ Las Mercedes was probably the most accessible such zone in Central America, if not Latin America.

2   This was included in a description of advantages offered by this FTZ, which I checked on March 11, 1998, at www.ibw.com.ni.

3   Some years later, some long-time promotoras became members of the Managua organizing team and received a salary from the organization. After MECs legal office was reestablished in the early 2000s, a major role of the promotoras was to accompany workers who had suffered rights violations to consult with MEC's lawyer and often to go with them to meetings with inspectors at the Ministry of Labor.

4   By 2002, when MEC underwent an external evaluation, organizers estimated that there were five hundred active promotoras with ties to the organization (Köpke 2002).

5   At the time of this writing, there are fifteen factories located in Nicaragua's state-owned free trade zone and ten privately operated zones located in Managua (6), San Marcos (1), Granada (1), Sebaco (1), and Mateare (1). In addition, there are twenty-three maquila factories that enjoy FTZ status but are not located in a FTZ. Recent estimates place the number of workers in the assembly factories of the state-owned FTZ at 37,143 (*Observador Económico* 2001-2; Comisión Nacional de la Zona Franca 2004).

6   As we saw in chapter 4, MEC's changed orientation and relations with organizations from the transnational women's movement also involved a change in vocabulary to coincide with participants' experiences within the CST and with organizational principles of personal autonomy within the collective.

7   Thus, Frundt's claim that "Nicaraguan women gained eight maquila unions in the late 1990s" (2002: 18) should be approached critically. Though certainly women made up much of the rank and file of these unions (Bellman 2003), what the experiences of MEC and the autonomous organizations of the Network highlight is, on the one hand, the difference between gender and women and, on the other hand, contestations around what constitutes an organization that works for women's interests. Unfortunately, in his analysis Frundt does not differentiate between Central American women maquila organizers who were working within traditional unions and those who left labor federations due to gender-based conflicts and oppression. For example, in a section entitled "Union Women" he quotes leaders from GRUFERPROFAM and AMES as well as Women's Movement Mélida Anaya Montes (MAM) of El Salvador, all of which are autonomous women's organizations and members of the Network, though their relationships with traditional union federations vary.

8   Indeed, even in the cases of factories in which codes of conduct and independent

monitoring have been used as a way to support unionization, the threat of factories closing is an ever-present one. See Molina and Quinteros 2000 for a discussion of the case of the Mandarin factory in El Salvador and Köpke 2000 for an account of the Kimi factory in Honduras.

9   The transnational movement to establish independent monitoring teams has experienced other internal conflicts as well. Some Central American unions came to see the independent monitoring groups as competing with their organizational space (Köpke 2000). For example, in the case of Honduras some conservative unions (which did not have representation in the maquilas) sided with state elites in invoking a nationalist "pro-foreign investment" ideology. This camp criticized the New York–based National Labor Committee (NLC) and the other organizations (among them a trade union affiliated with the Union of Needletrades, Industrial, and Textile Employees, UNITE, a U.S.-based union) that have worked to establish independent monitoring teams within the assembly factories, accusing them of betraying the "patria" and being motivated by foreign interests (Mendez and Köpke 1998). Later, considerable disagreement between UNITE and the NLC concerning the strategy of establishing independent monitoring teams emerged (Bissell 1998). UNITE began to articulate the view that this strategy is inappropriate for obtaining the long-term objectives of organized labor.

10 This research raises the issue of what constitutes a "women's organization." In chapter 4 we saw how, in their participation within the autonomous women's movement and even within their own organization, MEC organizers confronted essentialized categories of "women's" versus "workers'" organizations. As we saw, some MEC founders even left the organization to return to the labor movement or the Sandinista party to work on gender issues "from within." An interesting opportunity for further research would be to interview female union members in the FTZs of Nicaragua about gender issues in their organizations.

6. MEC AND THE POSTSOCIALIST STATE

1   *La Piñata* became the term used to refer to the private appropriation by Sandinistas of what had been state-owned property under the revolutionary government.

2   MEC did turn to the issue of wages in the early 2000s, after I had left the field, through a national strategy of lobbying to reform minimum wage laws.

3   The exception is discrimination based on sexual orientation, which is not codified in Nicaraguan law.

4   According to the Ministry of Social Action (MAS), in 1993 in the Pacific region of the country 33 percent of urban households were headed by women (quoted in Renzi and Kruijt 1997: 49). The Organization of American States reports the

figure for rural female-headed households to be 31 percent (quoted in Wilkie and Ortega 1997). The study conducted by MAS indicates that in Managua, of the total households in situations of chronic poverty, 52.4 percent are female-headed. In a 1996 study of urban households, Renzi and Agurto found that 38.3 percent of female-headed households were classified as being in a situation of "chronic poverty," and 34.8 percent of male-headed households were in this category. What is revealed is the widespread poverty in the country corresponding with the prevalence of female-headed households (1996: 184, 180).

5 The first head of this institution, Max Padilla, was quite vocal in his opposition to feminism and its concept of gender as a social structure, rather than a natural phenomenon. See Kampwirth 2003.

6 I am grateful to Roger Rouse, who pointed this out to me.

7 This point was hotly debated at a 1998 conference for the "Living Wage" held in Berkeley, California, and organized by Global Exchange. Activists discussed the pros and cons of framing their demands in this way, finding it difficult to employ a rights discourse—especially since a "living wage" is clearly different from legally defined "minimum wages."

7. RESISTANCE GOES GLOBAL

1 Such coalitions were comprised of U.S. groups like UNITE and the NLC in partnership with CENIDH and the Textile and Apparel Workers' Federation.

2 In 2000 CLR sponsored a speaking tour for a female Nicaraguan worker from the Mil Colores factory to attend the Kohl's shareholder meeting in Milwaukee. A CLR organizer and the worker were able to attend the meeting, as an order of nuns who owned shares in Kohl's offered her their proxy. The worker was not permitted to address the shareholders, but her prepared statement was read by one of the nuns who was a shareholder (Campaign for Labor Rights 2000).

3 See Kabeer 2004; Clawson 2003, esp. chap. 6; Seidman and Ross 2003; Scherrer and Grevin 2001; Bonacich and Appelbaum 2000.

ABBREVIATIONS AND ACRONYMS

AIP	Apparel Industry Partnership
AMES	Asociación de Mujeres en Solidaridad (Association of Women in Solidarity; Guatemala)
AMNLAE	Asociación de Mujeres Nicaragüenses, Luisa Amanda Espinoza (Association of Nicaraguan Women, Luisa Amanda Espinoza)
AMPRONAC	Asociación de Mujeres ante la Problemática Nacional (Association of Women Confronting the National Problem)
ATC	Asociación de Trabajadores Campesinos (Association of Rural Workers)
BANIC	Banco Nicaragüense de Industria y Comercio (Nicaraguan Bank of Industry and Commerce)
CAFTA	Central American Free Trade Agreement
CAUS	Central de Acción Unida Sindicalista (Confederation of Syndical Action and Unity)
CCIC	Canadian Council for International Cooperation
CDI	Centro de Desarrollo Infantil (Child Development Center)
CDS	Comites de Defensa Sandinista (Sandinista Defense Committees)
CEDAW	Convention on the Elimination of All Forms of Discrimination Against Women
CENIDH	Centro Nicaragüense de Derechos Humanos (Nicaraguan Center of Human Rights)
CEPAA	Council on Economic Priorities Accreditation Agency (United States)
CLR	Campaign for Labor Rights (United States)
CODEMUH	Colectiva de Mujeres Hondureñas (Honduran Women's Collective)
CONAPRO	Confederación Nacional de Asociaciones de Profesionales (National Confederation of Professionals)
CONPES	Consejo Nacional de Planificación Económica Social (National Commission for Economic and Social Planning)
CST	Central Sandinista de Trabajadores (Sandinista Workers' Central)

ESAF	Economic Structural Adjustment Facility
FIDEG	Fundación Internacional para el Desafío Económico Global (International Foundation for the Global Economic Challenge)
FLA	Fair Labor Association
FNT	Frente Nacional de Trabajadores (National Workers' Front)
FONIF	Fondo Nicaragüense Para la Niñez y la Familia (Nicaraguan Fund for Children and the Family)
FSLN	Frente Sandinista de Liberación Nacional (Sandinista National Liberation Front)
FTZ	free trade zone
ICIC	Inciativa Civil para la Integración Centroamericana (Civil Initiative for Central American Integration)
IDB	Inter-American Development Bank
ILO	International Labor Organization
IMF	International Monetary Fund
INIM	Instituto Nicaragüense de la Mujer (Nicaraguan Women's Institute)
JS-19	July 19th Sandinista Youth
MAM	Mélida Anaya Montes (women's movement; El Salvador)
MEC	"María Elena Cuadra," Working and Unemployed Women's Movement
MIFAMILIA	Ministerio de la Familia (Ministry of the Family)
NED	National Endowment for Democracy
Network	Red Centroamericana de Mujeres en Solidaridad con las Trabajadoras de la Maquila (Central American Women's Network in Solidarity with Maquila Workers)
NGO	nongovernmental organization
NLC	National Labor Committee (United States)
SAP	structural adjustment program
UNAG	Unión Nacional de Agricultores y Ganaderos (National Union of Farmers and Ranchers)
UNE	Unión Nacional de Empleados (Union of Public Employees)
UNITE	Union of Needletrades, Industrial, and Textile Employees
UNO	Unión Nacional de Oposición (National Union of Opposition)
USAID	U.S. Agency for International Development

BIBLIOGRAPHY

Abu-Lughod, Lila. 1990. "The Romance of Resistance: Tracing Transformations of Power through Bedouin Women." *American Ethnologist* 17 (1): 41–55.

———. 1993. *Writing Women's Worlds: Bedouin Stories*. Berkeley: University of California Press.

Acker, Joan. 1995. "Feminist Goals and Organizing Processes." In Myrna Marx Ferree and Patricia Yancy Martin, eds., *Feminist Organizations: Harvest of the New Women's Movement*, pp. 137–44. Philadelphia: Temple University Press.

Albrow, Martin. 1997. *The Global Age: State and Society Beyond Modernity*. Stanford, Calif.: Stanford University Press.

Alexander, M. Jacqui, and Chandra Talpade Mohanty. 1997. "Introduction: Genealogies, Legacies, Movements." In M. Jacqui Alexander and Chandra Talpade Mohanty, eds., *Feminist Genealogies, Colonial Legacies, Democratic Futures*, pp. xiii–xlii. New York: Routledge.

Alvarez, Sonia E. 1990. *Engendering Democracy in Brazil: Women's Movements in Transition Politics*. Princeton: Princeton University Press.

———. 1994. "The (Trans)formation of Feminism(s) and Gender Politics in Democratizing Brazil." In Jane S. Jaquette, ed., *The Women's Movement in Latin America: Participation and Democracy*, pp. 13–63. Boulder: Westview Press.

———. 1998. "Latin American Feminisms 'Go Global': Trends of the 1990s and Challenges for the New Millennium." In Sonia E. Alvarez, Evelina Dagnino, and Arturo Escobar, eds., *Culture of Politics, Politics of Cultures: Re-visioning Latin American Social Movements*, pp. 293–324. Boulder: Westview Press.

———. 2000. "Translating the Global Effects of Transnational Organizing on Local Feminist Discourses and Practices in Latin America." *Meridians* 1 (February): 29–67.

Alvarez, Sonia E., Evelina Dagnino, and Arturo Escobar. 1998a. "Introduction: The Cultural and the Political in Latin American Social Movements." In Sonia E. Alvarez, Evelina Dagnino, and Arturo Escobar, eds., *Culture of Politics, Politics of Cultures: Re-visioning Latin American Social Movements*, pp. 1–29. Boulder: Westview Press.

———, eds. 1998b. *Culture of Politics Politics of Cultures: Re-visioning Latin American Social Movements*. Boulder: Westview Press.

Ampié, Guillermo Fernández. 1996. "Vilma Núñez, precandidata presidencial del FSLN: Un liderazgo nuevo." *Barricada Internacional* (April–May): 14–16.

Andersson, Susanne. 1993. "New National Health Care Policy: Undercover Privatization." *Barricada Internacional* 13: 367/8: 12–13.

Anteproyecto de Ley. 1999. "Proyecto de Ley de Reformas y Adición al Decreto No. 46–91. Denominado Zonas Francas Industriales de Exportación." Managua.

Appadurai, Arjun. 1990. "Disjuncture and Difference in the Global Cultural Economy." *Theory, Culture and Society* 7: 295–310.

———. 1991. "Global Ethnoscapes: Notes and Queries for a Transnational Anthropology." In R. Fox, ed., *Recapturing Anthropology: Working in the Present*, pp. 191–210. Santa Fe: School of American Research Press.

Arnold, Gretchen. 1995. "Dilemmas of Feminist Coalitions: Collective Identity and Strategic Effectiveness in the Battered Women's Movement." In Myra Marx Ferree and Patricia Yancey Martin, eds., *Feminist Organizations: Harvest of the New Women's Movement*, pp. 276–90. Philadelphia: Temple University Press.

Babb, Florence E. 1996. "After the Revolution: Neoliberal Policy and Gender in Nicaragua." *Latin American Perspectives* 23 (1): 27–48.

———. 1997. "Negotiating Spaces: Gender, Economy, and Cultural Politics in Post-Sandinista Nicaragua. *Identities* 4 (1): 45–70.

———. 2001. *After Revolution: Mapping Gender and Cultural Politics in Neoliberal Nicaragua*. Austin: University of Texas Press.

Banco Central de Nicaragua. 1995. *La dinámica del mercado de trabajo urbano y sus implicaciones por género en Nicaragua*. Managua: Dirección General de Empleo y Salario, Ministerio del Trabajo, República de Nicaragua.

Banco Central de Reserva. 1998. *Reportaje Anual: 1997*. Managua: Banco Central de Reserva.

Bandy, Joe. 2004. "Paradoxes of Transnational Civil Society under Neoliberalism: The Coalition for Justice in the Maquiladoras." *Social Problems* 51 (3): 410–31.

Bandy, Joe, and Jennifer Bickham Mendez. 2003. "A Place of Their Own?: Women Organizers Negotiating the Local and Transnational in the Maquilas of Nicaragua and Northern Mexico." *Mobilization* 8 (2): 173–88.

Barber, Benjamin R. 2001. *Jihad vs. McWorld*. 2d. ed. New York: Ballantine Books.

Barreto, Pablo Emilio. 1997. "Porátil ante el MITRAB [Ministerio de Trabajo]." *La Barricada*. November 25.

La Barricada. 1994a. "CST: Secretaría de la Mujer reabre hoy sus puertas." June 6, p. 4.

———. 1994b. "Lideres CST rechazan cargos de corrupción." March 18, p. 4.

———. 1997a. "La Gran Zona Franca." June 18, p. 6A.

———. 1997b. "Obreros despedidos." November 19, p. 2A.

Basch, Linda, Nina Glick Schiller, and Cristina Szanton Blanc, eds. 1994. *Nations Unbound: Transnational Projects, Postcolonial Predicaments and Deterritorialized Nation-States*. Langhorne, Pa.: Gordon and Breach.

Basu, Amrita. 2000. "Globalization of the Local/Localization of the Global: Mapping Transnational Women's Movements." *Meridians* 1 (1): 68–84.

Basu, Amrita, ed. 1995. *The Challenge of Local Feminisms: Women's Movements in a Global Perspective*. Boulder: Westview Press.

Baumeister, Eduardo. 2002. "Nicaragua: migraciones externas." *El Observador Económico* 119 (December–January).

Bellman, Mary. 2003. "Factory Unions in Garment Industry Maquiladoras: Lessons from Central America." Paper presented at the Latin American Studies Association International Congress. March. Dallas.

Benería, Lourdes, and Shelly Feldman, eds. 1992. *Unequal Burden: Economic Crisis, Persistent Poverty, and Women's Work*. Boulder: Westview Press.

Bergeron, Suzanne. 2001. "Political Economy Discourses of Globalization and Feminist Politics." *Signs* 26 (4): 983–1006.

Beteta, Girlany Martínez. 1993. "Situación peligrosa en Zona Franca." *La Jornada de Nicaragua*, September 15, pp. 1, 4.

Bissell, Trim. 1998. "Analysis of Apparel Industry Partnership 'Preliminary Agreement.'" Listserv posting: Campaign for Labor Rights, November 8.

Blandón, María Teresa. 2001. "The Coalición Nacional de Mujeres: An Alliance of Left-Wing Women, Right-Wing Women, and Radical Feminists in Nicaragua." In Victoria González and Karen Kampwirth, eds., *Radical Women in Latin America: Left and Right*, pp. 111–31. University Park: Pennsylvania State University Press.

Blondet, Cecilia. 1995. "Out of the Kitchen and Into the Streets." In Amitra Basu, ed., *The Challenge of Local Feminisms: Women's Movements in a Global Perspective*, pp. 251–75. Boulder: Westview Press.

La Boletina. 1997a. "En las maquilas te sacan el jugo . . ." 31: 9–19.

——. 1997b. "Los puntos en agenda del 'Ministerio de la Familia.'" 30: 12–18.

——. 1997c. "Rayando el cuadro: Después de las elecciones." 29: 16–35.

Bonacich, Edna, and Richard P. Appelbaum. 2000. *Behind the Label: Inequality in the Los Angeles Apparel Industry*. Berkeley: University of California Press.

Bonacich, Edna, Lucie Cheng, Norma Chinchilla, Nora Hamilton, and Paul Ong. 1994. "The Garment Industry in the Restructuring Global Economy." In Edna Bonacich, Lucie Cheng, Norma Chinchilla, Nora Hamilton, and Paul Ong, eds., *Global Production: The Apparel Industry in the Pacific Rim*, pp. 3–18. Philadelphia: Temple University Press.

Booth, John A. 1985. *The End and the Beginning: The Nicaraguan Revolution*. Boulder: Westview Press.

Borge, Tomás. 1997. "'¡Qué se vayan!'" *La Barricada,* November 21, p. 4.

Bose, Christine E., and Edna Acosta-Belen, eds. 1995. *Women in the Latin American Development Process*. Philadelphia: Temple University Press.

Bourdieu, Pierre, and Loïc J. D. Wacquant. 1992. *An Invitation to Reflexive Sociology*. Chicago: University of Chicago Press.

Breaking Boundaries/Building Alliances. 2001. Conference Report. February. Managua.

Brecher, Jeremy, Tim Costello, and Brendan Smith. 2000. *Globalization from Below: The Power of Solidarity*. Cambridge, Mass.: South End Press.

Brodie, Janine. 1994. "Shifting the Boundaries: Gender and the Politics of Restructuring." In I. Bakker, ed., *The Strategic Silence: Gender and Economic Policy*. London: Zed Books.

Brown, L. D. and R. Tandon. 1983. "Ideology and Political Economy in Inquiry: Action Research and Participatory Research." *Journal of Applied Behavioral Sciences* 19: 277–94.

Brysk, Allison. 1993. "From Above and Below: Social Movements, the International System, and Human Rights in Argentina." *Comparative Political Studies* 26 (3): 259–85.

Burawoy, Michael. 2000. "Introduction: Reaching for the Global." In Michael Burawoy, Joseph A. Blum, Sheba George, Zsuzsa Gille, Teresa Gowan, Lynne Haney, Maren Klawiter, Steven H. Lopez, Sean Ó Riain, and Millie Thayer. *Global Ethnography: Forces, Connections, and Imaginations in a Postmodern World*, pp. 1–40. Berkeley: University of California Press.

Burawoy, Michael, Joseph A. Blum, Sheba George, Zsuzsa Gille, Teresa Gowan, Lynne Haney, Maren Klawiter, Steven H. Lopez, Sean Ó Riain, and Millie Thayer. 2000. *Global Ethnography: Forces, Connections, and Imaginations in a Postmodern World*. Berkeley: University of California Press.

Camacho, Alicia Schmidt. 1999. "On the Borders of Solidarity: Race and Gender Contradictions in the 'New Voice' Platform of the AFL-CIO." *Social Justice* 26 (3): 79–102.

Campaign for Labor Rights. 2000. E-mail alert, June 3. Printout in author's files.

Canales, Ernesto Garcia. 1998a. "Alemán llama a rescatar valores éticos." *La Prensa*, March 6, pp. 1A, 4A.

———. 1998b. "Mujeres dan apoyo total a Zoilamérica." *La Prensa*, March 5, p. 1A.

Canales, Ernesto Garcia, and Celso Canelo Candia. 1996. "Consejo confirma victoria de la Alianza Liberal." *La Prensa*, November 8, p. 1.

Castells, Manuel. 1993. "The Informational Economy and the New International Division of Labor." In Martin Carnoy, Manuel Castells, Stephen S. Cohen, and Fernando Henrique Carodoso, eds., *The New Global Economy in the Information Age*, pp. 15–43. University Park: Pennsylvania State University Press.

———. 1997. *The Power of Identity: The Information Age, Economy, Society and Culture*. Vol. 2. Oxford: Blackwell Publishers.

Centro de Estudios Internacionales (CEI). 1997. "Estrategias de Negociación en Procesos de Cabildeo." Managua: CEI.

Centro Nicaragüense de Derechos Humanos (CENIDH). 1996. "Investigación: El derecho a la libertad sindical y la actuación de las autoridades administrativas y judiciales." Managua: CENIDH.

Chamorro Barrios, Carlos F. 1997. "El estilo de un caudillo autoritario." *Envío* 182: 8–18.

Chigudu, Hope. 1997. "Establishing a Feminist Culture: The Experience of Zimbabwe Women's Resource Centre and Network." *Gender and Development* 5 (1): 35–42.

Chinchilla, Norma Stolz. 1990. "Revolutionary Popular Feminism in Nicaragua." *Gender and Society* 4: 370–97.

———. 1992. "Marxism, Feminism and the Struggle for Democracy in Latin America." In Arturo Escobar and Sonia E. Alvarez , eds., *The Making of Social Movements in Latin America: Identity, Strategy, and Democracy*, pp. 37–51. Boulder: Westview Press.

———. 1994. "Feminism, Revolution, and Democratic Transitions in Nicaragua." In Jane S. Jaquette, ed., *The Women's Movement in Latin America: Participation and Democracy*, pp. 177–97. Boulder: Westview Press.

Clark, Ann Marie, Elisabeth J. Friedman, and Kathryn Hochstetler. 1998. "The Sovereign Limits of Global Civil Society: A Comparison of NGO Participation in UN World Conferences on the Environment, Human Rights, and Women." *World Politics* 51 (October): 1–35.

Clawson, Dan. 2003. *The Next Upsurge: Labor and the New Social Movements*. Ithaca: ILR Press.

Clean Clothes Campaign. 1998. "Comments on SA 8000/Guidance." E-mailed report. Printout in author's files.

Close, David. 1999. *The Chamorro Years*. Boulder: Lynne Reinner Publishers.

Cohen, Jean. 1985. "Strategy or Identity: New Theoretical Paradigms and Contemporary Social Movements." *Social Research* 52 (4): 663–716.

Cohen, Jean L., and Andrew Arato. 1992. *Civil Society and Political Theory*. Cambridge, Mass.: MIT Press.

Colectiva de Mujeres Hondureñas. 1998. "Porque recorremos caminos similares, porque necesitamos lazos de solidaridad: Red Centroamericana de Mujeres en Solidaridad con las Trabajadoras de la Maquila." Choloma, Honduras: pamphlet.

Collins, Jane L. 2003. *Threads: Gender, Labor and Power in the Global Apparel Industry*. Chicago: University of Chicago Press.

Collins, Patricia Hill. 1990. *Black Feminist Thought*. London: HarperCollins Academic.

Comisión Nacional de la Zona Franca. 2002. Web site at www.czf.com.ni, accessed November 23, 2004.

Comité Nacional de Mujeres Sindicalistas de Nicaragua. 1996. "Diversas, pero unidas: en defensa de nuestros derechos." Managua: pamphlet.

Conroy, Michael. 1990. "The Political Economy of the 1990 Nicaraguan Elections." *International Journal of Political Economy* (fall): 5–33.

Cook, Rebecca J. 1994. *Human Rights of Women: National and International Perspectives.* Philadelphia: University of Pennsylvania Press.

Correa, Sonia, and Rosalind Petchesky. 1994. "Reproductive and Social Rights: A Feminist Perspective." In Gita Sen, Adrienne Germain, and Lincoln C. Cohen, eds., *Population Policies Reconsidered: Health, Empowerment, and Rights*, pp. 107–26. Cambridge, Mass: Harvard University Press.

Criquillon, Ana. 1995. "The Nicaraguan Women's Movement: Feminist Reflections from Within." In Minor Sinclair, ed., *The New Politics of Survival: Grassroots Movements in Central America*, pp. 209–37. New York: Monthly Review Press.

Dagnino, Evelina. 1998. "Culture, Citizenship, and Democracy: Changing Discourses and Practices of the Latin American Left." In Sonia E. Alvarez, Evelina Dagnino, Arturo Escobar, eds., *Culture of Politics, Politics of Cultures: Re-visioning Latin American Social Movements*, pp. 33–63. Boulder: Westview Press.

Della Porta, Donatella, Hanspeter Kriesi, and Dieter Rucht, eds. 1999. *Social Movements in a Globalizing World*. New York: Palgrave Macmillan.

Desai, Manisha. 2002. "Transnational Solidarity: Women's Agency, Structural Adjustment, and Globalization." In Nancy A. Naples and Manisha Desai, eds., *Women's Activism and Globalization: Linking Local Struggles and Transnational Politics*, pp. 15–33. New York: Routledge.

Dietz, Mary G. 1998. "Context Is All: Feminism and Theories of Citizenship." In Ann Phillips, ed., *Feminism and Politics*, pp. 378–400. New York: Oxford University Press.

Dijkstra, Geske. 1992. *Industrialization in Sandinista Nicaragua: Policy and Practice in a Mixed Economy*. Boulder: Westview Press.

Dirlik, Arif. 1994. *After Revolution: Waking to Global Capitalism*. Hanover, N.H.: University Press of New England.

——. 1997. "Critical Reflections on 'Chinese Capitalism' as Paradigm." *Identities* 3 (3): 303–30.

Dominguez, Edme R. 2002. "Continental Transnational Activism and Women Workers' Networks within NAFTA." *International Feminist Journal of Politics* 4 (2): 216–39.

Dore, Elizabeth, ed. 1997. *Gender Politics in Latin America: Debates in Theory and Practice*. New York: Monthly Review Press.

Drainville, Andre. 1998. "The Fetishism of Global Civil Society: Global Governance, Transnational Urbanism and Sustainable Capitalism in the World Economy." In

Michael Peter Smith and Luis Eduardo Guarnizo, eds., *Transnationalism from Below*, pp. 35–63. New Brunswick, N.J.: Transaction Publishers.

Economist Intelligence Unit. 1989. *Country Profile, 1989–90: Nicaragua*. London: Economist Intelligence Unit.

——. 1997. *Country Profile: Nicaragua, Honduras, 1997–8*. New York: Economist Intelligence Unit, Ltd.

Edelman, Marc. 2001. "Social Movements: Changing Paradigms and Forms of Politics." *Annual Review of Anthropology* 30: 285–317.

Edwards, Michael, and David Hulme, eds. 1996. *Beyond the Magic Bullet: NGO Performance and Accountability in the Post–Cold War World*. West Hartford, Conn.: Kumarian Press.

Eisenstein, Zillah. 1989. *The Female Body and the Law*. Berkeley: University of California Press.

——. 1993. *The Color of Gender: Reimaging Democracy*. Berkeley: University of California Press.

Elson, Diane, and Ruth Pearson. 1981. " 'Nimble Fingers Make Cheap Workers': An Analysis of Women's Employment in Third World Export Manufacturing." *Feminist Review* 7: 87–107.

England, Sarah. 1999. "Negotiating Race and Place in the Garifuna Diaspora: Identity Formation and Transnational Grassroots Politics in New York City and Honduras." *Identities* 6 (1): 5–53.

Enloe, Cynthia. 1989. *Bananas, Beaches, and Bases: Making Feminist Sense of International Politics*. Berkeley: University of California Press.

Eschle, Catherine. 2001. *Global Democracy, Social Movements, and Feminism*. Boulder: Westview Press.

Escobar, Arturo, and Sonia E. Alvarez, eds. 1992. *The Making of Social Movements in Latin America: Identity, Strategy, and Democracy*. Boulder: Westview Press.

Evans, Trevor. 1995. "Ajuste estructural y sector público en Nicaragua." In Trevor Evans, ed., *La transformación neoliberal del sector público: Ajuste estructural y sector público en Centroamérica y el Caribe*, pp. 179–261. Managua: CRIES [Coordinadora Regional de Investigaciones Económicas y Sociales].

Ewig, Christina. 1999. "The Strengths and Limits of the NGO Women's Movement Model: Shaping Nicaragua's Democratic Institutions." *Latin American Research Review* 34: 75–102.

Feijoó, Maria del Carmen, and Monica Gogna. 1994. "Women in the Transition to Democracy." In Elizabeth Jelin, ed., *Women and Social Change in Latin America*, pp. 79–114. Atlantic Highlands, N.J.: Zed Books, Ltd.

Feijoó, María del Carmen with Marecela María Alejandra Nari. 1994. "Women and Democracy in Argentina." In Jane S. Jaquette, ed., *The Women's Movement in Latin America: Participation and Democracy*, pp. 109–29. Boulder: Westview Press.

Ferguson, Ann. 1996. "Bridge Identity Politics: An Integrative Feminist Ethics of International Development." *Organization* 3 (4): 571–87.

———. 1998. "Resisting the Veil of Privilege: Building Bridge Identities as an Ethico-Politics of Global Feminisms." *Hypatia* 13 (3): 95–113.

Fernández-Kelly, María Patricia. 1983. "Mexican Border Industrialization, Female Labor Force Participation and Migration." In June Nash and María Patricia Fernández-Kelly, eds., *Women, Men and the International Division of Labor*, pp. 205–23. Albany: SUNY Press.

Fisher, Julie. 1993. *The Road from Rio: Sustainable Development and the Nongovernmental Movement in the Third World*. Westport, Conn.: Praeger.

Fisher, William. 1997. "Doing Good?: The Politics and Antipolitics of NGO Practices." *Annual Review of Anthropology* 26: 439–64.

Flora, Cornelia Butler. 1998. "Beyond Exploitation and Integration: New Scholarship on Women in Latin America." *Latin American Research Review* 33 (2): 245–52.

Fonseca Tincoco, Alí Ernesto. 1997. "La globalización: ¿De ángeles o demonios?" *Barricada Internacional* 17 (409): 22–25.

Foucault, Michel. 1980. *Power/Knowledge: Selected Interviews and Other Writings*. New York: Pantheon.

Freeman, Carla. 2000. *High Tech and High Heels in the Global Economy: Women, Work and Pink-Collar Identities in the Caribbean*. Durham: Duke University Press.

———. 2001. "Is Local : Global as Feminine : Masculine? Rethinking the Gender of Globalization." *Signs* 26 (4):1007–37.

Freeman, Carla, and Donna F. Murdock. 2001. "Enduring Traditions and New Directions in Feminist Ethnography in the Caribbean and Latin America." *Feminist Studies* 27 (2): 423–58.

Fröbel, Falker, Jurgen Heinriches, and Otto Kreye. 1980. *The New International Division of Labor: Structural Unemployment in Industrialized Countries and Industrialization in Developing Countries*. Cambridge: Cambridge University Press.

Frundt, Henry J. 2002. "Central American Unions in the Era of Globalization." *Latin American Research Review* 37 (3): 7–53.

Gabriel, Christina, and Laura MacDonald. 1994. "NAFTA, Women and Organising in Canada and Mexico: Forging a 'Feminist Internationality.' " *Millennium Journal of International Studies* 23 (3): 535–62.

Gille, Zsuzsa, and Sean Ó Riain. 2002. "Global Ethnography." *Annual Review of Sociology* 28: 271–95.

Glick Schiller, Nina. 1999. "Transmigrants and Nation-States: Something Old and Something New in the U.S. Immigrant Experience." In Charles Hirschman, Philip Kasinitz, and Josh Dewind, eds., *The Handbook of International Migration: The American Experience*, pp. 94–119. New York: Russell Sage Foundation.

Glick Schiller, Nina, Linda Basch, and Cristina Szanton Blanc. 1995. "From Immigrant to Transmigrant: Theorizing Transnational Migration." *Anthropological Quarterly* 68 (1): 48–63.

Gonzalez, David. 2000. "Nicaragua's Trade Zone: Battleground for Unions." *New York Times*, September 16, p. 3A.

Gonzalez, Mike, ed. 1990. *Nicaragua: What Went Wrong?* Chicago: Bookmarks Publishing Cooperative.

González, Victoria, and Karen Kampwirth. 2001a. Introduction. In Victoria González and Karen Kampwirth, eds., *Radical Women in Latin America: Left and Right*, pp. 1–28. University Park: Pennsylvania State University Press.

——, eds. 2001b. *Radical Women in Latin America: Left and Right*. University Park: Pennsylvania State University Press.

Gordon, Edmund T. 1998. "Cultural Politics of Black Masculinity." *Transforming Anthropology* 6 (1–2): 6–53.

Gorostiaga, Xabier. 1997. "La urgencia de un contrato social." *Envío* 182: 28–32.

Gould, Jeffrey. 1998. *To Die in This Way: Nicaraguan Indians and the Myth of Mestizaje 1880–1965*. Durham, N.C.: Duke University Press.

Grewal, Inderpal, and Caren Kaplan. 1994. "Introduction: Transnational Feminist Practices and Questions of Postmodernity." In Inderpal Grewal and Caren Kaplan, eds., *Scattered Hegemonies: Postmodernity and Transnational Feminist Practices*, pp. 1–33. Minneapolis: University of Minnesota Press.

Guarnizo, Luis E. 1994. "Los Dominicanyorks: The Making of a Binational Society." *Annals of the American Academy of Political and Social Science* 533: 70–86.

Guarnizo, Luis Eduardo, and Michael Peter Smith. 1998. "The Locations of Transnationalism." In Michael Peter Smith and Luis Eduardo Guarnizo, eds., *Transnationalism from Below*, pp. 3–34. New Brunswick, N.J.: Transaction Publishers.

Guattari, Félix. 1984. "Millions and Millions of Potential Alices." In Félix Guattari, ed., *Molecular Revolution*, pp. 236–41. London: Penguin.

Guidry, John A., Michael D. Kennedy, and Mayer N. Zald. 2000. "Globalizations and Social Movements." In John A. Guidry, Michael D. Kennedy, and Mayer N. Zald, eds., *Globalizations and Social Movements: Culture, Power, and the Transnational Public Sphere*, pp. 1–32. Ann Arbor: University of Michigan Press.

Hale, Charles. 1994. "Between Che Guevara and the Pachamama: Mestizos, Indians and Identity Politics in the Anti-Quincentenary Campaign." *Critique of Anthropology* 14: 9–39.

——. 1997. "Cultural Politics of Identity in Latin America." *Annual Review of Anthropology* 26: 567–90.

Hamilton, Cynthia. 1989. "Women in Politics: Methods of Resistance and Change." *Women's Studies International Forum* 12 (1): 129–35.

Hannerz, Ulf. 1996. *Transnational Connections: Culture, People, Places*. New York: Routledge.

Haraway, Donna. 1988. "Situated Knowledges: The Science Question in Feminism and the Privilege of Partial Perspective." *Feminist Studies* 14 (3): 575–99.

Hardy-Fanta, Carol. 1993. *Latino Politics, Latina Politics*. Philadelphia: Temple University Press.

Harris, Richard, and Carlos M. Vilas. 1995. "Introducción: La transformación revolucionaria de Nicaragua." In Richard Harris and Carlos M. Vilas, eds., *La Revolución en Nicaragua: Liberación nacional, democracia popular y transformación económica*, pp. 9–16. Mexico City: Ediciones Era.

Hellman, Judith Adler. 1992. "The Study of New Social Movements in Latin America and the Question of Autonomy." In Arturo Escobar and Sonia E. Alvarez, eds., *The Making of Social Movements in Latin America: Identity, Strategy, and Democracy*, pp. 52–61. Boulder: Westview Press.

Hondagneu-Sotelo, Pierrette. 2001. *Doméstica: Immigrant Workers Cleaning and Caring in the Shadow of Affluence*. Berkeley: University of California Press.

hooks, bell. 1990. *Yearning: Race, Gender and Cultural Politics*. Boston: South End Press.

Hossfeld, Karen J. 1990. " 'Their Logic Against Them': Contradictions in Sex, Race and Class in Silicon Valley." In Kathryn Ward, ed., *Women Workers and Global Restructuring*, pp. 149–78. Ithaca: Cornell University Press.

Instituto Nicaragüense de la Mujer (INIM). 1996a. "Documento de Acuerdo entre el INIM y el Movimiento de Mujeres." Managua, Nicaragua: Instituto Nicaragüense de la Mujer.

——. 1996b. "Informe: Encuentro con las organizaciones no gubernamentales dentro del proceso de desarrollo institucional del INIM." Managua: Instituto Nicaragüense de la Mujer, October 10.

International Labor Organization (ILO). 1996. *La situación sociolaboral en las Zonas Francas y maquiladoras de Centroamérica y República Dominicana*. San José, Costa Rica: Organización Internacional de Trabajo.

——. 2003a. "ILO Database on Export Processing Zones. Geneva: International Labor Organization." Web site at www.ilo.org accessed March 15, 2004. Printed copy in author's files.

——. 2003b. "Employment and Social Policy in Respect of Export Processing Zones." Report of ILO Governing Body. Geneva: International Labor Organization. March.

——. 2004. "More Women Are Entering the Global Labour Force Than Ever Before, but Job Equality, Poverty Reduction Remain Elusive." Press release, March 5.

Isbester, Katherine. 2001. *Still Fighting: The Nicaraguan Women's Movement, 1977–2000*. Pittsburgh: University of Pittsburgh Press.

Jackson, Cecile, and Ruth Pearson, eds. 1998. *Feminist Visions of Development*. New York: Routledge.

Jaquette, Jane S. 1994a. "Introduction: From Transition to Participation—Women's Movements and Democratic Politics." In Jane S. Jaquette, ed., *The Women's Movement in Latin America: Participation and Democracy*, pp. 1–11. Boulder: Westview Press.

——, ed. 1994b. *The Women's Movement in Latin America: Participation and Democracy*. Boulder: Westview Press.

——2001. "Regional Differences and Contrasting Views: Women and Democracy." *Journal of Democracy* 12 (3): 111–25.

Jelin, Elizabeth. 1994a. "Citizenship and Identity: Final Reflections." In Elizabeth Jelin, ed., *Women and Social Change in Latin America*, pp. 184–207. Atlantic Highlands, N.J.: Zed Books, Ltd.

——. 1994b. Introduction. In Elizabeth Jelin, ed., *Women and Social Change in Latin America*, pp. 1–11. Atlantic Highlands, N.J.: Zed Books, Ltd.

——. 1996a. "Citizenship Revisited: Solidarity, Responsibility, and Rights." In Elizabeth Jelin and Eric Herschberg, eds., *Constructing Democracy: Human Rights, Citizenship, and Society in Latin America*, pp. 101–19. Boulder: Westview Press.

——. 1996b. "Women, Gender and Human Rights." In Elizabeth Jelin and Eric Hershberg, eds., *Constructing Democracy: Human Rights, Citizenship, and Society in Latin America*, pp. 177–96. Boulder: Westview Press.

——. 1997. "Engendering Human Rights." In Elizabeth Dore, ed., *Gender Politics in Latin America: Debates in Theory and Practice*, pp. 65–83. New York: Monthly Review Press.

——. 1998. "Towards a Culture of Participation and Citizenship: Challenges for a More Equitable World." In Sonia E. Alvarez, Evelina Dagnino, and Arturo Escobar, eds., *Culture of Politics, Politics of Cultures: Re-visioning Latin American Social Movements*, pp. 405–21. Boulder: Westview Press.

Jelin, Elizabeth, ed. 1994c. *Women and Social Change in Latin America*. Atlantic Highlands, N.J.: Zed Books, Ltd.

Jelin, Elizabeth, and Eric Hershberg, eds. 1996. *Constructing Democracy: Human Rights, Citizenship, and Society in Latin America*. Boulder: Westview Press.

Johnston, Hank, and Bert Klandermans. 1995. *Culture and Social Movements*. Minneapolis: University of Minnesota Press.

Joseph, Suad. 1997. "The Public/Private—The Imagined Boundary in the Imagined Nation/State/Community." *Feminist Review* (57): 73–92.

Jubb, Nadine. 1995. "Women Organizing for Change in Nicaragua: Setting the Agenda for Social Transformation." *Latin American Working Group Letter Series* 47: 1–42.

Kabeer, Nalia. 1992. *Triple Roles, Gender Roles, Social Relations: The Political Subtext of Gender Training.* IDS Discussion Paper 313, Brighton, U.K.

——. 2004. "Labor Standards, Women's Rights, Basic Needs: Challenges to Collective

Action in a Globalizing World." In Lourdes Benería and Savitri Bisnath, eds. *Global Tensions: Challenges and Opportunities in the World Economy*, pp. 173–92. New York: Routledge.

Kampwirth, Karen. 2000. "Incest Strikes the Revolutionary Family: A Generation of Political Change in Nicaragua." Paper presented at the Latin American Studies Association International Congress. March. Miami.

——. 2002. *Women and Guerrilla Movements: Nicaragua, El Salvador, Chiapas, Cuba.* Pittsburgh: University of Pittsburgh Press.

——. 2003. "Antifeminism in Contemporary Nicaragua." Paper presented at the Latin American Studies Association International Congress. March. Dallas.

Kearney, Michael. 1995. "The Local and the Global: The Anthropology of Globalization and Transnationalism." *Annual Review of Anthropology* 24: 547–65.

Keck, Margaret, and Kathryn Sikkink. 1998a. *Activists Beyond Borders: Transnational Advocacy Networks in International Politics.* Ithaca: Cornell University Press.

——. 1998b. "Transnational Advocacy Networks in the Global Society." In David S. Meyer and Sidney Tarrow, eds., *The Social Movement Society*, pp. 217–38. Lanham, Md.: Rowman and Littlefield.

——. 2000. "Historical Precursors to Modern Transnational Social Movements and Networks." In John A. Guidry, Michael D. Kennedy, and Mayer N. Zald, eds., *Globalizations and Social Movements: Culture, Power, and the Transnational Public Sphere*, pp. 35–53. Ann Arbor: University of Michigan Press.

Kim, Seung-kyung. 1992. "Women Workers and the Labor Movement in South Korea." In Frances Abrahamer Rothstein and Michael L. Blim, eds., *Anthropology and the Global Factory*, pp. 220–37. New York: Bergin and Garvey.

King, Deborah. 1988. "Multiple Jeopardy, Multiple Consciousness: The Context of a Black Feminist Ideology." *Signs* 14 (1): 46–73.

Kondo, Dorinne. 1990. *Crafting Selves: Power, Gender and Discourses of Identity in a Japanese Workplace.* Chicago: University of Chicago Press.

Köpke, Ronald. 2000. "Las experiencias del equipo de monitoreo independiente de Honduras." In Ronald Köpke, Norma Molina, and Carolina Quinteros, eds., *Códigos de Conducta y Monitoreo en la Industria de Confección: Experiencias Internacionales y Regionales*, pp. 100–119. San Salvador, El Salvador: Fundación Böll.

——. 2002. "Informe de la evaluación del impacto del trabajo del Movimiento María Elena Cuadra (MEC) en las zonas francas de Nicaragua." Computer printout.

Labor Rights in China. 2000. "Derechos laborales en China: No nos hagamos ilusiones. Contra el cosmético global del SA 8000." In Ronald Köpke, Norma Molina, and Carolina Quinteros, eds., *Códigos de Conducta y Monitoreo en la Industria de Confección: Experiencias Internacionales y Regionales*, pp. 60–81. San Salvador, El Salvador: Fundación Böll.

252 Bibliography

Laclau, Ernesto, and Chantal Mouffe. 1985. *Hegemony and Socialist Strategy: Towards a Radical Democratic Politics*. London: Verso.

Lancaster, Roger N. 1992. *Life Is Hard: Machismo, Danger, and the Intimacy of Power in Nicaragua*. Berkeley: University of California Press.

Lebon, Nathalie. 1996. "Professionalization of Women's Health Groups in Sao Paolo: The Troublesome Road towards Organizational Diversity." *Organization* 3 (4): 588–609.

Lee, Ching Kwan. 1998. *Gender and the South China Miracle: Two Worlds of Factory Women*. Berkeley: University of California Press.

Lind, Amy. 2000. "Negotiating Boundaries: Women's Organizations and the Politics of Restructuring in Ecuador." In Marianne H. Marchand and Anne Sisson Runyan, eds., *Gender and Global Restructuring: Sightings, Sites and Resistances*, pp. 161–75. New York: Routledge.

——. 2002. "Making Feminist Sense of Neoliberalism: The Institutionalization of Women's Struggles for Survival in Ecuador and Bolivia." *Journal of Developing Societies* 18 (2–3): 228–58.

Lipschutz, Ronnie D. 1992. "Reconstructing World Politics: The Emergence of Global Civil Society." *Millennium* 21 (3): 389–420.

Lorde, Audre. 1984. *Sister Outsider: Essays and Speeches by Audre Lorde*. Freedom, Calif.: The Crossing Press.

Lowe, Lisa. 1996. *Immigrant Acts: On Asian American Cultural Politics*. Durham: Duke University Press.

Lowe, Lisa, and David Lloyd. 1997a. "Introduction." In Lisa Lowe and David Lloyd, eds., *The Politics of Culture in the Shadow of Capital*, pp. 1–32. Durham: Duke University Press.

——, eds. 1997b. *The Politics of Culture in the Shadow of Capital*. Durham: Duke University Press.

Luciak, Ilja A. 1995. *The Sandinista Legacy: Lessons for a Political Economy in Transition*. Gainesville: University Press of Florida.

MacDonald, Laura. 1997. *Supporting Civil Society: the Political Impact of NGO Assistance to Central America*. New York: Macmillan Press and St. Martin's Press.

——. 2002. "Globalization and Social Movements: Comparing Women's Movements; Responses to NAFTA in Mexico, the USA and Canada." *International Feminist Journal of Politics* 4 (2): 151–72.

MacEoin, Gary. 1999. "Maquila Neoslavery, Under Conditions from Bad to Inhuman." *National Catholic Reporter*, August 13, p. 12.

Mahler, Sarah J. 1998. "Theoretical and Empirical Contributions Toward a Research Agenda for Transnationalism." In Michael Peter Smith and Luis Eduardo Guarnizo, eds., *Transnationalism from Below*, pp. 64–100. New Brunswick, N.J.: Transactions Publishers.

——. 1999. "Engendering Transnational Migration: A Case Study of Salvadorans." *American Behavioral Scientist* 42 (4): 690–719.

Mansbridge, Jane. 1995. "What Is the Feminist Movement?" In Myrna Marx Ferree and Patricia Yancy Martin , eds., *Feminist Organizations: Harvest of the New Women's Movement*, pp. 27–34. Philadelphia: Temple University Press.

Mansbridge, Jane, and Aldon Morris, eds. 2001. *Oppositional Consciousness: The Subjective Roots of Social Protest*. Chicago: University of Chicago Press.

Marchand, Marianne H., and Anne Sisson Runyan. 2000a. "Introduction: Feminist Sightings of Global Restructuring: Conceptualizations and Reconceptualizations." In Marianne H. Marchand and Anne Sisson Runyan, eds., *Gender and Global Restructuring: Sightings, Sites and Resistances*, pp. 1–25. New York: Routledge.

——, eds. 2000b. *Gender and Global Restructuring: Sightings, Sites and Resistances*. New York: Routledge.

Marcus, George E. 1995. "Ethnography in / of the World System: The Emergence of Multi-Sited Ethnography." *Annual Review of Anthropology* 24: 95–117.

Marsh, Katherine. 2000. "Spring Break in Managua." *Rolling Stone*, October 26, pp. 85–88.

Mato, Daniel. 1998. "On Global and Local Agents and the Social Making of Transnational Identities and Related Agendas in 'Latin' America." *Identities* 4 (2): 167–212.

McAdam, Doug, John D. McCarthy, and Mayer N. Zald, eds. 1996. *Comparative Perspectives on Social Movements: Political Opportunities, Mobilizing Structures and Cultural Framings*. Cambridge: Cambridge University Press.

McAdam, Doug, Sidney Tarrow, and Charles Tilly. 2001. *Dynamics of Contention*. New York: Cambridge University Press.

McCarthy, John D. 1997. "The Globalization of Social Movement Theory." In Jackie Smith, Charles Chatfield, and Ron Pagnucco, eds., *Transnational Social Movements and Global Politics: Solidarity Beyond the State*, pp. 243–59. Syracuse, N.Y.: Syracuse University Press.

McRobbie, Angela. 1985. "Strategies of Vigilance: An Interview with Gayatri Chakravorty Spivak." *Block* 10: 5–9.

MEC, *see* Movimiento de Mujeres Trabajadoras y Desempleadas, "Maria Elena Cuadra" (MEC).

Meiselas, Susan. 1981. *Nicaragua: June 1978–July 1979*. New York: Pantheon Books.

Melucci, Alberto. 1985. "The Symbolic Challenge of Contemporary Social Movements." *Social Research* 52 (4): 789–816.

——. 1995. "The Global Planet and the Internal Planet: New Frontiers." In Marcy Darnovsky, Barbara Epstein, and Richard Flacks, eds., *Cultural Politics and Social Movements*, pp. 287–98. Philadelphia: Temple University Press.

———. 1996. *Challenging Codes: Collective Action the Information Age*. New York: Cambridge University Press.

Mendez, Jennifer Bickham. 2002a. "Creating Alternatives from a Gender Perspective: Central American Women's Transnational Organizing for Maquila Workers' Rights." In Nancy A. Naples and Manisha Desai, eds., *Women's Activism and Globalization: Linking Local Struggles and Transnational Politic*, pp 121–41. New York: Routledge.

———. 2002b. "Organizing a Space of their Own?: Global/Local Processes in a Nicaraguan Women's Organization." *Journal of Developing Societies* 18 (2–3): 196–227.

Mendez, Jennifer Bickham, and Ronald Köpke. 1998. *Mujeres y Maquila*. San Salvador, El Salvador: Fundación Böll.

———. 2001. *Mujeres y Maquila*. 2nd ed. San Salvador, El Salvador: Fundación Böll.

———. 2002. "Gender and Citizenship in a Global Context: The Struggle for Maquila Workers' Rights in Nicaragua." *Identities: Journal of Culture and Power* 9: 7–38.

Mendez, Jennifer Bickham, and Diane L. Wolf. 2001. "Where Feminist Theory Meets Feminist Practice: Outcomes and Processes in a Transnational Feminist Organization in Academia." *Organization: Interdisciplinary Journal of Organization, Theory and Society* 8 (4): 723–50.

Mertus, Julie. 1995. "State Discriminatory Family Law and Customary Abuses." In Julie Peters and Andrea Wolper, eds., *Women's Rights, Human Rights: International Feminist Perspectives*, pp. 135–48. New York: Routledge.

Metoyer, Cynthia Chavez. 2000. *Women and the State in Post-Sandinista Nicaragua*. Boulder: Lynne Rienner Publishers.

Meyer, Mark K., and Elisabeth Prügl, eds. 1999. *Gender Politics in Global Governance*. Lanham, Md.: Rowman and Littlefield.

Meza, Humberto. 1997. "Trabajadores apoyan Zona Franca Industrial." *La Tribuna* [Managua], November 25.

Mies, Maria. 1998. *Patriarchy and Accumulation on a World Scale: Women in the International Division of Labour*. 2d. ed. London: Zed Books, Ltd.

Miller, Francesca. 1991. *Latin American Women and the Search for Social Justice*. Hanover, N.H.: University Press of New England.

Mills, Mary Beth. 1999. *Thai Women in the Global Labor Force: Consuming Desires, Contested Selves*. New Brunswick, N.J.: Rutgers University Press.

Mindry, Deborah. 2001. "Nongovernmental Organizations, 'Grassroots,' and the Politics of Virtue." *Signs* 26: 1187–1211.

Ministerio de Trabajo. 1998. *Resolución Ministerial*. Managua: Ministerio de Trabajo.

Mohanty, Chandra Talpade. 1991. "Under Western Eyes: Feminist Scholarship and Colonial Discourses." In Chandra Talpade Mohanty, Ann Russo, and Lourdes Torres, eds., *Under Western Eyes: Feminist Scholarship and Colonial Discourses*, pp. 51–80. Bloomington: Indiana University Press.

Molina, Norma, and Aída Carolina Quinteros. 2000. "El monitoreo independiente en El Salvador." In Ronald Köpke, Norma Molina, and Carolina Quinteros, eds., *Códigos de conducta y monitoreo en la industria de confección: Experiencias internacionales y regionales*, pp. 82–99. San Salvador, El Salvador: Fundación Böll.

Molyneux, Maxine. 1985. "Mobilization Without Emancipation?: Women's Interests, State, and Revolution." *Feminist Studies* 11 (summer): 227–54.

——. 1998. "Analysing Women's Movements." In Cecile Jackson and Ruth Pearson, eds., *Feminist Visions of Development*, pp. 65–88. New York: Routledge.

Montoya, Ariel. 1998. "'FSLN nunca ha sido cívico,' afirma Bolaños." *La Prensa*, March 8, p. 4A.

Morley, David, and Kevin Robins. 1995. *Spaces of Identity: Global Media, Electronic Landscapes and Cultural Boundaries*. London: Routledge.

Morris, Aldon D., and Carol McClurg Mueller, eds. 1992. *New Frontiers in Social Movement Theory*. New Haven: Yale University Press.

Mouffe, Chantal. 1995. "Post-Marxism: Democracy and Identity." *Environment and Planning D: Society and Space* 13: 259–65.

Movimiento de Mujeres Trabajadoras y Desempleadas, "Maria Elena Cuadra" (MEC). 1995. Meeting report. Computer printout. Managua.

——.1996. *Zona Franca: Rostros de Mujer*. Managua: Movimiento de Mujeres Trabajadoras y Desempleadas, "María Elena Cuadra."

——. 1997a. "Campaña de Sensibilización." Computer printout.

——. 1997b. "Género, Discriminación y Derechos Humanos: Este es un Programa de Educación en Derechos de las Humanas." Managua: Movimiento de Mujeres Trabajadoras y Desempleadas, "María Elena Cuadra."

——. 1997c. "Género y Discriminación en la Zona Franca." Managua: Movimiento de Mujeres Trabajadoras y Desempleadas, "María Elena Cuadra."

——. 1998a. "Boletina del Movimiento de Mujeres Trabajadoras y Desempleadas, 'María Elena Cuadra.'" Managua: Movimiento de Mujeres Trabajadoras y Desempleadas, "María Elena Cuadra."

——. 1998b. *Manual de bolsillo de derechos laborales*. Managua: Movimiento de Mujeres Trabajadoras y Desempleadas, "María Elena Cuadra".

——. 1998c. MEC's Web page, http://apc.nicarao.org.ni/7Efamilias, accessed August 28.

——. 1999. "Diagnóstico sobre las condiciones socio laborales de las empresas de las Zonas Francas." Managua: Movimiento de Mujeres Trabajadoras y Desempleadas, "María Elena Cuadra."

Murguialday, Clara. 1990. *Nicaragua, Revolución y Feminismo, 1977–1989*. Madrid: Editorial Revolución.

Naples, Nancy A., and Manisha Desai, eds. 2002. *Women's Activism and Globalization: Linking Local Struggles and Transnational Politics*. New York: Routledge.

Nash, June. 1985. "Segmentation of the Work Process in the International Division of

Labor." In Steven E. Sanderson, ed., *The Americas in the New International Division of Labor*, pp. 253–72. New York: Holmes and Meier.

———. 1988. "Cultural Parameters of Sexism and Racism in the International Division of Labor." In Joan Smith, Jane Collins, Terrence Hopkins, and Akbar Muhammad, eds., *Racism, Sexism and the World System*, pp. 11–36. Westport, Conn.: Greenwood.

National Labor Committee (NLC). 1997. Website at http://www.nlc.org, accessed November 17, 1997.

National Public Radio (NPR). 2000. "Unions in Nicaragua." *All Things Considered*. August 18.

Navarro, Marysa. 1982. "First Feminist Meeting of Latin America and the Caribbean." *Signs* 8 (1): 154–57.

Neira, Oscar. 1997. "Política pro-agrícola: ¿Será posible?" *Envío* 182: 13–18.

Nelson, Paul J. 1997. "Conflict, Legitimacy, and Effectiveness: Who Speaks for Whom in Transnational NGO Networks Lobbying the World Bank?" *Nonprofit and Voluntary Sector Quarterly* 26 (4): 421–41.

New York Times. 1998a. "Officials Predict Hurricane's Toll Will Exceed 7,000." November 2, p. 1A.

———. 1998b. "Relief Efforts Reaching Rural Areas In Nicaragua." November 7, p. 3A.

Nicaragua Network. 2000. "Labor Crisis in Free Trade Zone Continues." Web site at www.infoshop.org/nicanet, accessed May 9, 2003. Printout in author's possession.

Nitlapán-Envío Team. 1997. "La crisis de los tranques." *Envío* 16 (182): 3–7.

El Nuevo Diario. 1993. "Trabajadores de Fortex denuncian." September 12, p. 7.

———. 1994. "Secretaría de la Mujer entregada en ruinas." June 4, p. 2.

Nuñez Soto, Orlando. 1986. "Ideology and Revolutionary Politics in Transitional Societies." In Richard R. Fagen, Carmen Diana Deere, and José Luis Coraggio, eds., *Transition and Development: Problems of Third World Socialism*, pp. 249–63. New York: Monthly Review Press.

O'Brien, Robert, Anne Marie Goetz, Jan Aart Scholte, and Marc Williams, eds. 2000. *Contesting Global Governance: Multilateral Economic Institutions and Global Social Movements*. Cambridge: Cambridge University Press.

El Observador Ecónomico. 2001–2. "Zonas francas industriales en Nicaragua: ¿Héroes o villanos?"119 (December-January).

O'Kane, Trish. 1995. "New Autonomy, New Struggle: Labor Unions in Nicaragua." In Minor Sinclair, ed., *The New Politics of Survival: Grassroots Movements in Central America*, pp. 183–207. New York: Monthly Review Press.

Ong, Aihwa. 1987. *Spirits of Resistance and Capital Discipline: Factory Women in Malaysia*. Albany: SUNY Press.

———. 1988. "Colonialism and Modernity: Feminist Re-Presentations of Women in Non-Western Societies." *Inscriptions* 3 (4): 79–93.

———. 1997. "The Gender and Labor Politics of Post-modernity." In Lisa Lowe and David Lloyd, eds. *The Politics of Culture in the Shadow of Capital*, pp. 61–97. Durham: Duke University Press.

Palmeri, Christopher. 1997. "Believe in Yourself, Believe in the Merchandise." *Forbes* 160 (5): 118–24.

Parreñas, Rhacel Salazar. 2001. *Servants of Globalization: Women, Migration, and Domestic Work*. Stanford, Calif.: Stanford University Press.

Pateman, Carole. 1988. *The Sexual Contract*. Cambridge: Polity.

Peña, Devon G. 1997. *The Terror of the Machine: Technology, Work, Gender, and Ecology on the U.S.-Mexico Border*. Austin: Center for Mexican American Studies, University of Texas, Austin.

Pérez Alemán, Paola. 1992. "Economic Crisis and Women in Nicaragua." In Lourdes Benería and Shelley Feldman, eds. *Unequal Burden: Economic Crisis, Persistent Poverty, and Women's Work*, pp. 239–58. Boulder: Westview Press.

Pérez Alemán, Paola, Diana Martínez, and Christa Windmaier. 1987. *Fuerza laboral feminina en la rama textil-vestuario: Segregación, salarios y rotación*. Managua: Oficina de la Mujer, Ministerio de la Presidencia.

Pérez-Stable, M. 1982. "The Working Class in the Nicaraguan Revolution." In Thomas Walker, ed., *Nicaragua in Revolution*, pp. 133–45. New York: Praeger.

Peters, Julie, and Andrea Wolper, eds. 1995. *Women's Rights, Human Rights: International Feministl Perspectives*. New York: Routledge.

Peterson, V. Spike, and Anne Sisson Runyan. 1999. *Global Gender Issues*. Boulder: Westview Press.

Petras, James. 1997. "Imperialism and NGOs in Latin America." *Monthly Review* 49 (7): 10–27.

Polakoff, Erica, and Pierre La Ramée. 1997. "Grass-Roots Organizations." In Thomas W. Walker, ed., *Nicaragua without Illusions: Regime Transition and Structural Adjustment in the 1990s*, pp. 185–201. Wilmington, Del.: Scholarly Resources Books.

Portes, Alejandro, Luis E. Guarnizo, L. Edwards, and P. Landolt. 1999. "Introduction: Pitfalls and Promise of an Emergent Research Field." *Ethnic Racial Studies* 22: 217–37.

La Prensa. 1996. "Arnoldo Presidente." October 22.

———. 2001. "Proponen reformas a Código Laboral." July 11.

———. 2002. "Vicepresidenta de Taiwan visita Zona Franca." January 12.

———. 2003. "Sobrevivientes del Casita construyendo vida y esperanza en El Tanque." October 28.

Prevost, Gary. 1997. "The Status of the Sandinista Revolutionary Project." In Gary Prevost and Harry E. Vanden, eds., *The Undermining of the Sandinista Revolution*, pp. 9–44. New York: St. Martin's Press.

Princen, Thomas, and Matthias Finger, eds. 1994. *Environmental NGOS in World Politics: Linking the Local and the Global*. New York: Routledge.

Quandt, Midge. 1993. "Nicaragua Unbinding the Ties: Popular Movements and the FSLN." *NACLA Report on the Americas* 26 (4): 11–14.

Radcliffe, Sarah A. 1993. "'People Have to Rise Up—Like the Great Women Fighters': The State and Peasant Women in Peru." In Sarah A. Radcliffe and Sallie Westwood, eds., *"Viva": Women and Popular Protest in Latin America*, pp. 147–218. London: Routledge.

Radcliffe, Sarah A., and Sallie Westwood, eds. 1993. *"Viva": Women and Popular Protest in Latin America*. London: Routledge.

Randall, Margaret. 1981. *Sandino's Daughters: Testimonies of Nicaraguan Women in Struggle*. New Brunswick, N.J.: Rutgers University Press.

——. 1992. *Gathering Rage: The Failure of Twentieth Century Revolutions to Develop a Feminist Agenda*. New York: Monthly Review Press.

——. 1994. *Sandino's Daughters Revisited: Feminism in Nicaragua*. New Brunswick, N.J.: Rutgers University Press.

Ray, Raka, and Anna C. Korteweg. 1999. "Women's Movements in the Third World: Identity, Mobilization, and Autonomy." *Annual Review of Sociology* 25: 47–71.

Red Centroamericana de Mujeres en Solidaridad con las Trabajadoras de la Maquila. 1997. "Acta de Conformacion de la Red." *Nuestra Ruta* 1: unpaginated.

Red de Mujeres contra la Violencia. 1995. "Algunas reflexiones . . ." Computer printout. Managua.

Renzi, María Rosa. 1996. "Las zonas francas en Nicaragua." *El Observador Económico* (52): 34–44.

Renzi, María Rosa, and Dirk Kruijt. 1997. *Los nuevos pobres: Gobernabilidad y política social en Nicaragua*. San José, Costa Rica: FLACSO [Facultad Latinoamericana de Ciencias Sociales].

Renzi, María Rosa, and Sonia Agurto. 1993. *¿Qué hace la mujer nicaragüense ante la crisis económica?* Managua: FIDEG.

——. 1996. *La mujer y los hogares urbanos nicaragüenses: Indicadores económicos y sociales*. Managua: FIDEG.

Rich, Adrienne. 1986. "Notes toward a Politics of Location." In Adrienne Rich, *Blood, Bread and Poetry: Selected Prose, 1979–1985*, pp. 210–31. New York: W. W. Norton.

Robinson, William I. 1997. "Maldesarrollo en América Central: Un estudio sobre globalización y cambio social." *Pensamiento Propio* (5): 33–65.

——. 2003. *Transnational Conflicts: Central America, Social Change and Globalization*. New York: Verso Press.

Romany, Celina. 1994. "State Responsibility Goes Private: A Feminist Critique of the Public/Private Distinction in International Human Rights Law." In Rebecca J.

Cook, ed., *Human Rights of Women: National and International Perspectives*,
pp. 85–115. Philadelphia: University of Pennsylvania Press.

Rosa, Kumudhini. 1994. "The Conditions and Organisational Activities of Women
in Free Trade Zones: Malaysia, Philippines and Sri Lanka, 1970–1990. In Sheila
Rowbotham and Swasti Mitter, eds., *Dignity and Daily Bread: New Forms of Economic Organizing Among Poor Women in the Third World and First*, pp. 73–99.
New York: Routledge.

Rosen, Ruth Israel. 2002. *Making Sweatshops: The Globalization of the U.S. Apparel
Industry*. Berkeley: University of California Press.

Ross, Andrew. 1997. Introduction. In Andrew Ross, ed., *No Sweat: Fashion, Free Trade
and the Rights of Garment Workers*, pp. 9–38. New York: Routledge.

Ross, Robert, and Charles Kernaghan. 2000. "Countdown in Managua." *The Nation*.
September 4, pp. 25–27.

Rouse, Roger. 1995. "Questions of Identity: Personhood and Collectivity in Transnational Migration to the United States." *Critique of Anthropology* 15 (4): 351–80.

Ruchwarger, Gary. 1987. *People in Power: Forging a Grassroots Democracy in Nicaragua*. South Hadley, Mass.: Bergin and Garvey.

Rushdie, Salman. 1987. *The Jaguar Smile: A Nicaraguan Journey*. London: Pan Books.

Saakes, Sylvia. 1991. "Particularidades del movimiento de mujeres en Nicaragua bajo
el gobierno Sandinista." In Ada Julia Brenes Peña, Ivania Lovo, Olga Lux Restrepo,
Sylvia Saakes, and Flor de María Zúñiga, eds. *La mujer nicaraguense en los años 80*,
pp. 169–88. Managua: Ediciones Nicarao.

Safa, Helen Icken. 1990a. "Women and Industrialization in the Caribbean." In Sharon
Stichter and Jean L. Parpart, eds., *Women, Employment, and the Family in the
International Division of Labor*, pp. 72–97. Philadelphia: Temple University Press.

———. 1990b. "Women's Social Movements in Latin America." *Gender and Society* 4
(3): 354–69.

———. 1994. *The Myth of the Male Breadwinner: Women and Industrialization in the
Caribbean*. Boulder: Westview Press.

———. 1995. "Economic Restructuring and Gender Subordination." *Latin American
Perspectives* 22 (2): 32–50.

———. 1996. "Beijing, Diversity and Globalization: Challenges to the Women's Movement in Latin America and the Caribbean." *Organization* 3 (4): 563–70.

Sagall, Sabby. 1995. "Report from Managua, August, 1989." In Mike Gonzalez, ed.,
Nicaragua: What Went Wrong?, pp. 119–29. Chicago: Bookmarks Publishing
Cooperative.

Sandoval, Chela. 1991. "U.S. Third World Feminism: The Theory and Method of
Oppositional Consciousness in the Postmodern World." *Genders* (10): 1–24.

———. 1995. "Feminist Forms of Agency and Oppositional Consciousness: U.S. Third
World Feminist Criticism." In Judith Kegan Gardiner, ed. *Provoking Agents: Gen-*

der and Agency in Theory and Practice, pp. 208–26. Chicago: University of Illinois Press.

Sassen, Saskia. 1991. The Global City: New York, London, Tokyo. Princeton: Princeton University Press.

Scheper-Hughes, Nancy. 1992. Death without Weeping: The Violence of Everyday Life in Brazil. Berkley: University of California Press.

Scherrer, Christoph, and Thomas Grevin, eds. 2001. Global Rules for Trade: Codes of Conduct, Social Labeling, Workers' Rights Clauses. Münster: Westfälisches Dampfboot.

Schild, Verónica. 1997. "New Subjects of Rights? Gendered Citizenship and the Contradictory Legacies of Social Movements in Latin America." Organization 4 (4): 604–19.

——. 1998. "New Subjects of Rights? Women's Movements and the Construction of Citizenship in the 'New Democracies.'" In Sonia E. Alvarez, Evelina Dagnino, and Arturo Escobar, eds., Culture of Politics, Politics of Cultures: Re-visioning Latin American Social Movements, pp. 93–117. Boulder: Westview Press.

Schirmer, Jennifer. 1993. "The Seeking of Truth and the Gendering of Consciousness: The CoMadres of El Salvador and the CONAVIGUA Widows of Guatemala." In Sarah A. Radcliffe and Sallie Westwood, eds., "Viva": Women and Popular Protest in Latin America, pp. 30–64. London: Routledge.

Scott, James. 1986. Weapons of the Weak. New Haven: Yale University Press.

Seidman, Gay. 1999. "Gendered Citizenship: South Africa's Democratic Transition and the Construction of a Gendered State." Gender and Society 13 (3): 287–307.

——. 2000. "Adjusting the Lens: What Do Globalizations, Transnationalism, and the Anti-apartheid Movement Mean for Social Movement Theory?" In John A. Guidry, Michael D. Kennedy, and Mayer N. Zald, eds., Globalizations and Social Movements: Culture, Power, and the Transnational Public Sphere, pp. 339–57. Ann Arbor: University of Michigan Press.

Seidman, Gay, and Robert Ross, eds. 2003. "Special Guest Edited Symposium: Would a Social Clause in Trade Treaties Help or Hinder?" PEWS News (fall): 1–10.

Sethi, Harsh. 1993. "Action Groups in the New Politics." In Ponna Wignaraja, ed., New Social Movements in the South: Empowering the People, pp. 230–55. Atlantic Highlands, N.J.: Zed Books, Ltd.

Sikkink, Kathryn. 1993. "Human Rights, Principled Issue-Networks, and Sovereignty in Latin America." International Organization 47 (3): 411–40.

——. 1996. "The Emergence, Evolution, and Effectiveness of the Latin American Human Rights Network." In Elizabeth Jelin and Eric Hershberg, eds., Constructing Democracy: Human Rights, Citizenship, and Society in Latin America, pp. 59–84. Boulder: Westview Press.

Slater, David, ed. 1985. *New Social Movements and the State in Latin America*. Amsterdam: CEDLA [Center for Latin American Research and Documentation].

Smith, Jackie. 1997. "Characteristics of the Modern Transnational Social Movement Sector." In Jackie Smith, Charles Chatfield, and Rong Pagnucco, eds., *Transnational Social Movements and Global Politics: Solidarity Beyond the State*, pp. 42–58. Syracuse, N.Y.: Syracuse University Press.

Smith, Jackie, Charles Chatfield, Rong Pagnucco, eds. 1997. *Transnational Social Movements and Global Politics: Solidarity Beyond the State*. Syracuse, N.Y.: Syracuse University Press.

Smith, Jackie, and Hank Johnston. 2002a. "Globalization and Resistance: An Introduction." In Jackie Smith and Hank Johnston, eds. *Globalization and Resistance: Transnational Dimensions of Social Movements*, pp. 1–10. New York: Rowman and Littlefield.

———, eds. 2002b. *Globalization and Resistance: Transnational Dimensions of Social Movements*. New York: Rowman and Littlefield.

Smith, Michael Peter. 1994. "Can You Imagine?: Transnational Migration and the Globalization of Grassroots Politics." *Social Text* 12 (39): 15–33.

Smith, Michael Peter, and Luis Eduardo Guarnizo, eds. 1998. *Transnationalism from Below*. New Brunswick, N.J.: Transaction Publishers.

Snow, David A., and Leon Anderson. 1993. *Down on Their Luck: A Study of Homeless Street People*. Berkeley: University of California Press.

Spalding, Rose J. 1987. *The Political Economy of Revolutionary Nicaragua*. Boulder: Westview Press.

Spivak, Gayatri C. 1988. "Subaltern Studies: Deconstructing Historiography." In Ranajit Guha and Gayatri C. Spivak, eds., *Selected Subaltern Studies*, pp. 3–44. New York: Oxford University Press.

Stacey, Judith. 1991. "Can There Be a Feminist Ethnography?" In Sherna Berger Gluck and Daphna Patai, eds., *Women's Words: The Feminist Practice of Oral History*, pp. 111–19. New York: Routledge, Chapman and Hall.

Staudt, Kathleen, ed. 1997. *Women, International Development, and Politics: The Bureaucratic Mire*. Philadelphia: Temple University Press.

Staudt, Kathleen, Shirin M. Rai, and Jane L. Parpart. 2001. "Protesting World Trade Rules: Can We Talk about Empowerment?" *Signs* 26 (4): 1251–63.

Stephen, Lynn. 1997. *Women and Social Movements in Latin America: Power from Below*. Austin: University of Texas Press.

Sternbach, Nancy Saporta, Marysa Navarro-Aranguren, Patricia Chuchryk, and Sonia E. Alvarez. 1992. "Feminisms in Latin America: From Bogotá to San Bernardo." In Arturo Escobar and Sonia E. Alvarez, eds., *The Making of Social Movements in Latin America: Identity, Strategy, and Democracy*, pp. 207–39. Boulder: Westview Press.

Stewart, Sheelagh, and Jill Taylor. 1997. "Women Organizing Women: 'Doing it Backwards and in High Heels.'" In Anne Marie Goetz, ed., *Getting Institutions Right for Women and Development*, pp. 212–22. New York: Zed Books.

Stienstra, Deborah. 2000. "Dancing Resistance from Rio to Beijing: Transnational Women's Organizing and United Nations Conferences, 1992–6." In Marianne H. Marchand and Anne Sisson Runyan, eds., *Gender and Global Restructuring: Sightings, Sites and Resistances*, pp. 209–24. New York: Routledge.

Sullivan, Donna. 1995. "The Public/Private Distinction in International Human Rights Law." In Julie Peters and Andrea Wolper, eds., *Women's Rights, Human Rights: International Feminist Perspectives*, pp. 126–34. New York: Routledge.

Sullivan, Kevin. 2002. "Former President's 'Hidden Treasure' Appalls Nicaragua; Successor Pursues Corruption Charges." *Washington Post*, September 12, A10.

Tarrow, Sidney. 2001. "Transnational Politics: Contention and Institutions in International Politics." *Annual Review of Political Science* 4: 1–20.

——. 2002. "From Lumping to Splitting: Specifying Globalization and Resistance." In Jackie Smith and Hank Johnston, eds., *Globalization and Resistance: Transnational Dimensions of Social Movements*, pp. 229–49. New York: Rowman and Littlefield.

Taylor, Verta, and Nancy E. Whittier. 1992. "Collective Identity in Social Movement Communities: Lesbian Feminist Mobilization." In Aldon D. Morris and Carol McClurg Mueller, eds., *Frontiers in Social Movement Theory*, pp. 104–29. New Haven: Yale University Press.

Teske, Robin L., and Mary Ann Tétrault eds., 2000. *Feminist Approaches to Social Movements, Community and Power: Conscious Acts and the Politics of Social Change*. Vol. 1. Columbia: University of South Carolina Press.

Thayer, Millie. 2000. "Traveling Feminisms: From Embodied Women to Gendered Citizenship." In Michael Burawoy, Joseph A. Blum, Sheba George, Zsuzsa Gille, Teresa Gowan, Lynne Haney, Maren Klawiter, Steven H. Lopez, Sean Ó Riain, and Millie Thayer. *Global Ethnography: Forces, Connections, and Imaginations in a Postmodern World*. Berkeley: University of California Press.

Tiano, Susan. 1994. *Patriarchy on the Line: Labor, Gender and Ideology in the Mexican Maquila Industry*. Philadelphia: Temple University Press.

Tirado, Silvia. 1994. "Weaving Dreams, Constructing Realities: The Nineteenth of September National Union of Garment Workers in Mexico." In Sheila Rowbotham and Swasti Mitter, eds., *Dignity and Daily Bread: New Forms of Economic Organizing Among Poor Women in the Third World and First*, pp. 100–113. New York: Routledge.

Trinh Minh-ha. 1989. *Women, Native, Other*. Bloomington: Indiana University Press.

——. 1990. "Not You/Like You: Post-Colonial Women and the Interlocking Questions of Identity and Difference." In Gloria Anzaldúa, ed., *Making Face, Making*

Soul: Creative and Critical Perspectives by Women of Color, pp. 371–75. San Francisco: Aunt Lute.

Tsing, Anna Lowenhaupt. 1993. *In the Realm of the Diamond Queen: Marginality in an Out-of-the-way Place*. Princeton: Princeton University Press.

Turner, Bryan S. 1990. "Outline of a Theory on Citizenship." *Sociology* 24 (2): 189–219.

United Nations Development Programme. 2000. *Human Development Report 2000*. New York: Oxford University Press.

——. 2003. *Human Development Report 2003*. New York: Oxford University Press.

Urla, Jacqueline. 1995. "Outlaw Language: Creating Alternative Public Spheres in Basque Free Radio." *Pragmatics* 5 (2): 245–61.

Valverde, Luis. 1993a. "Maquiladoras taiwanes intentan a callar a trabajadores." *La Barricada*, September 11, p. 1.

——. 1993b. "Organizan sindicato en la zona franca." *La Barricada*, October 6, p. 1.

Vanden, Harry E., and Gary Prevost. 1993. *Democracy and Socialism in Sandinista Nicaragua*. Boulder: Lynne Rienner Publishers.

Vargas, Virginia, and Cecilia Olea Mauleón. 1998. "Roads to Beijing: Reflections from Inside the Process." In *Roads to Beijing: Fourth World Conference on Women in Latin America and the Caribbean*. Lima; Santafé de Bogotá; Quito: Ediciones Flora Tristán; UNICEF; UNIFEM.

Vilas, Carlos M. 1986. *The Sandinista Revolution: National Liberation and Social Transformation in Central America*. New York: Monthly Review Press.

Wade, Peter. 1997. *Race and Ethnicity in Latin America*. Chicago: Pluto Press.

Walker, Thomas W. 1997. "Introduction." In Thomas W. Walker, ed., *Nicaragua without Illusions*, pp. 1–19. Wilmington, Del.: SR Books.

Westwood, Sallie, and Sarah A. Radcliffe. 1993. "Gender, Racism and the Politics of Identities in Latin America." In Sarah A. Radcliffe and Sallie Westwood, eds., *"Viva": Women and Popular Protest in Latin America*, pp. 1–29. New York: Routledge.

Whittier, Nancy. 1995. *Feminist Generations: The Persistence of the Radical Women's Movement*. Philadelphia: Temple University Press.

Wieringa, Saskia. 1994. "Women's Interests and Empowerment: Gender Planning Reconsidered." *Development and Change* 25: 829–48.

Wignaraja, Ponna, ed. 1993. *New Social Movements in the South: Empowering the People*. London: Zed Books.

Wilkie, James W., and José Guadelupe Ortega. 1997. *Statistical Abstract of Latin America*. Vol. 33. Los Angeles: UCLA Latin American Center Publications, University of California.

Wilson, Richard A. 1997. *Human Rights, Culture and Context: Anthropological Perspectives*. Chicago: Pluto Press.

Witness for Peace. 1997. "From the Maquila to the Mall." Washington: Witness for Peace.

Wolf, Diane Lauren. 1992. *Factory Daughters: Gender, Household Dynamics, and Rural Industrialization in Java*. Berkeley: University of California Press.

——. 1996a. "Situating Feminist Dilemmas in Fieldwork." In Diane L. Wolf, ed., *Feminist Dilemmas in Fieldwork*, pp. 1–55. Boulder: Westview Press.

——, ed. 1996b. *Feminist Dilemmas in Fieldwork*. Boulder: Westview Press.

World Bank. 2000. "Nicaragua at a Glance." Web site at www.worldbank. Accessed January 9, 2003.

Wright, Melissa. 2001. "The Dialectics of Still Life: Murder, Women and Maquiladoras." In Jean Comaroff and John L. Comaroff, eds., *Millennial Capitalism and the Culture of Neoliberalism*, pp. 125–46. Durham, N.C.: Duke University Press.

Yúdice, George. 1998. "The Globalization of Culture and the New Civil Society." In Sonia E. Alvarez, Evelina Dagnino, and Arturo Escobar, eds., *Cultures of Politics, Politics of Cultures: Re-visioning Latin American Social Movements*, pp. 353–79. Boulder: Westview Press.

Yuval-Davis, Nira. 1997a. *Gender and Nation*. Thousand Oaks, Calif.: Sage Publications.

——. 1997b. "Women, Citizenship and Difference." *Feminist Review* (57): 4–27.

Zuñiga, Carlos. 1995. Talk delivered to visitors at Nicaragua's Free Zone, "Las Mercedes." August 15.

INDEX

Page numbers in italics signify illustrations.

Association of Women Confronting the National Problem (AMPRONAC), 46. *See also* Association of Nicaraguan Women, "Luisa Amanda Espinoza" (AMNLAE)

Association of Women in Solidarity (AMES) (Guatemala), 147–49, 235 n.7

ATC. *See* Association of Rural Workers (ATC)

Atlantic Coast (of Nicaragua), 228 n.1

Austerity measures, 10, 28, 41

Authentic Workers' Front (FAT), 220

Autonomous Atlantic Northern Region (RAAN), 228 n.1

Autonomous women's movement: economic globalization and, 2; electoral democracies and, 73; feminist movement and, 50–51, 230 n.10; MEC and, 101–6, 109–10; Nicaraguan labor movement and formation of, 41; Nicaraguan revolution and formation of, 11, 17, 27; organizational structure of, 115–16; relationships of, with other women's groups, 50–51, 102–3, 230 n.11

Autonomy: feminism and, 104–10; MEC and, 88–92, 94, 99, 115, 217; in women's movement, 50–51, 71–72

Auxiliadora (pseud.), 91, 108–10

Baltodano, Mónica, 49

Barbados, 67

Barricada, La, 157, 170

Beijing Women's Conference (1995), 73, 98

Belli, Gioconda, 229 n.2

Bissell, Trim, 221, 236 n.9

Blandón, María Teresa, 91, 103

Blondet, Cecelia, 120

Bolaños, Enrique, 11, 36, 203

Boletina, La, 157

Bonacich, Edna, 218

Boomerang effect, 173

Borge, Tomás, 48, 170

Bourdieu, Pierre, 228 n.9

Boycotts, 63, 167, 218–19, 221; MEC position on, 168, 174

Breadwinners: female, 3, 39, 220; male, 193, 199–200

"Breaking Boundaries/Constructing Alliances" conference, 210

Bush, George H. W., 28, 30

Cadres, 85, 95, 142, 152, 183, 216

CAFTA. *See* Central American Free Trade Agreement (CAFTA)

Campaign for Labor Rights (CLR), 15, 164, 173, 209, 220–22, 237 n.2

Campaigns, transnational: of anti-sweatshop movement, 208–9, 211; of the Network, 8, 143, 150–51

Canadian Council for International Corporation (CCIC), Human Rights Award of, 160, 208

Canadian International Development Agency, 207

Capitalism: flexible accumulation and, 151; systems of subordination in, 67; transnational interests and, 115, 152, 195, 197. *See also* Economic Globalization

Carazo, department of, *xvi,* 2, 19, 27

Cardenal, Ernesto, 229 n.2

Catholic Church, 33, 198, 203

CAUS. *See* Confederation of Syndical Action and Unity (CAUS)

CDS. *See* Sandinista Defense Committees (CDS)

CEDAW. *See* Convention on the Elimination of all Forms of Discrimination Against Women (CEDAW)

Documentation and Research Center (of MEC), 97, 100, 113, 180–81; information politics and, 143, 145

Domestic sphere, 76, 190; male bread-winners and, 193, 198–99; state intervention in, 193, 197–98, 200–201, 204; public sphere vs., 196, 214, 220; social reproduction within, 193–94, 201. *See also* Separation of spheres

Domestic violence, 19–20; campaigns against, 158; FSLN mass organizations and, 93; MEC programs on, 1, 77, 105–6, 201, 211 political violence and, 72

Domestic workers, unionization of, 12; MEC and, 100

Domestic Workers' Union, "Rigoberta Menchú," 53, 231 nn.14–15

ECCO, 166

Economic globalization: Central America under, 9–10; gender and, 2–3; information politics under, 144, 150; mobility of capital under, 150; nation-state and, 202; networks and, 70; Nicaragua under, 6, 10–11, 30, 179; resistance to, 67–70; transnational organizing strategies under, 133–35; women of color under, 66–70; women workers under, 67–69

Educational programs (of MEC), 105, 134–35, 141, 201, 206

Elections: 1990, 10, 30, 33; 1996, 11, 33–35, 117; 2001, 11, 36

Eloisa (pseud.), 80, 87–88

El Salvador, *xvi*, 1, 10, 209; the Network and, 146, 149, 151

El Viejo, *xvi*, 2, 11, 91, 100, 108, 207

Encuentros (conferences): encuentro of autonomous women's organizations (1992), 104; Latin American and Caribbean Feminist Meeting, 49

Enhanced Structural Adjustment Facility (ESAF), 30, 229 n.4

Estelí, *xvi*, 2, 54, 56–57, 111, 207–8; effects of Hurricane Mitch on, 208

Ethnography, 8, 12–14; *See also* Research methods

Evelyn (pseud.), 80, 180, 210; autonomy and, 101, 103; class-based divisions in women's movement and, 96–98; Documentation and Research Center and, 113, 145, 181; institutionalization of MEC, 84, 87; oppositional networks of, 159; self-limiting radicalism and, 168

Export-oriented production, 11–12, 38

Fair Labor Association (FLA), 160

Family: female caretakers of, 37, 191–92; FONIF and, 35, 198; liberal ideology and, 200; neoliberalism and, 197, 200; nuclear, 198–99; protected by nation-state, 193, 198. *See also* Breadwinners; Domestic sphere; Female-headed households; Ministry of the Family (MIFAMILIA)

Family values, 198, 200, 202–4; in the Catholic Church, 199; Liberal Alliance party and, 199, 202–3

FAT. *See* Authentic Workers' Front (FAT)

Female-headed households, 198–99, 236 n.4

Feminism, 103–4; class consciousness and, 107–8; challenges to class-based notion of, 120; globalization of, 73–74, 92–93, 120; Latin American, 70–77, 92–93; MEC and 24, 77, 83, 92–100, 104–6, 107, 109, 120, 225; the Network and, 148; popular, 69–70, 72, 95

Feminist identity: las feministas and, 102; las institucionalizadas and, 95; of Managua collective (of MEC), 104–7, *131*, *132*; of regional leaders (of MEC), 107–10

Feminist movement: in Latin America, 24, 72–73, 92–93, 231 n.12; in U.S., 70–71, 72; Marxism and, 71; racism in, 233 n.15; women's movement and, 230 n.10

Feminist perspective vs. gender perspective, 231 n.12

Feminist research, 17–24. *See also* Research methods

Feminists of color, 233 n.15; multiple jeopardy and, 214–15

Ferguson, Ann, 119

Festival of 52 Percent, 49

FESTRAS. *See* Syndical Federation of Food, Agricultural, and Related Workers (FESTRAS) (Guatemala)

FIDEG. *See* International Foundation for the Global Challenge (FIDEG)

FLA. *See* Fair Labor Association (FLA)

Flexible strategies of production, 144–45

FNT. *See* National Workers' Front (FNT)

FONIF. *See* Nicaraguan Fund for Children and the Family (FONIF)

Formal labor market, women in, 3, 27, 38, 227 n.2

FORTEX Group factory: 1993 strike at, 54–55, 135–36, 162, 195; unions in, 162, 165–66

Foucault, Michel, 232 n.9

Freeman, Carla, 67

Free radio movement, 158

Free Trade Zones (FTZS), vii, 8, 210; conditions for women workers in, 38–40; food practices in, 39, 230 n.6; Free Trade Zone Corporation and, 45, 139, 160, 164, 170; as global patriarchy, 105;

labor force of, 38; "Las Mercedes," 11, 44–45, 54, *128*, 139, 234 n.1; legislation creating, 10–11; in Nicaragua, 11–12; 1991 transnational apparel industry and, 10; wages in, 40, 230 n.7

Fröbel, Falker, 66–67

Frundt, Henry J., 235 n.7

FSLN. *See* Sandinista National Liberation Front (FSLN)

FTZS. *See* Free Trade Zones FTZS

GAP, 168

Garifuna (Honduras), 232 n.6

Garment assembly, vi–viii, 227 n.1; factories, 10–11, 38

Gender: analysis, 3, 225; awareness training, 206; blindness, 169, 174–75, 223; claims, 47, 52; consciousness, 52, 225; difference, 191–92, 196, 204; economic globalization and, 2–3, 66–70; human rights and, 74; in labor movement, 5, 205–6, 213–14, 220–23; politics of, 27; privatization and, 37–38; roles, 3, 37, 105–6, 192–94; segregation in textile industry, 229 n.5; vision of MEC, 100

Gender perspective, 59, 105, 150, 169, 172, 225; of MEC, 6, 52, 100; feminist perspective vs., 231 n. 12

Generalizability, 4

Global capitalism. *See* Economic globalization

Global ethnography, 6–8, 16–17. *See also* Research methods

Global Exchange, 9, 15, 210, 237 n.7

Global Fund for Women, 113

Globalization, vii–viii, 7; from above and below, 59, 63, 175, 205, 212; from below, 150, 173, 175, 216, 223; contentious politics under, 65–66, 233 n.11; creating spaces for resistance in, 67;

Globalization (*continued*)
gender and, 66–67; local politics under, 74, 141; power and, 214; social movements and, 60–64; women's agency under, 67–68

Gramsci, Antonio, 225

Granada, *xvi*, 2, 12, 14–15, 18, 19, 54, 84, 183, 207; department of, *xvi*, 2, 85, 103, 107, 111

Grassroots, 206, 215–17; AMNLAE and, 47; feminists (feministas de base) and MEC, 94–99, 216; MEC and, 6, 82, 120–122, 227 n.5; National Women's Secretariat (of CST) and, 52–53; NGOs and, 122; politics and globalization, 134

Great Britain, 25

Gringa, 18–19, 22, 177

GRUFERPROFAM, 235 n.7

Grupo Factor X/Casa de la Mujer (Mexico), 210

Guatemala, *xvi*, 1, 10, 15, 156, 169, 228 n.1; child labor in, 151; the Network and, 146–49

Guerilla movements: women's participation in, 70

Guerra, Carlos, 184–86

Guevara, Che, 27, 229 n. 3

Hard Copy, 170–72, 175, 213, 222–24

Hegemony, 225

Honduran Women's Collective (CODEMUH), 9, 169

Honduras, *xvi*, 1, 10, 15, 25, 27, 169, 209, 236 n.9; effects of Hurricane Mitch on, 208; Garifuna, 232 n.6; the Network and, 146, 148, 151

Hossfeld, Karen, 67

Human rights: gender equality and, 196; under globalization, 179–80; liberal ideology in, 191, 202; MEC's use of, 8,

93–94, 193; reformulation of, 233 n.17; transnational strategies for, 174; women's rights and, 74, 182, 191–92, 132, 201, 204

Hurricane Mitch, 36, 208

ICIC. *See* Civil Initiative for Central American Integration (ICIC)

Identity politics: in labor movements, 70; in social movements and, 61–62

Illiteracy rates, 62

ILO. *See* International Labor Organization (ILO)

IMF. *See* International Monetary Fund (IMF)

INATEC. *See* National Technical Institute (INATEC)

Independent monitoring of maquiladoras, 172, 209–10, 214, 235 n.8, 236 n.9; gender perspective and, 169–70, 172; members of the Network and, 156, 169, 171–72, 209

Indigenous ancestry, 227 n.7

Indigenous population, 228 n.1

Infant mortality: in Nicaragua, 32

Informal economic sector, 37, 40–41

Information politics, 65–66, 113, 134–35, 174, 219, 222; Documentation and Research Center and, 145; "Jobs, Yes . . . But with Dignity" campaign and, 144–46; professionalization and, 215; promotoras and, 143; reformist vs. transformative and, 65–66; strategies of production and, 144, transnational, 218

Information technology: under globalization, 9, 61, 63, 134–35, 219; international fax campaign, 173; MEC offices and, 180; the Network and, 114, 150; professionalization and, 114; strategies of production and, 144

Leafleting campaigns, 209, 221–22; MEC
position on, 168
Legal offices (of MEC), 206, 235 n.3
Leninism, 29, 95, 229 n.3
León, *xvi*, 1, 2, 12, 86, 112, 207–8; depart-
ment of, 27, 54, 84
Leverage politics, 167, 173, 188. *See also*
Accountability politics
Liberal Alliance, 184; active citizenship
and, 202; antifeminist agenda of, 198–
99; Catholic Church and, 35, 198, 203;
neoliberalism and, 11, 197; 1996 elec-
tion and, 11, 33–35; pro-family posi-
tion of, 198–200, 202–3; 2001 election
and, 11. *See also* Alemán, Arnoldo
Liberal ideology: and the family, 200;
and human rights, 187, 191, 202
Liberation theology, 229 n.3
Literacy campaign, 32, 140
Living wage, 204, 237 n.7
Lola (pseud.), 44, 57, 85–86, 107, 183
Lombriz, 5–6

Madres de la Plaza de Mayo (the Madres;
Argentina), 75, 141, 203, 214
Malaysia: maquiladoras in, 68–69
Malinches, Las, 96, 103, 141, 199, 203, 234
n.3
MAM. *See* Women's Movement Mélida
Anaya Montes (MAM) (El Salvador)
Managua, *xvi*, 1, 2, 11–12, 14, 18, 19, 33,
207–8; as residence for maquila
workers, 139; department of, 27
Maquiladoras, 1, 227 n.1, 235 n.5; conditions for workers, 166; information
politics and, 145; MEC position on, 155,
167–68, 171; the Network and, 5, 146–
51; threat of relocation and, 145, 167–
68, 174, 235 n.8
Maquila workers, 12–13, 37–38; agency

of, 67–69; gender/race and, 67; MEC
and, 1–2, 6; the Network and, 146–51;
organized resistance in, 68–69
Maquila Solidarity Network (Canada), 210
María Luisa (pseud.), 85–86, 90, 102–3,
107–8, 112, 183
Marxism: class reductionism in, 68, 92;
feminism and, 71; FSLN and, 27, 41,
229 n.3; MEC's integral approach and,
162
Master's tools, 201
Matagalpa, *xvi*, 2, 54, 87–88; department
of, *xvi*, 2, 84; effects of Hurricane
Mitch on, 208
Matrices of domination, 212–13
Mayra (pseud.), 140–41
MEC. *See* Working and Unemployed
Women's Movement, "María Elena
Cuadra" (MEC)
Media, 8, 33–34, 58, 177–79, 184; under
globalization, 178; radio, 158, 177–78;
Textile and Apparel Workers' Federa-
tion's campaign and, 164–66; transna-
tional anti-sweatshop movement
campaign and, 208–9. *See also* "Jobs,
Yes . . . But with Dignity" campaign:
media strategy of
Meiselas, Susan, 229 n.2
Mestizaje, 228 n.1
Mestizo, 228 n.1
Mexico City women's conference (1975)
73
Microcredit, 2, 216, 231 n.13; MEC provi-
sion of, 76, 105, 107, *127*, 141, 207–8
Microenterprises, 53, 99, 107, *127*, 207, 231
n.13
MIFAMILIA. *See* Ministry of the Family
(MIFAMILIA)
Mil Colores, 208–9, 222, 237 n.2
Minimum wage: 211, 236 n. 2, 237 n. 7

Minimum Wage Commission, 212

Minister of Construction and Transport, 45

Minister of Economy and Development, 45

Ministry of Finance, 43, 45

Ministry of Labor (MITRAB): Center of Documentation, 97–98; CST and, 46; Fortex Group strike and, 136; MEC and, 8, 142–43, 151, 159, 173; ministerial resolution of, 161, 189–90, 210

Ministry of the Family (MIFAMILIA), 35, 117, 198–201

Ministry of Social Action, 236 n.4

Miskitu, 228 n.1

MITRAB. *See* Ministry of Labor (MITRAB)

Mixed organizations, 99, 108–10, 113

Mobilization for Global Justice, 15

Molyneux, Maxine, 75–77, 229 n.2

MRS. *See* Sandinista Reform Party (MRS)

Mujer y Cambio (Women and Change), 96

Multiple jeopardy, women of color and, 214–15

NAFTA. *See* North American Free Trade Agreement (NAFTA)

Nairobi women's conference (1985), 73

Narváez Murillo, Zoilamerica, 202–3

National Assembly of Nicaragua, 30, 33, 35–36, 184, 188, 193, 198; bill to regulate FTZs and, 209–10; Commission on Peace and Human Rights, 184, 186

National campaign (of MEC). *See* "Jobs, Yes . . . But with Dignity" campaign

National Catholic Reporter, 209

National Coalition of Women, "March 8th," 103–4

National Committee of Women Syndicalists of Nicaragua, 146

National Confederation of Professionals (CONAPRO), women's secretariat of, 47, 230 n.11

National Confederation of Professionals—Heroes and Martyrs (CONAPRO H-M), women's secretariat of, 230 n.11

National Day of the Domestic Workers, 53, 231 n.15

National Endowment for Democracy (NED), 30

National Executive (of CST), women members of, 55

National Guard, 26

Nationalism: the family and, 193; gender and, 193–96, 213

National Labor Code, 8, 165, 189; MEC workshops on, 138, 183, 201; proposed reforms to, 211

National Labor Committee (NLC), 164, 169–70, 173, 209, 213, 236 n.9, 237 n.1

National Public Radio (U.S.), 209

National Technical Institute (INATEC), 140–41

National Union of Farmers and Ranchers (UNAG), 29; women's secretariat of, 47, 102

National Union of Opposition (UNO), 10, 30, 43

National Women's Secretariat (of CST), 4, 47, 51–52, 102, 135–36, 211; CST conflicts with, 3–4, 54–57, 79–80; dependence on external funding, 118; development projects of, 53; Documentation and Research Center, 145; FORTEX Group factory strike and, 54–55; MEC leadership and, 79–80, 83, 100, 139

National Workers' Front (FNT), 43–44

Nation-state: active citizenship in, 179–80; civic responsibility of, 186, 188–89;

Nation-state (*continued*)
dismantling of the welfare state, 64,
82; economic globalization and, 202;
the family and, 193, 198; gender difference and, 193–96; liberal assumptions
about, 187; as patriarch, 193, 196, 198,
200, 213; racism and, 194–95; social
movements and, 179–80, 182–85; sovereignty and, 188, 193; transnational
capitalist interests and, 195, 197; use of
language of citizenship and, 179–80,
182–83; use of language of rights and,
179–80, 182–85; women as reproducers of, 193–94, 200–201, 203, 213

Navarro, Wilfredo, 161

Negotiation techniques: effectiveness of,
161; as gendered, 153–54; language of,
152–53, 166; Network of Women
against Violence and, 117; as political
strategy, 154–55; workshops on, *130*,
133–34, 152–53, 160

Negrito/a, 227 n.7

Neocolonialism, external dependency
and, 119, 122

Neoliberalism, 9–10, 31, 193–94, 215;
active citizenship under 179–80, 185–
86; Alemán and, 11, 179, 197; Chamorro administration and, 197; and
consequences for women, 3, 37–38,
182; definition of citizenship under,
185, 226; demise of the welfare state
under, 64, 82; democracy under, 2, 10,
179, 183, 204, 226; development projects under, 11, 38, 82; the family and,
197, 200; human rights under 187–88;
in Nicaragua, 179–80, 197; NGOs and,
121; rights vs., 183–88; sandinismo vs.,
182; social conservatism and 197–98,
200

Network-like organizational structure,
152; of MEC, 101, 110–12, 115–18, 120; of
the Network, 148, 150–52

Network of Documentation Centers
Concerning Women and Children,
97–98, 103–4

Network of Women Against Violence, 15,
50, 103–4, 117, 158, 190

Networks: oppositional, 8, 138–43, 146,
157, 159; as new form of resistance
under economic globalization, 70;
and transnationalization of feminism,
73–74. *See also* Transnational Advocacy Networks (TANs)

Network, The. *See* Central American
Women's Network in Solidarity with
Maquila Workers (the Network)

New social movements, 73, 89–90, 115,
232 nn.4–5, 10; identity politics and,
62; in Latin America, 62. *See also*
Social movement theory

New York Times, 209

NGO-ization, 215–17; class differences
and, 113; of Latin America, 64; of MEC,
82; of women's movements, 112–13,
121. *See also* Nongovernmental organizations (NGOs); Professionalization

NGOS. *See* Nongovernmental organizations (NGOs)

Nicaragua: Atlantic and Pacific Coasts
of, 228 n.1; citizenship and rights in,
182–84, 202; contra war in, 28, 30, 42;
economic globalization and, 6, 10–11,
30; effects of Hurricane Mitch on, 208;
foreign investment in, 197; GDP of, 41–
42; history of, 25–37, 228 n.1; infant
mortality rates in, 32; inflation, 31–32;
literary tradition of, 229 n.2; neoliberalism and, 31, 179, 197; 1990 election, 10, 30, 33; 1990 national strike,
43; 1991 FTZ legislation, 10–11; 1997

Nicaragua (*continued*)
national budget, 230 n. 9; 1997
national strike, 35–36, 158, 197; 1997
transportation strike, 19; 1996 election, 11, 33–35, 117; political and economic transitions in, 2, 6, 10–11, 16–
17; poverty in, 12, 33, 199, 263 n.4;
public spending and, 31; SAPS and, 31–
32, 37; 2001 election, 11, 36; unemployment in, 32, 38; U.S. intervention in,
25–26, 30, 33; U.S. trade embargo, 28–
29, 32, 42
Nicaraguan Bank of Industry and Commerce (BANIC), 36
Nicaraguan Center of Human Rights
(CENIDH), 169, 211, 237 n. 1
Nicaraguan Commission for Economic
and Social Planning (CONPES), 212
Nicaragua Network (Washington, D.C.),
209
Nicaraguan Fund for Children and the
Family (FONIF), 35, 198
Nicaraguan labor movement: conflicts
with MEC, 161–66, 175, 211–12; discrimination against women in, 77, 93–
94, 103; gendered leadership of, 51;
gender issues in, 165–66; history of,
41–46, 162–63; during the Sandinista
period, 155; sexual harassment in, 103,
221. *See also* Sandinista National Liberation Front (FSLN); Sandinista
Workers' Central (CST)
Nicaraguan Network of Women Against
Violence, 158
Nicaraguan revolution, viii, 2, 10, 25–28,
229 n. 2; formation of autonomous
women's movement and, 11, 17, 27;
women combatants in, 70–71
Nicaraguan Women's Conference
"Diverse but United," 49–50

Nicaraguan Women's Institute (INIM),
35, 96–97, 117, 198, 199
Nineteenth of September National
Union of Garment Workers, 69
NLC. *See* National Labor Committee
(NLC)
Nongovernmental organizations (NGOS),
ix, 7–9, 215; accountability and, 217;
categorizations of, 234 n.1; connection
to grassroots, 216–17; development
strategies of, 53, 206, 231 n.13; globalization and, 82; social movements vs.,
64–66, 82, 121–22, 234 n.1;
North American Free Trade Agreement,
69–70
North/South relationship: collaborations and, 218–19; external dependency in, 119–20, 215–16; power
dynamics of, 175, 206, 215
Nuclear family, 198–99
Núñez, Vilma, 34

Obando y Bravo, Miguel, 203
Oppositional alternatives, 138–39
Oppositional strategies: cooperation vs.
competition, 134
Ortega, Daniel, 42, 116; 1996 elections,
33–35; support of AMNLAE, 48,
Zoilamérica Narváez Murillo and,
202–3
OXFAM, 53, 86, 147, 207, 210

Pacific Coast (of Nicaragua), 228 n.1
Padilla, Max, 237 n.5
Participant observation, 12–24. *See also*
Research methods
"Patria libre o morir," 116, 172
Patricia (pseud.), 79–80
Pérez Alemán, Paola, 229 n.5
"Personal as political, the," 94, 104, 138

Personal responsibility, 202

Petition drive, MEC and, 160. *See also* "Jobs, Yes . . . But with Dignity" campaign

Petrolina (pseud.), 114, 153

Philippines, organized female resistance in maquiladoras in, 68

Piñata, La, 44, 182, 202, 236 n.1

Plan of Occupational Conversion, 31–32

Political agency, 225

Polyarchy, 73, 178–79

Popular feminism, *See* Feminism: popular

Poverty. *See* Nicaragua: poverty in

Power: Foucault on, 232 n.9; from above and below, 59, 62–63; in transnational politics, 213

Prensa, La, 27, 203

Private sphere. *See* Domestic sphere; Separation of spheres

Privatization, 10, 30, 43–44, 197; effects of, on women, 37–38, 53; of textile industry, 38

Professionalization, 98–99, 112–13; information politics and, 215; las institucionalizadas, 95; MEC and, 113–15, 121, 216–17; NGOS and, 121, 215–16. *See also* NGO-ization

Promotoras (promoters), 212, 235 n.4; cadres and, 142, 216; "Jobs, Yes . . . But with Dignity" campaign and, 159–60; role of, in MEC, 39, 141–43, 145 235 n.3

Public services: reduction of, 3, 9–11, 31, 37, 66, 120, 215

Public sphere: as a male domain, 175, 214, 220; media as a, 158, 177–79; transnational, 135, 175. *See also* Domestic sphere; Separation of spheres

Puntos de Encuentro (Points of Encounter), 93, 98, 102

RAAN. *See* Autonomous Atlantic Northern Region

Race: blindness, 223; economic globalization and, 66–70; external dependency and, 119–20, 234 n.6; nationalist discourse and, 194–95

Racial categories, 227 n.7, 228 n.1

Radcliffe, Sarah, 193

Radical reformism, 167, 201–2. *See also* Self-limiting radicalism

Radio. *See* Media

Radio Ya, 158, 177–78

Ramírez, Sergio, 35

Randall, Margaret, 91, 229 n.2

Reagan, Ronald, 28

Reformist strategies: MEC and, 135; transformative strategies vs., 65–66, 202, 224. *See also* Radical Reformism; Self-limiting Radicalism

Representation, politics of, 22–23

Reproductive health: MEC programs on, 1, 105–6, 195, 201

Reproductive rights, 51, 203, 206

Research methods: ethnography, 8, 12–14, feminist, 17–24; global ethnography, 6–8, 16–17; interviewing, 12–15, 18, 21; participant observation, 12–24

Resistance, 202, 225; accommodation and, 213; cultural politics and, 62; gendered reconceptualization of, viii, 63–64; as social transformation, 225; women workers and, 67–70

Revolution. *See* Nicaraguan Revolution

Reyna (pseud.), 80, 100, 110, 145, 177–78

Rich, Adrienne, 105, 229 n.2

Rights, 203; active citizenship and, 185; gender difference and, 191, 193, 196; under globalization, 179–80, 186; MEC use of language of, 180–81, 183–85, 189–90; MEC code of ethics and, 189;

Taft, William Howard, 26

Taiwan: Alemán visit to, 197; maquila factories and, 166, 194–95

Tamara (pseud.), 81, 84, 100, 108, 110

Target, 209, 222

Tarrow, Sidney, 65–66, 231 n.3

TELCOR, 80

Téllez, Dora María, 34–35, 136–37

Textile and Apparel Workers' Federation (of the CST), 162–66, 173, 209, 211, 213, 221–22, 237 n.1; conflicts with MEC, 161–66; MEC leadership and, 80; unionization in the FTZ, 162–66; unionizing campaign, 164–66

Third World feminists, 22, 233 n.15

Tijerino, Doris, 49

Tipitapa, *xvi*, 2; effects of Hurricane Mitch on, 208; maquila workers and, 18, 139, 208

Transnational advocacy networks (TANS), 64, 147; favorable conditions for, 147; the Network and, 146; resistance and, 232 n.8; TSMS vs., 64–66

Transnationalism, 60; migration and, 60–61

Transnational social movements (TSMS), 61, 65, 232 n.10; institutional approach to, 231 n.3; TANS vs., 64–66. *See also* New social movements; Social movement theory

Transnational strategies, 172–74

Transportation, public, 18–19, 97

Turner, Brian, 185

U.S. Agency for International Development (USAID), 30–31

U.S. intervention in Nicaragua, 25–26, 30, 33; trade embargo, 28–29, 32, 42

U.S.-Mexico border, women's activism and maquiladoras along, 69–70

UNAG. *See* National Union of Farmers and Ranchers (UNAG)

UNE. *See* Union of Public Employees (UNE)

Union August 16, 165

Union of Needletrades, Industrial, and Textile Employees (UNITE), 236 n.9, 237 n.1

Union of Public Employees (UNE), women's secretariat of, 230 n.11

UNITE. *See* Union of Needletrades, Industrial, and Textile Employees (UNITE)

United Nations, 6; conferences and summits of, 9, 61, 73, 92

United Students Against Sweatshops (USAS), 209

Universal Declaration on Human Rights, 8, 157, 189

University of Central America (Managua), 158, 177

UNO. *See* National Union of Opposition (UNO)

Vilas, Carlos, 41

Wages: in FTZS, 40, 230 n.7; living wages, 204, 237 n.7; minimum wages, 211, 236 n. 2, 237 n. 7; in Nicaragua, 42

Walker, William, 26

Wal-Mart, 144, 230 n.9

War of the Comuneros, (1881), 25

Weapons of the weak, 232 n.8. *See also* Resistance

Westwood, Sallie, 193

WID. *See* Women in Development (WID)

Witness for Peace, 170, 209, 213

Women: as breadwinners, 39, 220; child care and, 38–39; as family caretakers, 37, 75; 191–92; in formal labor market;

Women (*continued*)

    3, 38, 227 n.2; in informal economy, 37, 40–41; issues of, as apolitical, 195–96; nationalism and, 193–94; and nation-state control of sexuality, 198, 203; privatization and, 37–38; second shift and, 40; triple shift and, 40

Women in Development (WID), 120

Women of color, economic globalization and, 66–70

Women's Health Network, 50

Women's issues: workers' issues vs., 5, 96, 195–96, 214, 218, 220, 222, 223, 236 n.10

Women's Movement Mélida Anaya Montes (MAM) (El Salvador), 220, 235 n.7

Women's movements: autonomy and Latin American, 71–72; class and Latin American, 72–73, 148; class and Nicaraguan, 96–99, 102; divisions within, 104; in Europe, 182; globalization of, 73–74; human rights and, 74; NGO-ization of, 112–13, 120, 216; race and Latin American, 72–73; strategic/practical gender interests in, 72, 75–77, 120; in United States, 23–24, 182; along U.S./Mexico border, 69

Women's rights: human rights and, 74, 182, 191–92, *132*, 201, 203; MEC and, 1, 8, 93–94, 190; Nineteenth of September National Union of Garment Workers and, 69

Women's secretariats, 51–54; of ATC, 47, 102; of CONAPRO H-M, 47, 230 n.11; formation of, 47; relationships with other women's groups and, 50–51, 102–3, 230 n.11; of UNAG, 47, 102; of UNE, 230 n.11. *See also* National Women's Secretariat (of CST)

Women Syndicalists of Central America and the Caribbean, 146

Women/worker dichotomy, 5, 96–99, 195–96, 214, 218, 220, 222, 223, 236 n.10

Women Working Worldwide (U.K.), 210

Workers' issues, *See* Maquiladoras: conditions for workers; Maquila workers; Women's issues: workers' issues vs.; Women/worker dichotomy

Working and Unemployed Women's Movement, "María Elena Cuadra" (MEC): activism vs. professionalism, 113–15, 121; alternative political strategies, 136–41, 166; autonomy and, 72, 89–92, 99–112, 119, 172; autonomy from labor movement, 72; breaks from CST, 1, 3–4, 57–58, 79, 87, 103–4, 107; categorization of, 59–60, 64–66, 77, 206; centralized organizational structure of, 83–88, 100–101, 110–12; class position in women's movement, 96–99; conditions for maquila workers, 2; conflicts with labor movement, 7, 161–66, 175, 211–12; Doble militantes (double militants), 108–12; external dependency and, 7–8, 22, 84, 86–87, 115, 118–20, 172, 215–17, 234 n.6; feminism and, 24, 77, 83, 92–100, 104–9, 120, 225; gender difference and, 193–96; gender perspective of, 6, 225; globalization and, 16; grassroots identity of, 6, 52–53, 82, 95–99, 120–22, 206, 216, 227 n.5; institutionalization of, 80, 82–88; "Jobs, Yes . . . But with Dignity" campaign, 145–46, 157, 208; job-training programs of, 1–2, 76, 105–7, 134, 140–41, 206–8; legal status of, as nonprofit (personería jurídica), 83; legal support of maquila workers and, 211–12; logo of, 81, *123*; Managua Collective of, 100–106; naming of, 4, 181; National Women's Secretariat (of

Working and Unemployed (*continued*)
CST) leadership and, 79–80, 83, 86,
100, 102, 139; network-like organizational structure, 101, 110–12, 115–18,
120; NGO-ization of, 82, 113–52; 1995
anniversary congress and commemoration, "United and Strong Against
Discrimination Against Women," 88–
89, 94, 135; organizational autonomy,
88–92, 99–112; personal autonomy,
88–92, 104, 107, 119, 172; position of,
on maquiladoras, 155, 167–68, 171;
professionalization of, 216; organizational alternative to labor movement,
8, 94–112, 116–17; petition drive, 160;
program for maquila workers, 134–41;
programs for women, 1–2, 76–77,

105–7, 134–35, 140–41, 201, 206–7, 225;
regional leaders of, 107–8; strate-
gic/practical gender interests of, 76–
77, 120; transformative potential of,
201–2; transnational anti-sweatshop
movement and, 15, 169; transnational
practices of, 5, 8–9, 16, 83, 102, 118;
transnational networks in Asia, 210;
uses language of citizenship, 179–80,
183–85, 189–90; uses rights discourse,
8, 93–94, 180–81, 183–85, 189–90, 193
World Bank, 6, 9–10, 28, 30, 219–20
World Trade Organization (WTO), ix,
219

Zamorra, Daisy, 229 n.2
Zapatistas (Mexico), 232 n.6

Jennifer Bickham Mendez is an associate professor in the
Department of Sociology at The College of William and Mary.

Library of Congress Cataloging-in-Publication Data

Mendez, Jennifer Bickham.
From the revolution to the maquiladoras : gender, labor, and
globalization in Nicaragua / Jennifer Bickham Mendez.
p. cm. — (American encounters/global interactions)
Includes bibliographical references and index.
ISBN 0-8223-3552-2 (cloth : alk. paper)
ISBN 0-8223-3565-4 (pbk. : alk. paper)
1. Movimiento de Mujeres Trabajadoras y Desempleadas "María Elena Cuadra."
2. Women's rights—Nicaragua—Societies, etc.
3. Women offshore assembly industry workers—Nicaragua.
4. Globalization—Economic aspects—Nicaragua—Sex differences.
I. Title. II. Series.
HQ1236.5.N5M46 2005   305.43'338097285–dc22
2005004620